ANGELA THIRKELL'S WORLD

ANGELA THIRKELL'S WORLD

A Complete Guide to the People and Places of Baretshire

by Barbara Burrell

 MOYER BELL

Wickford, Rhode Island & London

Published by Moyer Bell

First Edition

LIBRARY OF CONGRESS
CATALOGING-IN-PUBLICATION DATA

Burrell, Barbara, 1952–
    Angela Thirkell's world: a guide to the people and
places of Barsetshire / by Barbara Burrell. — 1st ed.
    p. cm.
    1. Thirkell, Angela Mackail, 1890–1961 —
Characters — Dictionaries.   2. Thirkell, Angela
Mackail, 1890–1961 — Settings — Dictionaries.
3. Barsetshire (England: Imaginary place.) —
Dictionaries.   4. Pastoral fiction, English —
Dictionaries.   I. Title.
    ISBN 1-55921-289-6
    PR6039.H43.Z58   2001
    823'.912 — dc21   00-052548
                                             CIP

Printed in the United States of America
Distributed in North America by Publishers Group
West, 1700 Fourth Street, Berkeley, California 94710,
800-788-3123 (in California 510-528-1444) and in
Europe by Gazelle Book Services Ltd., Falcon House,
Queen Square, Lancaster LA1 1RN England 524-68765

To
HOLT PARKER
with love

Works of the Barsetshire Cycle of
Angela Thirkell with original first
publication dates (all by Hamish Hamilton)

HR	*High Rising*	1933
WS	*Wild Strawberries*	1934
DH	*The Demon in the House*	1934
AF	*August Folly*	1936
SH	*Summer Half*	1937
PT	*Pomfret Towers*	1938
TB	*The Brandons*	1939
BL	*Before Lunch*	1939
CBI	*Cheerfulness Breaks In*	1940
NR	*Northbridge Rectory*	1941
MH	*Marling Hall*	1942
GU	*Growing Up*	1943
TH	*The Headmistress*	1944
MB	*Miss Bunting*	1945
PBO	*Peace Breaks Out*	1946
PE	*Private Enterprise*	1947
LAR	*Love Among the Ruins*	1948
OBH	*The Old Bank House*	1949
CC	*County Chronicle*	1950
DD	*The Duke's Daughter*	1951
HRt	*Happy Return*	1952
JC	*Jutland Cottage*	1953
WDIM	*What Did It Mean?*	1954
ESR	*Enter Sir Robert*	1955
NTL	*Never Too Late*	1956
ADA	*A Double Affair*	1957
CQ	*Close Quarters*	1958
LAAA	*Love At All Ages*	1959
TSAT	*Three Score and Ten*	1961
	(completed by C.A. Lejeune)	

FOREWORD

"I've written the same story so many times that I'm never quite sure now which book I'm in, and I find I'm always making people the wrong age, or mixing up their names, or forgetting whether they know each other or not."

These are the words of Mrs. Morland, Angela Thirkell's literary *alter ego*, in Thirkell's last work, *Three Score and Ten* (completed by C. A. Lejeune, and published posthumously in 1961). Though Mrs. Morland was referring to her Madame Koska novels, Angela Thirkell knew the problem too well. Since beginning to populate her mythical Barsetshire (before 1933), she wrote about a book per year, twenty-nine in all, each containing hundreds of vividly realized characters. It is no wonder that she occasionally lost track of what she had done with a few of them.

This book is designed to help readers find their way through the thicket of Thirkell's creations. It is alphabetical, for ease of reference. Under the name of every character, readers will find a chronological list of all the books in which they appeared (*see* "Works"), and what we learned about them in each. Page numbers are not given, as there are too many varying editions.

Here are the basic elements of a biographical entry for a denizen of Thirkell's Barsetshire:

NAME.   All names appear in **bold type**. This also includes listings of incorrect names, variants, and other names that the character is known by. So, if you are stumped by a character in *Pomfret Towers*, looking up **the Screaming Girl** will send you to her proper name, **Faraday-Home, Miss**. From that point, you can find her boisterous friends **Peter** and **Micky**, despite the fact that they never are given any last names at all. When Thirkell herself mistook a name, it is noted here; if you look up a mysterious **Mr. Twitcher**, you will be told: *see* **Mr. Twicker**. You will also find out in which book Thirkell got it wrong, and at what point she chose to add more information about the person, such as a full name.

The main entry for a person is generally under the name by which they are first known: under the maiden name for women who later marry (**Kate Keith** Carter), or under the married name for women who are already wives or widows, even if you later learn their maiden names (**Mrs. Lavinia Brandon**, née Oliver). In fact, women's names have been my greatest problem. Since the inhabitants of Barsetshire are fictional, they are listed here under the names Thirkell used for them, not as they would have appeared on their visiting cards. After **Susan Dean** marries, she is called Susan Belton, but also Mrs. Freddy.

Some characters (such as **Tubby Fewling**) are best known by their nicknames, while other Reverends and Rectors are addressed as "Mr." Terms of address also distinguish the older generation from their descendants: the unadorned "Mr. Marling" always means the patriarchal **William Marling**, while his wife, the Honourable Amabel, is almost always **Mrs. Marling**; and "Mr." makes it easier to distinguish the senior **Henry Leslie** from his two grandsons and namesakes.

I have made judicious use of parentheses, but they are not used in main entries except for a nickname, or an actual first name if the nickname is more commonly used. Some characters (such as **S. Wheeler** and **Miss Merriman**) are secretive about their first names, so rather than proclaiming the name in every reference, I have hidden it within the main entry.

There are lots of repeated names: just look under **Wheeler**, or **Brown**, or **Pollett**. That's because there are lots of big, intermarried families in Thirkell's Barsetshire. I have tried to be precise in distinguishing which one is which. The list order is: first just **Wheeler** (unmodified); when there are several, I list the ones from the earliest books first. Then I go alphabetically by first names, with less attention to titles unless there are no first names or the first names are the same. **Mr. Wheeler** comes before **Mrs. Wheeler**, then **Old Wheeler**, **Old Mrs. Wheeler**, **S. Wheeler**, and **Young Wheeler**, alphabetically.

"Le" or "la" are treated as "the," so **le Capet** is under C; but "de" or "du" are treated alphabetically; **de Courcy** is under 'D.'

Some characters are known by their organizations:

Barabbas, Master of
Barchester Chronicle, Young Man from the

Others are known by adjectives or modifiers:

Brick-Red Face, Man with the
Screaming Girl, the
Dull Girl in the Upper Fifth
Fair Girl from the Lower Sixth

Some are known by their relatives or affinities:

Archdeacon's Daughter, the
Bishop's Wife, the
Head Chief of Mngangaland, the Eightieth Son of the
Note: **Mrs. Turner** has two nieces: Their main entries are
under **Betty** and **Other Niece, the**.

You can also look people up under their positions:

Bishop, the
Captain of Rowing, the
Head Chief of Mngangaland, the
Prime Minister of Mngangaland, the
Head Witch Doctor of Mngangaland

PROFESSION AND RESIDENCE.   Also titles, if any. I have
tried to be accurate about the titles though, as an American, I
don't come by it naturally. Thus, the wife of the Eighth Earl
of Pomfret is Sally, Lady Pomfret, never Lady Sally Pomfret.

I have tended to stick in last names where they wouldn't normally be, otherwise you would never know to look the aforementioned up under the name **Sally Wicklow**, and her married name is Foster! Thirkell herself was sometimes slap-dash with titles: Watch **Lord Stoke** turn from an earl and a husband to a baron and a bachelor.

RELATIONS. Children of a family are listed in age order, eldest first, as Thirkell herself tended to give them. Family entries tend to be repetitive, but each one had to be complete.

AGES. This is where Thirkell trips up most frequently: It's a difficult thing to have a county full of fictional characters all aging naturally over the years.

"Not that it matters greatly in this Cloud-Cuckoo-Land of Barsetshire; and it is just as perplexing in our own lives; everyone is older or younger than one thinks they are." (LAAA 59)

SOME USEFUL ABBREVIATIONS.

q.v.: *quod vide*, "which see".

See sends you to a main entry in this book.

"*Cf.*" means "compare," and is used for citations of other authors, especially Anthony Trollope, who first invented and peopled Barsetshire. Full references to individual works are not given, mainly because Trollope's characters also kept turning up in his various books. Anybody who enjoys Thirkell would probably enjoy Trollope as well.

If I am inconsistent, I follow an inconsistent author. That is
one of her delights. Also, errors and misspellings have either
persisted in or been introduced by the various editions that
Thirkell's works have gone through. That is not so delightful,
but those who use this book should keep it in mind, and be
forgiving. If any attentive reader finds me to be in error, please
contact me and I will correct it in subsequent editions.

"It is much the same in ordinary life, and never shall we
remember who is who—or was who. Life is a vain show and as
we get older we find it simpler to sit back and look at it—not
without pleasure—and let our children do some of the remem-
bering for us." (LAAA 59)

ANGELA THIRKELL'S WORLD

A Complete Guide
to the People and
Places of Barsetshire

Aberfordbury, Lord: *See* **Hibberd, Sir Ogilvy.**

Accompanist to Aubrey Clover
- ❖ An expressionless man of no particular age; he always goes back to his mother's in Ealing after a performance, if possible. (PE 47)

- ❖ Swears horribly when he finds that **Aubrey Clover** and **Denis Stonor** will play two pianos themselves in their new revue. (CC 50)

- ❖ Plays for their sketch of *Two-Step for Three* for Northbridge Coronation Entertainment, and stays on to ad-lib for the Pageant of History. (WDIM 54)

Adams, Amabel Rose
- ❖ Baby daughter of **Lucy Marling** Adams and **Sam Adams**. (DD 51)

- ❖ She has a little brother. (NTL 56)

✤ Her brother is **William**, and little sister **Leslie**. She is now nine or ten, attending Barchester High School, and is friends with **Eleanor Leslie** and **Robin Morland**. (TSAT 61)

Adams, (Mrs.) Lucy: *See* **Marling, Lucy.**

Adams, Heather

✤ Daughter of **Sam Adams**, slightly lumpish at sixteen years old; her mother died when she was seven. Attends the Hosiers' Girls' Foundation School at Harefield Park, where she excels in mathematics, plays Audrey in *As You Like It*, and has a crush on **Freddy Belton**, who saves her when she falls into the lake while skating, and tells her about his lost love, the **Wren**. (TH 44)

✤ In her last term at the Hosiers' Girls' School, she sits for a scholarship to Newton College. After she wins it, she and **Miss (Cicely) Holly** stay with **Mrs. Merivale** and study before she leaves for college. She becomes friends with **Anne Fielding** and has a crush on **Jane Gresham**. Her mother died seven or eight years previously (but *see* TH 44 above). (MB 45)

✤ Now at Cambridge, gets engaged to **Young Ted Pilward**. (PBO 46)

✤ Studying for exams, will be married in a year. Puts her foot in it by telling **Susan Dean** about Freddy Belton's lost love. (LAR 48)

✤ Due to be married in September, she moves into the Old Bank House with her father. The wedding, however, is to be in Hogglestock, where she and Ted will live after the honeymoon. (OBH 49)

* Her very costly wedding. (CC 50)

* Her first child, **Edward Belton Pilward**, born. (DD 51)

* She and Ted go to the Riviera with her father and Lucy. (HRt 52)

* She and Ted now have two children. (TSAT 61)

Adams, Leslie

* Third child of **Lucy Marling** Adams and **Sam Adams**, little sister of **Amabel Rose** and **William**. She is named after the Rushwater family. (TSAT 61)

Adams, Sam

* Ironmaster, owner of Hogglestock Rolling Mills. Widower, one daughter, **Heather Adams**. Serves as Justice of the Peace and as magistrate with **Mr. (Fred) Belton**. Lower class and a loud dresser, but no

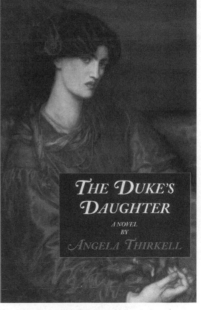

fool. His grandfather was in the Crewe railway shops; his father served under Admiral Hornby (father of **Christopher Hornby**) as chief engineer of H.M.S. *Carraway*. Speaks to the War Agricultural Committee so that Mr. Belton can sell the Church Meadow to the Hosiers' Girls' Foundation School. (TH 44)

* Taking more of a part in County affairs, under the guidance of **Mrs. (Lucy) Belton**. Benefactor to Barchester

Cathedral, elected to County Club, chairman of **Admiral Palliser's** Board of Directors. Attends the Barsetshire Archaeological Society's excavations of Bloody Meadow. Becomes fond of **Jane Gresham** and finds out about her missing husband for her. (MB 45)

* Stands for Parliament as a Labour candidate, and wins. (PBO 46)

* As an M.P., is a thorn in the side of his party. (PE 47)

* Offers a job to **Lucy Marling** as well as buying Marling land. (LAR 48)

* Buys the Old Bank House from **Miss (Hilda) Sowerby**. His father, while drunk, had been hit by a lorry and killed; his mother and three siblings died before he married. His wife died at thirty. He renovates the Old Bank House, gives a garden party as a housewarming, and gets engaged to Lucy Marling. (OBH 49)

* Presides over Heather's marriage to **Young Ted Pilward**, then marries Lucy. Leaves the Labour party. (CC 50)

* Now a justice of the peace (but *see* TH 44, above). He and Lucy name their new baby **Amabel** (for her mother) **Rose** (for his first wife).

* His mother's name was Hilda, and she had been in service at Hartletop Priory (and walking out with the third footman) until she married. (DD 51)

* Leaves Parliament. He and Lucy visit the Riviera with Heather and Ted Pilward. (HRt 52)

* Subsidizes Coronation festivities at his own Works and at Barchester General Hospital. His father was "a good

tradesman" (*see* TH 44, OBH 49 above). Going into business with **Mr. (Donald) MacFadyen** and **Old (Ted) Pilward**, so wants to rent most of Pomfret Towers for offices and an experimental station for Amalgamated Vedge. (WDIM 54)

* His and Lucy's second child a boy. (NTL 56)

* They put the boy's name down for Harefield House School. (CQ 58)

* There's a rumor that he'll be offered a knighthood. (LAAA 59)

* He forms a Syndicate with **Sir Robert Fielding, Sir Robert Graham**, Mr. Pilward, **Mr. (Frank) Dean**, and **Gradka Bonescu** the Mixo-Lydian Ambassador to buy **Wiple** terrace to keep it from being purchased by **Lord Aberfordbury**, and give it to Southbridge School. He and Lucy host **Mrs. (Laura) Morland's** Seventieth Birthday Tea at the Old Bank House. (TSAT 61)

Adams, William
* Unnamed second child of **Lucy Marling** Adams and **Sam Adams**. Little brother of **Amabel Rose**. (NTL 56)

* They put the boy's name down for Harefield House School. (CQ 58)

* His name is given, after his mother's father. His little sister's name is **Leslie**. (TSAT 61)

Addison
* Boy at the Priory School, friend of **Pickering** and **Young Dean**. Stung by wasp. (LAR 48)

❖ Forgets to blow up **Charles Belton's** bicycle tires. (OBH 49)

❖ In his last term, to go on to Southbridge School. (DD 51)

Admiral of the Mixo-Lydian Fleet: *see* **Prsvb, Admiral.**

Aella, Saint

❖ Rude Saxon swineherd who refused to drive out the Monastery pigs at Lent; when they died, he was killed by the bailiff, and, ultimately, canonized. May have given his name to St. Hall Friars, Hallbury, where **Dr. Dale** presides. (MB 45)

❖ Patron saint of the Home for Stiffnecked Clergy. (PE 47)

❖ Dr. Dale's successor as Rector of St. Hall Friars celebrates St. Aella's canonization in "a positively Romish way." (OBH 49)

Aelthwithric, Bishop of Barchester

❖ According to the doubtful testimony of a fragment of manuscript attributed to **Brother Diothermic** of **Saint Aella,** he went on pilgrimage to the Holy Land, taking with him most of the new Cathedral's cash and plate. He was never heard from again. His seat went unfilled for fifteen years, while the Cathedral's estates and revenues were looked after by **Lord Toothbane.** (HRt 52)

Aggie

❖ A small girl, named after **Lady Agnes Graham.** Her parents are cottagers for **the Leslies** at Rushwater, and her father, a laborer, is one of the best hedge-layers in the country. There are also three younger children, the last an illegitimate child of a sergeant at Brandon Abbas. (PBO 46)

Alberfylde, Bunyan, First Baron

❖ Father of **"Fifi," Mrs. C. Augustus Fortescue.** (BL 39)

Albert

❖ **Mr. Knox's Annie's** (and presumably also **Flo's**) brother, a footman for **Lord Stoke** at Rising Castle. Plays the mouth-organ and has a double-jointed thumb. (DH 34)

❖ Now Lord Stoke's coachman, drives the brougham. (ESR 55)

❖ Now butler/valet; his cousin is **Mrs. Panter,** who does laundry at Hatch End. (NTL 56)

❖ Was still a footman, and laughed out loud, when **Tony Morland** came to lunch at Rising Castle and kept all the pits from the cherry pie in his mouth. His mother won a prize at the Barchester Palais de Danse. (TSAT 61)

Alcock, Mrs.

❖ Housekeeper for **Lord and Lady Bond,** Staple Park. (BL 39)

Alcock, Ruby

❖ A showoff at Barchester High School when **Grace Grantly** was there. (TSAT 61)

Alf

❖ Village idiot of High Rising, result of a union between a nice girl (though distinctly wanting) and a small traveling salesman she knew as "the gentleman." Serves as odd man to **George Knox,** and made skipjacks for **Sibyl Knox** when she was small. (TSAT 61)

Allen, Nannie

✤ Mother of **Selina Allen**, retired nanny of the **Waring**
family. Daughter of a small farmer, she married a commercial traveller named Albert Allen very young. He drank
himself and his business into the grave in a couple of years.
As well as **Cecil and Leslie Waring**, she nursed the **Lufton**
children and **Octavia Crawley**. Now retired for ten years,
she lives at No. 1 Ladysmith Cottages near Beliers Priory,
and takes in **Tommy Needham** as a lodger. Her great-
niece is **Nurse** for the Marlings, and her great-nephew Sid
is a sergeant-major. (GU 43)

✤ Was known as Allie when she was temporary nurse to **Lord
Gerald Palliser**; his younger sister, **Lady Glencora Palliser**, remembers her. (DD 51)

✤ Had planned to move along with Selina when **Philip**
and **Leslie Waring Winter** take their school to Harefield,
but really commutes between there and her old cottage.
(JC 53)

Allen, Selina

✤ Daughter of **Nannie Allen**, who left her at the farm with
her grandparents while she went into service. Widow of a
Mr. Crockett, a middle-aged greengrocer in Blackheath.
She is nearer fifty than forty, with wildly curling hair.
Though pursued by **Private Tom Jenks** and by **Jasper
Margett**, she turns them down for **Sergeant Ted Hop-
kins**. (GU 43)

✤ Becomes cook for **Leslie and Philip Winter** at the Beliers
Priory School. (LAR 48)

* **Lydia Merton** gave her the silver button she'd gotten back from Jasper Margett; she told Hopkins, who threw it in the Dipping Pond. (DD 51)

* She, Hopkins, and her mother (part time) move to Harefield with the School. (JC 53)

Amanda

* An "exquisite creature," former receptionist at Maidenhair, the best hairdresser in Barchester; now works at the Regional Commissioner's Office with **John Leslie**. (MH 42)

Angus

* Gamekeeper to Lord and **Lady Ellangowan**; he amused **Ludovic, Lord Mellings**, when the **Pomfrets** visited during shooting season. (OBH 49)

Annie, Mr. Knox's

* Housekeeper to **George Knox**. Her sister, **Flo**, obliges at High Rising; her **Aunt** is **Mrs. Mallow, Dr. Ford's** housekeeper. (HR 33)

* Her younger brother **Albert** is footman to **Lord Stoke**. (DH 34)

* Mr. Knox had hoped she'd give notice after he married, but after a few difficulties, she recognized **Anne Todd** Knox as one of the ruling class and settled down. Her niece is **Odeena Panter**, who is as bad a parlormaid as she is a cook. (NTL 56)

* Her niece obliges for **Mrs. (Laura) Morland** when **Stoker** is out. Albert's mother (and so presumably hers) won a prize at the Barchester Palais de Danse. (TSAT 61)

Annie's Aunt, Mr. Knox's: *See* **Mallow, Mrs.**

Apperley, Miss
❖ Games mistress, Hosiers' Girls' Foundation School. (TH 44)

Appleyard, Mr.
❖ London landlord to **Aubrey Clover** and **Jessica Dean**. (WDIM 54)

Arabin, Dean and Mrs.
❖ Installed a bathroom in the Barchester Deanery ca. 1876 (*cf.* Trollope). (CBI 40)

Arbuckle, Imogen
❖ Student at Barchester High School. When told by **Miss Pettinger** to take the red polish off her nails, she does, but then puts blue ink on them. (OBH 49)

Arbuthnot, Mrs. Colonel (née Lily Elliman)
❖ Had a liaison with **Captain Frederick Brandon**, who gave her a diamond bracelet at Poona in 1876. (TB 39)

❖ Her son by him was probably named **Fred Arbuthnot**, and was the father of **Captain Fred** and **Miss (Effie) Arbuthnot**. Mr. Wickham knew her as the mother of a World War I Arbuthnot who was still good-looking in her late seventies. (PE 47)

Arbuthnot, Miss Effie (F.E., for Florence Edith)
❖ Older sister of **Captain Fred Arbuthnot** and sister-in-law of his widow **Peggy Arbuthnot**, with whom she moves into Editha Cottage, **Wiple** Terrace. A bird expert and painter, author of *Coot and Hern* and of a series of articles for *Country Life*. Now thirty-seven, she spent a year up-

country near her brother's regiment in India. Looks just like her father, who was probably named **Fred Arbuthnot**, and was the child of **Mrs. Colonel Arbuthnot** and **Captain Frederick Brandon**, which is why she also has a look of **Miss (Amelia) Brandon**. She turns down **Mr. Wickham** and accepts a proposal from **Colonel Crofts**. (PE 47)

❖ Doing pictures of birds for **Mr. Johns'** natural history series. (CC 50)

Arbuthnot, Captain Fred
❖ Left ten thousand pounds in **Miss (Amelia) Brandon's** will; he is under thirty. (TB 39)

❖ His mother and father died when he was young; the latter was probably also **Fred Arbuthnot**, and the son of **Mrs. Colonel Arbuthnot** and **Captain Frederick Brandon**. He and **Peggy** were engaged at his grandmother's, **Mrs. Colonel Arbuthnot**. Served in an Indian regiment, the 462nd. He played polo and ran through all his money, then borrowed his sister **Effie's**. But settled his ten thousand pounds from Miss Brandon's will on Peggy before he could spend it. Killed in a random shooting in Burma when he and Peggy had only been married a year. (PE 47)

Arbuthnot, Fred
❖ Military colleague of **Sir Harry Waring**, who was attached to his regiment in 1893, under **Colonel Bare**. Probably the same World War I Arbuthnot known by **Wickham**; he was the illegitimate son of **Mrs. Colonel Arbuthnot** and **Captain Frederick Brandon**, and father of **Captain Fred** and **Miss Effie Arbuthnot**. (PE 47)

Arbuthnot, Peggy

* Twenty-seven-year-old daughter of a retired Indian judge and an admiral's daughter, from Devonshire. Married to **Captain Fred Arbuthnot** for less than a year when he was killed; now living on the income from his ten thousand pound inheritance, which he settled on her. **Colin Keith** finds Editha Cottage in **Wiple** Terrace for her and her sister-in-law **Effie Arbuthnot** to share. When she had been at Umbrella in India, met **Aubrey Clover** and **Jessica Dean** on one of their wartime tours, when she took over the part of Mrs. Lupton in *Attitude to Life* from "**that dreadful Sonia**." Takes the dancing lead in the Red Cross Fete production of Aubrey's *Out Goes She*, opposite **Francis Brandon**, who afterwards proposes; she accepts. (PE 47)

* She is pregnant. (LAR 48)

* Again pregnant. (OBH 49)

* They married in autumn 1946, almost three years before; their first child was **Effie**, then came twins soon after. She and Francis repeat their Argentina Tango from *Out Goes She* for the Conservative Do at Gatherum. She cannot make him behave well toward his mother, however, with whom they are living. (CC 50)

* Francis is behaving badly toward her, but he is told off by **Lady Glencora Palliser**. Peggy gets rid of the Brandons' old nurse, **Miss Vance**, by sending her to Lady Cora, and gets **Bessie Thatcher** from Grumper's End as a replacement. (HRt 52)

* Pregnant yet again. (JC 53)

Archdeacon, the

* From Plumstead Episcopi. He has a **Daughter**. He served as English chaplain at Buenos Aires (where he knew the **Juan Robinsons**) for two years before coming to Barchester. Attends a weekend party at Pomfret Towers, where he argues with **Professor Milward**, criticizes **Mrs. (Hermione) Rivers'** book on Buenos Aires, and almost reads aloud from *The Pickwick Papers*. (PT 38)

* Dines with the **Crawley**s and complains about the West Barsetshire Pack. (CBI 40)

* His wife was a Rivers, as it turns out. (MH 42)

* Never loses his temper except when frost stops the hunting. (PE 47)

* He publishes the three hundred-page *Short Survey of the Religious and Lay Aspects of Glebe Land*, which neither people nor libraries buy, but Plumstead is a good living, and he has private means. (DD 51)

* He is renowned for having no sense of humor. (HRt 52)

Archdeacon's Daughter, the

* From Plumstead. An acquaintance of **Guy Barton's**, she meets him again at the weekend party at Pomfret Towers, where she gives tea and whiskey to his sister **Alice Barton** and tells about taking **Julian Rivers** to her club for drinks. (PT 38)

* Working on the land and training land girls. Engaged to Guy Barton. (CBI 40)

* Now married to Guy. Her mother was a Rivers. (MH 42)

Arden, the Reverend (by courtesy) Enoch
- ⁺ Pastor of Hallbury Ebenezer. He believes Greek and Latin to be works of the devil. Gives a Communist sermon that alienates **Sam Adams**. (MB 45)

- ⁺ While preaching a guest sermon at Hogglestock Beulah, compares the Hogglestock Anglican church to the Gates of Hell. (LAR 48)

- ⁺ Claims the right to christen **Amabel Rose Adams**, which Sam Adams refuses, but he gives him a check for his League of Christian Soviet Endeavor "made payable to bearer, as he looked half starved." (DD 51)

- ⁺ Loses Barchester for **Jeffrey Palliser** by leading his small party of Independent Cranks to vote Labour. (HRt 52)

Aunt, Miss Hopgood's: *See* **Hopgood, Mrs. Helen.**

Aunt, Mr. Knox's Annie's: *See* **Mallow, Mrs.**

Aurelio: *See* **Marco Aurelio.**

Badger, Miss
* ✣ Secretary to **John Leslie** in London. (WS 34)

Baker
* ✣ Maid to the **Warings**, Beliers Priory. (GU 43)

Baker, Major F.C.
* ✣ Secretary of the Ullathorne Golf Club. The card on his church pew has "M.C. with bar" after his name. (HRt 52)

Baker, Mrs.
* ✣ Former housekeeper to the **Leslies** at Rushwater, famed for her bad temper. Now retired to Folkestone, where she has **Conque** to visit for the holidays. Conque plans to move in with her. (OBH 49)

* ✣ She and Conque are apparently quarreling, but that is usual. (ESR 55)

Balder
 * Former estate plumber to the **Pallisers**, Gatherum Castle. (CC 50)

Banister, Mr.
 * Vicar of St. Mary's Church, Rushwater; lets his house to the **Boulles** for August. (WS 34)

 * Canon of Barchester. (MH 42)

 * His mother was a paying guest at **Mrs. Merivale's**. (MB 45)

 * Goes everywhere on a bicycle. (PBO 46)

Bank Manager, a Local
 * Pompous, self-satisfied, and too ready to divulge his bank's concerns. Addresses the rally to save **Wiple** Terrace and reveals that Paul's College does intend to sell it, with the prospective buyer being **Sir Ogilvy Hibberd's** (a.k.a. Lord Aberfordbury's) National Rotochrome Polychrome Universal Picture Postcard Company. The Bank Manager later turns out to have invested heavily in that company, but Wiple Terrace is saved by **Sam Adams'** syndicate. (TSAT 61)

Banks, Miss
 * Due to the wartime shortage of teachers, she teaches elementary Latin at Southbridge School, but hasn't got the slightest idea about Latin metrics or quantities (and is notorious for mispronouncing "Uranus"). Alienates everyone and is ultimately fired. (PBO 46)

 * Now in a highly lucrative job with UNESCO in Paris. She bullies her secretary, who adores her. (PE 47)

❖ Joined the Pan European Union for General Interference, but had an argument with **Geoffrey Harvey** and was fired. (LAR 48)

Banton, Old Mrs.

❖ A permanent invalid, gone gaga; cared for by **Nurse Ward**. (NTL 56)

Barabbas College, the President (or Master) of

❖ Of Oxford; attends **Rose Birkett's** wedding. He is the husband, of course, of the **Wife of the President of Barabbas**. (CBI 40)

❖ Now he is Master of the College. (TH 44)

Barabbas College, the Wife of the Master of

❖ Of Oxford. She has a practice of sleeping outdoors on a camp bed in warm weather; in his student days, **Mr. (Bill) Birkett** stumbled over her one morning and had to report to the Dean of his College about it. (CBI 40)

❖ She does folk dancing and gets a special chair in Romano-Lydian culture created for **Dr. (Ph.) Professor Kropóv**. (TH 44)

❖ She wears a mackintosh (much like the **Wife of the Master of Lazarus**). (JC 53)

Barchester Chronicle, the Young Man from the

❖ Reporting on the wedding of **Miss Merriman** and **Mr. Herbert Choyce**, he tries to keep notes in his head and has to be straightened out by **Sir Robert Graham**, whom he misidentifies as **Caxton**. (ADA 57)

Barclay, (Mrs.) Lettice: *See* **Watson, Mrs. Lettice.**

Barclay, Captain Tom
* From Yorkshire. His mother, **Dora Stoke**, is a distant relation of **Lord Stoke**; his father died recently. He has sisters. His unit disarms unexploded bombs. **Lucy Marling** brings him home, but he proposes to her widowed sister **Lettice Watson** and is accepted. (MH 42)

* Unable to lecture on bombs to convalescents at Beliers Priory. (GU 43)

* They are living in Yorkshire with her children, **Diana** and **Clare Watson**. (MB 45)

* He is now a farmer, and they have two more children, both boys. (CC 50)

Bare, Colonel
* Commander of **Fred Arbuthnot's** regiment in '93; **Sir Harry Waring** remembers them as the Polar Bears. (PE 47)

Barton, Alice
* Younger daughter of **Mr. (Walter) and Mrs. (Susan) Barton**. A painter, delicate and nervous; her parents make her go to the weekend party at Pomfret Towers, where she falls in, and later out of, love with **Julian Rivers**, and is befriended by **Phoebe Rivers**. She is informally engaged to **Roddy Wicklow**. (PT 38)

* Engaged to Roddy. (BL 39)

* Married. (CBI 40)

* They have two children. (GU 43)

* Now three small children, several dogs and some puppies. (PE 47)

* The **Wicklow** children are **Guy, Phoebe**, and **young Alice** in the pram. They live at Nutfield. (OBH 49)

* Phoebe and young Alice have measles. Their Nanny's brother used to be the butler at Pomfret Towers (**Peters**). (WDIM 54)

* Their Nutfield house is the one his parents lived in. All the children are currently at **Miss Vance's** Small Child Hotel at the seaside (though Guy and Phoebe must be at least sixteen!) (LAAA 59)

* She illustrates the remembrance album presented to **Mrs. (Laura) Morland**. All the children are now young adults. (TSAT 61)

Barton, Guy

* Elder son of **Mr. (Walter)** and **Mrs. (Susan) Barton**. Works in his father's architectural firm, Barton and Wicklow. Due to his mother's enthusiasms, almost christened Ippolito. Attends the weekend party at Pomfret Towers with his sister **Alice**; becomes engaged, then unengaged, to **Phoebe Rivers**. (PT 38)

* Now in the R.A.F. Once Phoebe Rivers married, he got engaged to the **Archdeacon's daughter** from Plumstead. (CBI 40)

* Married to the Archdeacon's daughter. (MH 42)

* Now an architect, in partnership with his father. (LAAA 59)

Barton, Mrs. Susan

❖ Wife of **Mr. (Walter) Barton**, of Mellings (the Pomfret dower house). Mother of **Guy** and **Alice**. Author of erudite historical novels, mainly on Renaissance themes. Before her marriage and his death, she was a close friend to **Harry, Lord Mellings**. (PT 38)

Barton, Mr. Walter

❖ Husband of **Mrs. (Susan) Barton**, of Mellings (the Pomfret dower house). Father of **Guy** and **Alice**. Senior partner of the architectural firm Barton and Wicklow. The family owns an old Scotch terrier, Penny. (PT 38)

❖ He is doing the repairs to Hiram's Hospital. (BL 39)

❖ The opening ceremonies for his new building there are soon to occur. (CBI 40)

❖ His father was also an architect, and renovated Boon's Benefit in Winter Overcotes for the railway company. (GU 43)

❖ He writes *Minor Domestic Architecture of East Barset*. (PE 47)

❖ He and Mrs. Barton go to Italy. (OBH 49)

❖ His father and he have been architects to the **Beltons** at Harefield House. (CQ 58)

Bateman

❖ **Colonel Crofts'** former batman, now factotum. A farmer's son and Associate Member of the Loyal Band of Old Juvenile Bellboys. Succeeds **Old Propett** as sexton of Southbridge, though forbidden to ring the passing bell for him. Walking out with **Eileen** of the Red Lion. (PE 47)

* Now married to Eileen, but misidentified as "ex-corporal Jackson" (*see* **Corporal Arthur Fishguard Jackson**). (CC 50)

* Learns cricket in a few weeks, so as to oblige at the Southbridge School Cricket Match. (NTL 56)

B

Beak, Miss
* Of the Morleena Domestic Enquiry Bureau, Winter Overcotes. (GU 43)

Bear, Colonel: *See* **Bare, Colonel**.

Beasley, Commander
* Royal Navy (retired). Now of Tork Cottage. Plays a victim of gas attack for **Mrs. (Minnie) Paxon's** casualty practice drill. (NR 41)

* His service was during World War I. A member of the British Needlers. To play Sir Walter Raleigh in the Northbridge Pageant of History for the Coronation celebrations. (WDIM 54)

Beckett, the Reverend Anselm
* Husband of **Tertia Crawley**, daughter of **Dean** and **Mrs. Crawley**. (HRt 52)

Bedale, Lisa
* Anagrammatic pseudonym used by **Isabel Dale** to write thrillers (such as *Aconite at Night*) featuring the detective **Gerry Marston**. (CC 50)

Beedle
* His uncle was **Mr. Beedle** the stationmaster. He was taken on by **Sir Harry Waring** as knife-and-odd-job man at

Beliers Priory. After Sir Harry's death, he went as a kind of
butler to Pomfret Towers, where his aunt worked. (LAAA
59)

Beedle, Henry

❖ Son of **Mr.** and **Mrs. Beedle**, made a prisoner of war after
Dunkirk. His godfather is **Sir Harry Waring**. (GU 43)

❖ Formerly of the Barsetshires, now returned from five years
of farm work while a prisoner; gets a job with **Lucy Marling** on **Sam Adams'** land. (OBH 49)

Beedle, Mr.

❖ Husband of **Mrs. Beedle**, father of **Henry**, and Station
Master of Winter Overcotes. They live in River Rising
cottage on Boon's Benefit, which was bought by the railway company. His mother is still alive. Bemoans the theft
of the station Cup, but gets it back when he lets **Bill
Morple** off. (GU 43)

❖ Retired. (OBH 49)

❖ His nephew is **Beedle**. (LAAA 59)

Beedle, Mrs.

❖ Wife of **Mr. Beedle**, and mother of **Henry**, of River Rising
cottage, Boon's Benefit. Was once nurserymaid under
Nannie Allen for **George Waring**. Her mother died at
ninety-five and would never wear her false teeth. (GU 43)

Beeton, Mrs.

❖ Cook to **Lord Stoke**. Has a leg, and a sister in Eastbourne.
Her leg gets so bad that she has to go to Barchester General
in an ambulance. (TSAT 61)

Bellenden, Esmé

* Author of *Men of Harlech*, a Banned Book of the Month. When asked if Esmé is a man or a woman, **Miss Bent** says "I couldn't possibly say, and what is more, I don't suppose anyone could." (CBI 40)

Bellinger

* Boy at Southbridge School. Keeps a dormouse. (PE 47)

Belton, Charles Thorne

* Youngest son of **Mr. (Fred)** and **Mrs. (Lucy) Belton**. In army artillery, doing Triple-A (anti-anti-anti-tanks) at Shrimpington-on-Sea. His Aunt Mary (presumably his father's sister), who changed her will every year, left him two hundred pounds. He leaves for the front. (TH 44)

* Now around twenty-five, he left the army as a Captain. Gets a job teaching at the Beliers Priory School, where he moons over **Lady Agnes Graham** and bosses her daughter **Clarissa Graham**. His great-uncle **Old Charles** left him a hundred pounds. (LAR 48)

* He helps Clarissa upon the death of her grandmother, **Lady Emily Leslie**. (OBH 49)

* He becomes informally engaged to Clarissa. (CC 50)

* Formally engaged to Clarissa. (DD 51)

* His father makes over some capital to him; he and Clarissa are married by special license on New Year's Day. They go to the **Pomfrets'** villa at Cap Ferrat for their honeymoon. (HRt 52)

* Clarissa is pregnant. (ESR 55)

❖ They have one child. (NTL 56)

❖ They have a fat little boy and an excellent small girl. (CQ 58)

Belton, Mrs. Clarissa: *See* **Graham, Clarissa.**

Belton, Elsa

❖ Middle daughter of **Mr. (Fred)** and **Mrs. (Lucy) Belton.** Twenty-five years old, doing hush-hush war work in Dept. ZQY83. Engaged to **Christopher Hornby,** and wants him to lend her father the money to get the Hosiers' Girls' Foundation School out of Harefield Park, but both of them discourage her. She and Christopher are married by special license. (TH 44)

❖ Pregnant, with **Nurse Chiffinch** in attendance. (MB 45)

❖ They have a girl, **Catriona,** and a boy, **Freddy.** (LAR 48)

❖ She has a third child, again with Nurse Chiffinch for the month. (DD 51)

Belton, Mr. Fred

❖ Husband of **Mrs. (Lucy) Belton,** father of **Freddy, Elsa,** and **Charles.** Of Harefield Park. He is the sixth Belton since **(Belton) the Nabob,** one hundred fifty years before. Sisters **Elsa** and **Mary.** His mother lived to age ninety-three. The family moves to Arcot House and rents Harefield Park to the Hosiers' Girls' Foundation School. (TH 44)

❖ His little pigs win at the Pig Breeders' Show and Conservative Rally at Staple Park. Considers selling some land to **Sam Adams.** His mother, while in her dotage, mistook him for his uncle **Old Charles.** (LAR 48)

* They hold the August meeting of the Barsetshire Archaeological at Harefield. He sells land for a new school to the
Hosiers' Girls' Foundation; when they move, **Philip Winter** will move his school from Beliers Priory into Harefield
House. (DD 51)

* His father built a dower house for *his* bullying old mother.
He makes over some capital to his children, mainly to
Charles, as the others are well-off. (HRt 52)

* He went to Rugby and then to King's, where he got a
second. (CQ 58)

Belton, Freddy

* Eldest son of **Mr. (Fred)** and **Mrs. (Lucy) Belton**. Commander in the Royal Navy, first of H.M.S. *Gridiron*, then
H.M.S. *Barsetshire*. Was engaged to a **Wren**, but she was
killed in an air raid. He tells **Heather Adams** about this
after he rescues her from her fall through the ice in the lake.
(TH 44)

* Now thirty-eight and a Captain, working at the Admiralty.
Courts and wins **Susan Dean**. (LAR 48)

* Now married, they live on second floor of Arcot House
with his parents. They expect a baby in August. (OBH 49)

* The baby is very satisfactory. (CC 50)

* He is still at Admiralty in London. They moved to Dowlah
Cottage after **Mrs. Hoare** died. Their son is named **Frederick**, but called Baby to avoid confusion. (DD 51)

* They now have a daughter as well. (HRt 52)

* He is now a rear admiral with several letters after his name.
(CQ 58)

B

✦ They live at Harefield and have another baby, a boy. (TSAT 61)

Belton, Mrs. Freddy: *See* **Dean, Susan**.

Belton, Frederick
  ✦ Proper name of the eldest son of **Susan Dean** and **Freddy Belton**, though he is called Baby to avoid confusion. (DD 51)

Belton, Mrs. Lucy (née Thorne)
  ✦ Wife of **Mr. (Fred) Belton**, mother of **Freddy, Elsa**, and **Charles**. Of Harefield Park. Of the Thornes of Ullathorne, she is a distant relation of **Lady Edith Pomfret**. The family moves to Arcot House and rents Harefield Park to the Hosiers' Girls' Foundation School. (TH 44)

  ✦ She has some connection to **Lucy Marling**'s maternal grandfather, **Lord Nutfield**. (DD 51)

Belton, the Nabob
  ✦ Founder of the Belton family fortune and buyer of Harefield Park from the **Milburds**, one hundred fifty years ago. The present **Mr. (Fred) Belton** is sixth in line from him. In his old age he took a French mistress, who hired a French architect to build the Garden House at Harefield, then ran away with him and a lot of jewelry. (TH 44)

  ✦ The Nabob had dissipated most of his fortune on her. (CC 50)

  ✦ He also built "the Nabob" (or "Nabob's Head"), now a pub, as a house for her. His son used to write him begging letters from the Continent. (HRt 52)

❖ If he is the one for whom Harefield House was built, his name was Frederick Belton, Esq., Armiger; but *see* above, and **the Milburds**. (CQ 58)

Belton, (Mrs.) Susan: *See* **Dean, Susan.**

Benny

❖ Former boxing instructor at Upper School, Southbridge; once a great army boxer. (HR 33)

Benson

❖ A man **Colin Keith** and **Robin Dale** knew at Sadd-el-Bakk in Africa; he collected butterflies and had hair growing out of his ears. (PE 47)

Benson, Mr.

❖ Vicar of Southbridge for thirty years, about sixty years ago; a port-drinking, fox-hunting parson. (PE 47)

Bent, Miss

❖ She and her dear friend **Miss Hampton** share Adelina Cottage, **Wiple** Terrace. They change their dog's name according to who's being gallant in the war. (CBI 40)

❖ They bring their nanny goat Pelléas to the Hallbury Cottage Hospital Bring and Buy Sale. (MB 45)

❖ They give a farewell party for **Mr.** and **Mrs. Bissell** of the Hosiers' Boys' Foundation School. (PBO 46)

❖ Now the dog is just named Gallant. (PE 47)

❖ Now he's Amethyst (but still gallant). (CC 50)

❖ After having been Churchill twice, the dog is No Name. They cruise the Greek islands, having learned that Paphos is an anagram for Sappho. (JC 53)

* She directs efforts to defend Wiple Terrace from being absorbed by **Sir Ogilvy Hibberd**, now Lord Aberfordbury. (TSAT 61)

Benton, Mr.

* London dentist who made false teeth for **Mr. (Harold) Downing, Colonel Passmore**, and **Mr. (Gregory) Villars**. (NR 41)

Bertha

* Was head housemaid (of three) at Rushwater in **Mr. (Henry) Leslie's** days, and is still there. (PBO 46)

Bertha

* Middle-aged, in service at Pomfret Towers; sister of a former boot-and-knife boy there (perhaps **Finch**?). (ADA 57)

Betterton, Lady

* Dowdy but immensely rich customer of **Scatcherd's** Stores. (NR 41)

Betts, Mrs.

* She rents out a room for the Clothing Exchange, thus provoking the ire of **Madame Tomkins**. (PBO 46)

Betty

* Young friend of **Francis** and **Delia Brandon**; says "ack-cherly" a great deal. (TB 39)

* Turns out to be the niece of **Mrs. (Poppy) Turner**. She and her sister, the **Other Niece**, were taken in by Mrs. Turner when their parents died of influenza. She becomes engaged to **Captain Topham**. (NR 41)

❖ Married and living in Hacken's Fen, Norfolk. Mrs. Turner goes to live with her, and **Effie Arbuthnot** comes for the birdwatching. (PE 47)

Beverley, Fritz
❖ Naval friend of **Wickham**, with whom he exchanged grips. (LAAA 59)

le Biau, Guibert
❖ Author of the *Andalhou*, edited by "**Numa Garagou**"; see **M. Bontemps**. (CC 50)

Bill
❖ A young man in the Navy; recently torpedoed, plays the ocarina. Visits the **Phelps'** house with **Tubby Smith-Hetherington**. (CBI 40)

Bill, Mrs.: *See* Marling, Mrs. Bill.

Billie
❖ Model and all-round slave for **Julian Rivers'** idol, the great artist **Bolikoff**. She died before she could see his great work representing her emotional effect upon him. (PT 38)

Bingham, Bobby
❖ **Dorothy Bingham** was offended when he gave his niece (presumably one of her twin daughters) a corkscrew as a wedding present. (HRt 52)

Bingham, Dorothy ("Dodo")
❖ A widow, daughter of a Duke; mother of twin girls **Rose** and **Hermione,** and of three sons in the Army. A cousin of **Lady Emily Leslie.** A stalwart gardener and fox-hunter. Her nephew can't go to Munich because of the Nazis. (WS 34)

* She is the second daughter of the **Duke of Towers** and of a Miss Foster, who was cousin of the **Sixth Earl of Pomfret**. (PBO 46)

* Her husband was in big business. Rose's first child is named for her. (LAR 48)

* She was offended when **Bobby Bingham** gave his niece a corkscrew as a wedding present. (HRt 52)

* Now deceased. (ESR 55)

* She had been **David Leslie's** second cousin once removed as well as his mother-in-law. (ADA 57)

Bingham, Hermione

* Younger twin daughter of **Dorothy "Dodo" Bingham**, fair-haired while her sister **Rose** is dark. Married **Lord Tadpole**, of Tadpole Hall, Tadcaster, just before the war. Has one daughter. (PBO 46)

* Now four babies; the most recent to be christened at Tadcaster, where his cousin has a living. (LAR 48)

* One of the children, a girl, was a seven-month preemie; **Nurse Chiffinch** came in to help. (CC 50)

* They have Nurse Chiffinch for the holidays in Shropshire. (HRt 52)

* They have **Rose** and **David Leslie's** children to stay with them. (ESR 55)

Bingham, Rose

* Elder twin daughter of **Dorothy "Dodo" Bingham**, dark-haired while her sister **Hermione** is fair. Works in the Foreign Office, at the Embassy in Paris. Traveled abroad extensively during the war, while her faithful maid kept her

flat in Paris. Has also gone out intermittently with **David Leslie**; now she is posted home, and they become engaged. (PBO 46)

❖ Now living in Paris; two children, **Dorothy ("Dodo")** and **Henry**. (LAR 48)

❖ Now in America, where they can leave Dodo (now seven) and Henry (six) with **Martin Leslie's** mother when they travel. They invite **Edith Graham** to stay with them. (ESR 55)

❖ The children, aged about ten, are at camp. They all live a very rootless life in America. (ADA 57)

Birkett, Mrs. Amy ("Ma Birky")
❖ Wife of **Mr. (Bill) Birkett**, mother of **Rose** and **Geraldine**. Presides over Southbridge School, and has a dog, Sylvia. She routs **Una Grey**. (HR 33)

❖ They get Rose married. (CBI 40)

❖ They bring **Robin Dale** back to Southbridge to teach. (MB 45)

❖ They host a school sports day; Rose comes back to visit. (PBO 46)

❖ They retire to the Dower House, Worsted. She has a niece in Kensington. (PE 47)

❖ They are now living at the Dower House. (LAR 48)

Birkett, Mr. Bill
❖ Husband of **Mrs. (Amy) Birkett**, father of **Rose** and **Geraldine**. Headmaster of Southbridge Lower School. **Una Grey** was formerly his secretary. (HR 33)

* The year before, he was promoted to become headmaster of the Upper School. He hires **Colin Keith**. He and his wife spend the holidays and summer at the **Villars'** Northbridge Rectory. He is the author of *Determination of Logical Causality*. His name is given as Henry. (SH 37)

* They finally get Rose married. He was at Oxford with **Dean Crawley**. (CBI 40)

* Brings **Robin Dale** back to Southbridge to teach. (MB 45)

* They host school sports day; Rose comes back to visit. (PBO 46)

* He presides over his last Speech Day; they retire to the Dower House, Worsted, where he will work on his edition of the *Analects* of **Procrastinator**. (PE 47)

* Now at the Dower House. (LAR 48)

* His book due out in autumn. (HRt 52)

* Book published by Oxbridge. (JC 53)

* **Mrs. (Laura) Morland** tells **Everard Carter** that "whoever it was that wrote a book about the *Analects* of Procrastinator whoever he was" had his name put down for a Lloyd George knighthood, but made a row about it till they gave him an O.M. (LAAA 59)

Birkett, Geraldine
* Younger daughter of **Mr. (Bill)** and **Mrs. (Amy) Birkett**, "off somewhere to learn the language," along with her sister **Rose**. (HR 33)

* In **Lydia Keith's** form at Barchester High School. (SH 37)

* Bridesmaid at Rose's wedding; does Red Cross with **Delia Brandon** at the Barchester Infirmary. She is infatuated with the unworthy **Fritz Gissing**, but gets engaged to **Geoff Fairweather**. (CBI 40)

* Living in an out-of-the-way cottage while Geoff is in Libya; unhappy because she can't get a nurse for her son **John** and so can't go back to the Red Cross. (GU 43)

* Now has a good nanny. (PBO 46)

* Now has two babies and again can't get any help. (PE 47)

Birkett, Rose Felicity
* Elder daughter of **Mr. (Bill)** and **Mrs. (Amy) Birkett**, "off somewhere to learn the language," along with her sister **Geraldine**. (HR 33)

* A handful. At sixteen, engaged to **Mr. Smalley**, the art master of Barchester High School. When sent to school in Munich, she got engaged to an officer (**Lieutenant von Storck**) and a band conductor (**Herr Lob**) at the same time. She comes home and gets engaged to **Philip Winter**, but breaks it off by throwing her ring at him. (SH 37)

* Engaged and finally married to Lieutenant **John Fairweather**. They go to Las Palombas. News soon follows of a baby due in August. (CBI 40)

* They are in Washington. Their children are **Henry** and **Amy**, and another is due in June. (GU 43)

* They are now in Portugal, and have had their third child. (MB 45)

* Now back in England, with a flat in Lowndes Square. (PBO 46)

* She can't attend her father's last Speech Day due to the imminent birth of their fourth child, who is named **Mary** (not, as Rose wished, Glamora). (PE 47)

* Stayed with the **Luftons** and left a terrible mess in her bedroom; hears **Eric Swan's** lecture and confuses Sir Walter Scott with Scott of the Antarctic. (HRt 52)

* Now renting the **Umblebys'** house at Greshamsbury. Organizes the Friends of the **Phelpses**. Her boys (but *see* above) are at school, her two youngest (both girls) at home with a nanny. (JC 53)

* She will play the role of Britannia in the Naval Pageant at Greshamsbury. (WDIM 54)

* Her first child was born in 1940, the last in 1946; despite the names above (Henry, Amy, ?, and Mary), the two youngest are girls, "the two elder are probably boys." (CQ 58)

Bishop of Barchester, the

* Both he and his **Wife** are wrong in every way; low church, pink and stingy. Gives a reception for colonial bishops at which he allots ten to every bottle of champagne. As in 1936, his cellar floods. (CBI 40)

* Presides at dedication of Barchester High School hall as a recreation hall for convalescent soldiers. (GU 43)

* Makes an anti-classics speech in the House of Lords; skips Bobbin Day at the Hosiers' Girls' Foundation School. (TH 44)

* He disciplines the **Precentor** for using extra petrol. (MB 45)

* They have one depressing **son** in the Mission Field, with an office in Westminster. He gives a radio broadcast on "Our Duty to a Penitent Foe." They turn the Palace wine cooler into a planter. (PBO 46)

* He gives a broadcast about Sweden entitled "Germans in Human Shape." Goes to Zurich to promote unity between Mixo- and Slavo-Lydia. (LAR 48)

* They have no children (but *see* PBO 46, above). He has celebrated his twenty-fifth year as a clergyman. They have to go away while the Palace cesspool is repaired. (OBH 49)

* They give their usual summer garden party, then go to the Casa Higginbottom in Florence. While at college with **Isabel Dale's** father, he was known as Old Gasbags. (CC 50)

* Their planned cruise to Madiera is put off until after the general election. They finally sail on the *Anubis*, which runs into rough weather off North Africa, but unfortunately arrives safely. (HRt 52)

* They put on a mystery play in the Cathedral crypt for the Coronation. They go to dinner at the **Crawleys'**; this is their first actual, rather than rumored, appearance. (WDIM 54)

* She has the old blackout curtains made into extra aprons for him. (NTL 56)

* He gives a second-hand copy of his book about their cruise to Madiera to **Miss Merriman** as a wedding present. He gets a cold at **Grace** and **Jane Crawley's** wedding. (ADA 57)

* He gives shipboard talks on "The Mediterranean Culture" so that they can get a cheap Hellenic cruise. Their lawyers are **Stringer**, not **Keith** and Keith. (CQ 58)

* Rumored to be thinking of resigning and taking the sine-cure of **St. Aella's** Home for Stiff-Necked Clergy. (LAAA 59)

* Will be away for a Diocesan Conference at Easter, so **Ludovic Foster, Lord Mellings,** plans his wedding for that time. They skip the Crawleys' dinner party to make a ceremonial visit to Nkrumah in Ghana, and then are detained there. (TSAT 61)

Bishop of Mngangaland, the: *See* **Joram, Bishop.**

Bishopess, the: *See* **Bishop's Wife, the.**

Bishop's Son, the
* He is depressing, and works in the mission field, with an office in Westminster. (LAR 48)

* Now his parents are said to be childless. (OBH 49)

Bishop's Wife, the
* A true counterpart of her husband, the **Bishop of Barchester**. Attends dedication of the Barchester High School hall as a recreation hall for convalescent soldiers; she and **Miss Pettinger** are bosom friends. (GU 43)

* She gives the prizes at Barchester High School. (MB 45)

* They have one depressing **son** in the Mission Field, with an office in Westminster. They turn the Palace wine cooler into a planter. (PBO 46)

* When she is rude to **Aubrey Clover** at the Perpetual Curates' Benefit Fund Charity Matinee, he extemporizes a song, "I took my husband's gaiters off and put them on myself." (LAR 48)

* They have no children (but *see* PBO 46, above). They have to go away while the Palace cesspool is repaired. (OBH 49)

* They give their usual summer garden party, then go to the Casa Higginbottom in Florence. (CC 50)

* Their planned cruise to Madiera is put off until after the general election. They finally sail on the *Anubis*, which runs into rough weather off North Africa, but unfortunately arrives safely. (HRt 52)

* They put on a mystery play in the Cathedral crypt for the Coronation. They go to dinner at the **Crawleys'**. (WDIM 54)

* She has the old blackout curtains made into extra aprons for him. (NTL 56)

* They go on a cheap Hellenic cruise. (CQ 58)

* She opposed **Lord William Harcourt's** taking his current clerical living. (LAAA 59)

* They skip the Crawleys' dinner party because she wants to make a ceremonial visit to Nkrumah in Ghana, and they are detained there. (TSAT 61)

Bissell, Mrs. Elaine

* Wife of **Mr. Bissell**, Headmaster of the Hosiers' Boys' Foundation School. No children; of 27 Condiment Road, E48, London. She was a teacher and studied psychology.

When the school is evacuated to Southbridge, they rent
Maria Cottage, **Wiple** Terrace. They keep a feeble-
minded niece of a niece, **Edna**. Their London circle includes **Mr. and Mrs. Lefroy** of the Technical School, **Mr.
and Mrs. Jobson** of the Chemical Works, **Mr. Pecker** from
the Free Library and his daughter. (CBI 40)

٭ As **"Mr. and Mrs. Bissett"** they are given a farewell party
by **Miss Hampton** and **Miss Bent**, as the school is returning to London. (PBO 46)

٭ They return for **Mr. Birkett's** final Speech Day. Now
described as a great-niece, Edna is in the Ada Clotworthy
Mental Institution. (PE 47)

٭ They become tenants of **Joyce Perry Smith**. (CC 50)

٭ She attends the rally to defend Wiple Terrace from being
bought by **Lord Aberfordbury**. (TSAT 61)

Bissell, Mr.

٭ About thirty-five, husband of **Mrs. (Elaine) Bissell**, no
children; of 27 Condiment Road, E48, London. Headmaster of the Hosiers' Boys' Foundation School. When the
school is evacuated to Southbridge, they rent Maria Cottage, **Wiple** Terrace. They keep a feeble-minded niece of a
niece, **Edna**. Member of the Isle of Dogs Left Wing
Athenaeum. Their London circle includes **Mr. and Mrs.
Lefroy** of the Technical School, **Mr. and Mrs. Jobson** of
the Chemical Works, **Mr. Pecker** from the Free Library
and his daughter. He calls on the **Birketts** on **Rose's**
wedding day, but **Geraldine** keeps calling him **"Mr.
Gristle."** (CBI 40)

❖ As **"Mr. and Mrs. Bissett"** they are given a farewell party by **Miss Hampton** and **Miss Bent**, as the school is returning to London. (PBO 46)

❖ They return for **Mr. (Bill) Birkett's** final Speech Day. Now described as a great-niece, Edna is in the Ada Clotworthy Mental Institution. As a youth, he raced earwigs at the Isle of Dogs Polytechnic. (PE 47)

❖ They become tenants of **Joyce Perry Smith**. (CC 50)

Bissett, Mr.: *See* **Mr. Bissell.**

Black, Miss
❖ Serves at the lending library, Gaiters; tells **Lord Crosse's** secretary all about the **Bishop's wife's** bad taste in books. (NTL 56)

Blackstone, Mr.
❖ Master of the prep school attended by **Oliver Marling** and **Ludovic, Lord Lufton**. He took orders and is now a Rural Dean in Loamshire. Has tufts of hair in his ears. (DD 51)

Blumenfeld, Nat
❖ New York producer of **Denis Stonor's** musical shows. (LAR 48)

❖ There is a film offer for their latest show. (TSAT 61)

Bob, Mrs.: *See* **Bronson-Hewbury, the Honourable Clara.**

Bobbums: *See* **Spender, Major.**

Bobby: *See* **"Copper."**

Boccafiume, Cardinal

✤ Descendant of the Borgia family; friend of **Mrs. (Susan) Barton**. (PT 38)

✤ Helped **Professor Milward** with the Italian side of the **Pomfret** history. (LAAA 59)

Bodger, Mrs. (presumably)

✤ The **Millers'** cook at St. Ewold's is a Bodger from Grumper's End. She lives in, and locks her door at night, taking precautions in case anyone should try to Get Her; but this scenario is unlikely, as she is very plain and the same size all the way down. (HRt 52)

Bodger, Old

✤ Of Starveacres Hatches. Ratcatcher to the gentry and to Pomfret Towers, as was his father before him. (TH 44)

✤ Now of Harefield. (MB 45)

✤ Now almost seventy-five. He is a cousin of **Miss Hoggett's** mother's half-brother. (OBH 49)

Bodger, Old Percy

✤ Son of **Old Bodger** and father of **Young Percy Bodger**; now dead. He was an expert on wells. (OBH 49)

Bodger, Young Percy

✤ Grandson of **Old Bodger** and son of **Old Percy Bodger**. Gets bricks out of the Hallbury Rectory well for the Barsetshire Archaeological meeting. (MB 45)

✤ With assistance from **the Boy**, cleans out the well at the Old Bank House. He got **Nannie Twicker's** cat out of a well at Northbridge, and **Horace Tidden's** body from one on Pomfret land. (OBH 49)

Bohun, the Rev. Thomas

❖ Canon of Barchester from 1657 to 1665, Doctor of Divinity and erotic poet. Author of "The Worme of the Flesh and the Worme of the Spirit" and "To his Mistress, on Seeing Sundrie Worme-castes." Died as a result of his rash journey to London to observe the Plague. Subject of a study by **Oliver Marling**. (MH 42)

❖ He willed money to Boon's Benefit foundation for old vergers, sextons, and cathedral servants in Winter Overcotes (Overcotes Palace was the pre-reformation summer residence of the Bishops of Barchester). (GU 43)

❖ There is a proposal to erect a small chapel in the Cathedral in his honor. (PE 47)

❖ There is now a commemorative tablet to him, composed by **Dean Crawley**, in the Cathedral. (LAR 48)

❖ He studied Rosicrucianism. Oliver Marling collates his 1665 edition with the **Duke of Omnium's** 1668 edition, with special attention to the "Sonnet on his Mistress's Pox." Oliver's work is being considered for publication by **Adrian Coates**. (CC 50)

❖ Oliver's opuscule is printed privately. (DD 51)

❖ The object of his verses turns out to have been **Mistress Pomphelia Tadstock**. (ESR 55)

Bolikoff

❖ Russian artist, now of Camden Town. Had been supported by his late model, **Billie**. Unique object of **Julian Rivers'** respect, he did a rather disgusting book jacket for **Sasha Menski's** *Worm that Eateth the Flesh*. **Mrs. (Susan) Barton**

knew and disliked him in Florence, where he borrowed lots
of money in small sums and never paid it back. (PT 38)

* Does the determinist decor for a ballet, "Les centaures et
les Lapithes." (TB 39)

Bolton, the Marquess and Marchioness of
* Parents of Lady Iris and lady Phyllis, whom **Miss Bunting**
had to keep out of the way the week the Budget came out.
He dislikes **Mr. Holt** and won't let him come see the
garden. (MB 45)

Bolton Abbey, the Lady who lived at
* A nice dull woman who lived in an ugly red-brick house
and had working parties during the war; owned a cat,
Milly. (PE 47)

Bond, Alured, Lord
* Husband of **Lucasta, Lady Bond**; father of **the Honourable
Cedric Weyland Bond**. Of Staple Park. Famous for voting
against the third clause of the Root Vegetables Bill. He
keeps **Mr. (Henry) Leslie's** bull overtime, and it frightens
Jessica Dean. (AF 36)

* His family's line of Saxon names is the result of his great-
great-grandfather **Jedediah Bond's** conviction that he was
a direct descendant of King Alfred. He has more money
than he knows what to do with. Bought Laverings Farm
out from under **Sir Ogilvy Hibberd**, and rented it on a long
lease to **Mr. (John) Middleton**. Backs **Denis Stonor's**
ballet. (BL 39)

* Lectures convalescent soldiers on the Middle East. (GU
43)

* Staple Park is now let to a school, while they live in a small house on the estate. (MB 45)

* He is now a Liberal. (PBO 46)

* Now living in part of Staple Park's servants' wing, so he could fire his tyrannous butler, **Spencer**. They give a combined Conservative Rally and Pig Breeders' Show, where he has a reunion with Denis Stonor. (LAR 48)

* Reference to a "young Lady Bond" should indicate that he has died, but *see* the following. (CC 50)

* As Lord Bond, "the great cow magnate," attends the Barsetshire Archaeological. (DD 51)

* Has a grandson, **Young Bond**, about whom he and Lady Bond are great worriers. (HRt 52)

* Must have died, as his wife is identified as "Lord Bond's mother." (WDIM 54)

Bond, Athelstane
* Son of **Ivanhoe Bond**, elected to parliament due to his philanthropy. Father of **Ethelwulf**. (BL 39)

Bond, the Honourable Cedric Weyland ("C.W.")
* Son and heir of **Alured, Lord Bond** and **Lucasta, Lady Bond**. **Richard Tebben** catches him out in the Skeynes versus Worsted cricket match. Fills in in the title role in

Mrs. (Louise) Palmer's production of *Hippolytus*, where he is impressed by **Betty Dean**. (AF 36)

❖ Working in New York. He returns on a job and becomes engaged to **Daphne Stonor**. (BL 39)

❖ They are married and live at the White Cottage, near the **Middletons**. Their two little boys are six and four years old. (LAR 48)

❖ Their sons are at **Philip Winter's** Priory School, where the elder, **Young Bond**, may be sickening for whooping cough. (HRt 52)

❖ He has succeeded to the title and to Staple Park. (WDIM 54)

❖ As the present Lord Bond, he and his wife are breaking his family's chain of Saxon names with each new baby. (ESR 55)

Bond, (Mrs.) Daphne: *See* **Stonor, Daphne.**

Bond, Ethelwulf, Lord
❖ Son of **Athelstane Bond**. Married money and was made a peer in 1907. Father of **Alured, Lord Bond**. (BL 39)

Bond, Ivanhoe
❖ Son of **Jedediah Bond**, he became a Member of Parliament for one of the **Earl of Pomfret's** rotten boroughs. Father of **Athelstane**. (BL 39)

Bond, Jedediah
❖ Yorkshire woolens manufacturer, determined to be a descendant (at eight hundred years' remove) of King Alfred.

Father of **Ivanhoe**, grandfather of **Athelstane**, great-grandfather of **Ethelwulf**, and great-great-grandfather of **Alured, Lord Bond**. Built Staple Park. (BL 39)

Bond, Lucasta, Lady (née Stoke)

❖ Wife of **Alured, Lord Bond**, of Staple Park; mother of **the Honourable Cedric Weyland Bond**. Has a famous feud with **Mrs. (Louise) Palmer**. (AF 36)

❖ Half-sister of **Lord Stoke**. Organizes protest meeting at **the Middletons'** to save Pooker's Piece. (BL 39)

❖ She and her husband dine at seven on patriotic but unappetizing food. (GU 43)

❖ Staple Park is now let to a school, while they live in a small house on the estate. (MB 45)

❖ Now living in part of Staple Park's servants' wing, they give a combined Conservative Rally and Pig Breeders' Show. (LAR 48)

❖ Has a grandson, **Young Bond**, about whom she is an especially great worrier. (HRt 52)

❖ Identified as Lord Bond's mother, so her husband must have died. (WDIM 54)

❖ After Lord Bond's death, she wanted to live in the village near her brother, but he hadn't a house empty, so she moved to Bath. (ESR 55)

❖ Dislikes the title Dowager Lady Bond, and tries to be called Lucasta, Lady Bond instead, but it's popularized as Lady Lucasta or even Lady Luke (the latter not to her face). Went to Bournemouth, where Lord Stoke would prefer that she live (rather than with him?). (NTL 56)

❖ Now going to Cheltenham to stay with **old Lady Norton** in her private hotel suite and to look for a house. (TSAT 61)

Bond, Young

❖ Son of **Daphne Stonor** Bond and **the Honourable C.W. Bond**; source of worry for his grandparents, **Lord and Lady Bond**. Now at **Philip Winter's** school, along with his younger brother; may have whooping cough. (HRt 52)

Bond, Young Lady: *See* **Stonor, Daphne**.

Bones, Jimmy

❖ Son of **Mr. Bones** the butcher, for whom he does deliveries. Sees **Guy Barton** and **Phoebe Rivers** kissing, and is sent to bed for saying so. (PT 38)

Bones, Mr.

❖ Butcher of Nutfield, son **Jimmy**. He and his wife win a cruet at the village whist drive. (PT 38)

Bonescu, Gradka

❖ Mixo-Lydian refugee working as cook and housekeeper for the **Fieldings**, Hallbury; recommended by **Mrs. Perry**. Her surname is not given, as it is supposed to be impossible to say or memorize. Daughter of a university professor, she is studying for the exams of the Society for the Propagation of English, and passes them with honors thanks to **Miss (Maud) Bunting's** coaching. She goes back to Mixo-Lydia. (MB 45)

❖ Returns as member of the Mixo-Lydian trade delegation. (LAR 48)

❖ Now **Mixo-Lydian Ambassador,** and her surname is given. She sublets the London flat of **Aubrey Clover** and **Jessica Dean,** though they don't recognize her when they meet her with **Frances Harvey** at the Gatherum Conservative Do. (CC 50)

❖ After she passed her exams, she became head of the Bunting College in Mixo-Lydia, and translated *Bleak House* into Mixo-Lydian (*Hroj Czandik*). She snubs the **Brownscus** at the Barsetshire Archaeological, and the **Harveys** everywhere. (DD 51)

❖ Her late mother and **Dumka's** father's late sister were cousins; she gets Dumka a job with the **Richard Carters.** (NTL 56)

❖ Visits the Fieldings. (ADA 57)

❖ Now a "very large well-dressed woman" at the Bring and Buy Sale for Mixo-Lydian miners. (CQ 58)

❖ She is in England to defend a Mixo-Lydian clerk (and graduate of the Bunting College) from being fired by Frances Harvey, and to set up a memorial to Miss Bunting. She joins **Sam Adams'** Syndicate to buy **Wiple** Terrace, and sets up her "tabloid" to Miss Bunting there, as well as an exchange student program between Mixo-Lydia and Southbridge. (TSAT 61)

Bontemps, M.
❖ Mayor of a small commune in Lille and ardent *Félibriste.* Under the *nom de plume* **Numa Garagou,** edited the *Andalhou* of **Guibert le Biau.** Invites **Mr. (Harold) Downing**

and **Miss (Ianthe) Pemberton** to Lille to celebrate their publication of the *Féau–Filhz* volume of the *Biographical Dictionary of Provence*. (CC 50)

Bostock, Mr.

* ❖ New Vicar of St. Mary's Church, Rushwater, succeeding **Mr. Banister**. He comes from potato country, so he is not used to the rampant cow-mindedness exemplified by the **Leslies**. **Mrs. Poulter** does for him, but soon her son **Ted** and his wife-to-be **Lily Brown** will take over (by **Emmy Graham's** arrangement). (PBO 46)

* ❖ He gives a thanksgiving service for **Lady Emily Leslie's** birthday reunion. (LAR 48)

* ❖ Now a canon of Barchester. (OBH 49)

* ❖ He loses the key to the vestry. (DD 51)

* ❖ Marries **Clarissa Graham** to **Charles Belton**. (HRt 52)

* ❖ He and **Dean Crawley** marry **Miss Merriman** and **Mr. (Herbert) Choyce**. (ADA 57)

Boulle, Prof. Henri

* ❖ Husband of **Mme. Boulle**, father of **Pierre**, **Ursule**, and **Jean-Claude**. From Touraine, of an Alsatian family. His mother was English. They take **Mr. Banister's** house in Rushwater for August. (WS 34)

Boulle, Jean-Claude

* ❖ Youngest son of **Prof. Henri** and **Mme. Boulle**, brother of **Ursule** and **Pierre**. A spotty boy scout and reactionary royalist. Unable to pull off a royalist demonstration at **Martin Leslie's** seventeenth birthday party. (WS 34)

Boulle, Madame

 ❖ Wife of **Prof. Henri Boulle**, mother of **Pierre, Ursule**, and **Jean-Claude**. Of Touraine. A former governess, her great-grandfather was the Count de Florel. They take **Mr. Banister's** house in Rushwater for August. (WS 34)

Boulle, Prof. Pierre

 ❖ Eldest son of **Prof. Henri** and **Mme. Boulle**, brother of **Ursule** and **Jean-Claude**. About twenty-five, a romantic royalist. He tutors **Martin Leslie** in French. During their stay at Rushwater, he falls in love with **Lady Agnes Graham** and rescues her daughter **Emmy Graham** from the pond in the kitchen garden. (WS 34)

 ❖ He is referred to as **M. Duval** or **Durand**. (PBO 46)

 ❖ Now at the French Embassy in London. He meets Agnes Graham on a plane from Mixo-Lydia. (ADA 57)

 ❖ Referred to as Maitre Pierre Boulle, a legal friend of **Noel Merton's** who might take **Lavinia Merton** for a year's visit. He has a wife and teenage family in Paris. (LAAA 59)

 ❖ Professor, of the *Académie Francaise*; he and his wife did have Lavinia to stay with them. (TSAT 61)

Boulle, Ursule

 ❖ Middle daughter of **Prof. Henri** and **Mme. Boulle**, sister of **Jean-Claude** and **Pierre**. About twenty, with a crush on **Joan Stevenson**. Sews flag for the royalist demonstration at **Martin Leslie's** seventeenth birthday party. (WS 34)

Boy, the

 ❖ Aged about seventy; helps **Young Percy Bodger** clean out the well at the Old Bank House. (OBH 49)

* At Rushwater; has done nothing on weekly wages for many years. (DD 51)

Boy, the
* The new pantry boy for **Lord Crosse**, Crosse Hall; being trained by the butler, **Peters**. (NTL 56)

* He is thinking of going into catering. (ADA 57)

Bradford, Mr.
* Former Classics master at Southbridge School, who lapsed into senility and was replaced by **Colin Keith**. (SH 37)

Brandon, Miss Amelia ("Aunt Sissie")
* Mistress of Brandon Abbey. Daughter of **Old Mr. and Mrs. Brandon**, younger (by twelve years) sister of **Frederick Brandon**. A temperamental and wealthy invalid. Her other connections include the late **Henry Brandon**, either a nephew or first cousin once removed, his widow **Lavinia** and children **Francis** and **Delia; Hilary Grant**, a first cousin twice removed; an uncle of Cedric Brandon's who lives in Putney; and a cousin in New Zealand. When she dies, she leaves all her money to charity except for small legacies to Francis, Delia, and Hilary; ten thousand pounds to her companion **Ella Morris**; ten thousand pounds to **Captain Fred Arbuthnot**. (TB 39)

* The government takes Brandon Abbey as a military hospital. (CBI 40)

* The Ministry of General Interference has taken over Brandon Abbey, so the charity it was meant for never got it. A picture of the gorilla statues in the Abbey reveals the relationship between the Brandons and the Arbuthnots. (PE 47)

* Miss Brandon would have been ninety-one this summer. (CC 50)

Brandon, Delia

* Younger daughter of **Mr. (Henry)** and **Mrs. (Lavinia) Brandon**; sister of **Francis**. Nineteen, strong-willed, fond of accidents and disasters; friend of **Lydia Keith**. Carves **Hilary Grant's** name into a vegetable marrow. (TB 39)

* Doing Red Cross at Barchester General; she is a bridesmaid for **Rose Birkett**, and is engaged to Hilary Grant. (CBI 40)

* Married to Hilary. (MH 42)

* Her little boy **Freddie** has chicken pox, they come to Stories, and she works at W.V.S. while Hilary is in Washington. (GU 43)

* Her new baby is a girl. (TH 44)

* She is having another baby in August. (PBO 46)

* The latest baby is a girl named **Felicia**, but now she has only two babies. She, like Francis, will inherit half her father's money. (PE 47)

* She now has twins, "darling little boys," and they are staying at Stories in old **Turpin's** cottage. During their holidays, the boys will fly out and stay with their parents on excavation. (HRt 52)

Brandon, Effie

* Eldest daughter of **Peggy Arbuthnot** Brandon and **Francis Brandon**. (CC 50)

Brandon, Francis Oliver

❖ Elder son of **Mr. (Henry)** and **Mrs. (Lavinia) Brandon**; brother of **Delia**. Twenty-three years old, and doesn't want to jump through **Miss (Amelia) Brandon's** hoops in order to inherit her wealth. (TB 39)

❖ Overage for the military (at twenty-four? *see* below), and working in an office at Barchester. (CBI 40)

❖ Now about thirty. Was stationed in Jerusalem with the Barsetshires; fought in the Near and Middle East (and/or in Africa and Italy), and won the M.C. Now out of the army and back at work as director of a firm in Barchester. He will eventually inherit half his father's money. He dances the "Argentina Tango" with **Peggy Arbuthnot** in **Aubrey Clover's** show for the Red Cross Fete, and they become engaged. (PE 47)

❖ They married in autumn 1946, almost three years before, and now have three children: a girl **Effie**, and twins born soon after. They repeat their dance from *Out Goes She* for the Conservative Do at Gatherum. He is quite selfish, especially toward his mother, with whom they are living, but she escapes the situation by getting engaged to **Bishop Joram**. (CC 50)

❖ He is a chartered accountant, financier, churchwarden, and the Treasurer of the Conservative Committee for something. His business gets into trouble, but eventually comes right. Now he behaves badly towards Peggy, but he is told off for his own good by **Lady Glencora Palliser** Waring. (HRt 52)

❖ Peggy is pregnant again. (JC 53)

Brandon, Mrs. Francis *or* **Peggy:** *See* **Arbuthnot, Peggy.**

Brandon, Frederick
* Son of **Old Mr. and Mrs. Brandon**, older (by twelve years) brother of **Miss (Amelia) Brandon**. In the Army in India; when stationed in Poona in 1876, gave a diamond bracelet to **Mrs. Colonel Arbuthnot**. Killed while pig-sticking in Jubilee year (TB 39)

* Due to the Arbuthnot scandal, had to exchange into another regiment. Mrs. Colonel Arbuthnot had a son by him (probably **Fred Arbuthnot**) who became the father of **Captain Fred** and **Effie Arbuthnot**. (PE 47)

Brandon, Mr. Henry
* The late husband of **Mrs. (Lavinia) Brandon**, father of **Francis** and **Delia**. Nephew or first cousin once removed of **Miss (Amelia) Brandon**. Only married six or seven years before dying of pneumonia at Cannes. (TB 39)

* They married just after World War I. Had he lived, would have been almost seventy this year (his wife was almost fifteen years younger). (CC 50)

Brandon, Mrs. Lavinia (née Oliver)
* Widow of **Mr. (Henry) Brandon**, mother of **Francis** and **Delia**. Of Stories, near Pomfret Madrigal. An object of (somewhat tiresome) devotion to **Mr. (Justin) Miller, Ella Morris, Hilary Grant**, and her faithful Nurse (**Miss Vance**) and maid **Rose. Sir Edmund Pridham** is her trustee and watchdog. (TB 39)

* She billets a small nursery school at Stories. (CBI 40)

* In charge of the local Land Girls. (GU 43)

* **Miss Feilding** and the last three babies of her nursery school leave. Mrs. Brandon organizes the Red Cross Fete play; Francis will continue to live with her after he marries **Peggy Arbuthnot**. (PE 47)

* She is now fifty-five; her husband would have been almost seventy (they married just after World War I). Francis is not treating her well; she becomes engaged to **Bishop Joram**. (CC 50)

* They are married and spend a month in France. (DD 51)

* She gives a party in honor of Sir Edmund Pridham (which is delayed for as long as **the Bishop and his wife** are in Barchester). (HRt 52)

Brandon, Old Mr. and Mrs.

* Parents of **Frederick** and **Amelia "Sissie" Brandon**. He was a jute merchant and built Brandon Abbey; she was a **Morton** from Cheshire. Her youngest sister **Miss Morton** married Robert Grant of the Barsetshires, and their son was **Edward Grant**. (TB 39)

Brandon, Aunt Sissie: *See* Brandon, Miss Amelia.

Brentwood, Jim

* Of Garoopna, Australia. He, **Mr. Wickham**, and a fellow named **Troubridge** put up the money for the fine (and a few drinks afterward) when **Tom Buckley** was penalized for not voting in the Federal Election. (HRt 52)

Brick-Red Face, the Man with the

* Sporting gent, weekend guest at Pomfret Towers. **Alice Barton** tells him that they changed the sluices at Starve-

acres Hatches. He may also be the **M.F.H.** who offers to mount **Sally Wicklow**. (PT 38)

Bronson-Hewbury, the Honourable Clara

❖ Unnamed doctor's daughter, the fiancée of **Dr. Robert Perry**. (LAR 48)

❖ Now given a first name and title. (DD 51)

❖ She is now **Mrs. Bob,** and is alienating her husband from his family. Her father is a titled consultant with a place in Berkshire. (HRt 52)

Bronwen

❖ Slave Friend acquired by **Barbara Dunsford** at the Pension **Ramsden** at Menton; named "Wendy" to her "Friendy." (ADA 57)

Brown

❖ Head gardener to the **Leslies,** Rushwater. (WS 34)

❖ In charge of **Ted Poulter** as gardener. (PBO 46)

Brown, Abner

❖ A dairyman, grazes one of the Southbridge School fields; also carts coal. Nephew of **Mr. Brown** of the Red Lion. (CBI 40)

Brown, Arthur

❖ He let a Rushwater pig drown in the pond and was told off by **Mr. Macpherson**. (DD 51)

Brown, Ernie

❖ Son of **Police Constable** and **Mrs. Haig Brown**. One brother. (JC 53)

Brown, Farmer

❖ Owns Parsley Island opposite Northbridge Rectory, rents sites there to campers (e.g., **Eric Swan** and **Tony Morland**). (SH 37)

Brown, Mrs. Haig

❖ Wife of **P.C. Haig Brown**, mother of **Ernie** and one other boy. Her aunt was in temporary service at Omnium Castle. (JC 53)

❖ She launders and chars for the **Phelpses**. (CQ 58)

Brown, Police Constable Haig

❖ Of Southbridge; husband of **Mrs. Haig Brown**, with two boys (one named **Ernie**). Nephew of **Mr. Brown** of the Red Lion. Named for a general of World War I, in which his father served, but known as "Scotch and Splash" or "Neat Scotch" in the village. (JC 53)

❖ Was to stand in for his uncle as umpire at the Southbridge School cricket match, but was called off on special duty. (NTL 56)

❖ His mother is a cousin of **S. Wheeler**, housekeeper to the **Beltons**. (CQ 58)

Brown, Henry

❖ Cousin of **Sid Brown**, near Low Rising. Due to a broken ankle, he rents his bicycle to **Tony Morland**. (DH 34)

Brown, Lady

❖ Of Les Mouettes, Mentone. She picks up a Russian dancer from the Pension **Ramsden**; he gambles on her *carte blanche* and loses everything, including his gold anklet. (NR 41)

Brown, Lily

❖ Daughter of **Mrs. Brown of Rushwater Parva** and the late **Old Brown**; walking out with **Ted Poulter**. By **Emmy Graham's** arrangement, after they marry, they'll live in with **Mr. Bostock**. (PBO 46)

❖ Her mother-in-law **Mrs. Poulter** is dying at home, and she's helping out. (OBH 49)

❖ According to **Edith Graham**, Ted beat her, but they got married, so it's all right. (ADA 57)

Brown, Miss

❖ Fitter at Bostock and Plummer, Barchester. (CC 50)

Brown, Mr.

❖ Owns the garage in High Rising. (HR 33)

❖ Rents and repairs bicycles, owns a boathouse, and rents boats on the canal. (DH 34)

❖ His old mother in the Rising cottage hospital has no teeth and won't use her false ones because of graven images. (TSAT 61)

Brown, Mr.

❖ Of the Red Lion pub, Southbridge. His grandfather **Smith** kept a tied house in Camden Town, and his mother sent him there on visits. He attended the Old Sewerworks Road Board School. His nephew is **Abner Brown**. (CBI 40)

❖ He owns a taxi allowed petrol for station work. (GU 43)

❖ Belongs to a Masonic lodge, and still drives the taxi. (PBO 46)

* He is a churchwarden; his brother is a coal-merchant; his uncle is eighty-seven; another nephew, **Young Brown**, is a jobbing gardener. (PE 47)

* Another nephew is **P.C. Haig Brown**. (JC 53)

* His sciatica, and the brandy, keeps him from umpiring the Southbride School cricket match. (NTL 56)

* As a small businessman, speaks against **Lord Aberford-bury's** plans for **Wiple** Terrace, and is rewarded with increased custom. (TSAT 61)

Brown, Mrs., of Rushwater Parva
* Widow of **Old Brown** and mother of **Lily Brown**. If Lily and **Ted Poulter** marry, she plans to live with her sister in Rushwater Parva. (PBO 46)

* Along with his housekeeper, helps lay out **Mr. Macpherson**. (DD 51)

Brown, Old
* The late husband of **Mrs. Brown of Rushwater Parva** and father of **Lily Brown**. (PBO 46)

Brown, Sid
* Porter, High Rising station. Brother of **Mr. Brown** of the High Rising garage, and cousin of **Henry Brown**. (HR 33)

Brown, Sid, Young
* Handles the mail, High Rising; also delivers the milk. Helps out in the house when his Dad (**Sid Brown?**) goes to Blackpool for his holiday. (LAAA 59)

Brown, Young
* Jobbing gardener, nephew of **Mr. Brown** of the Red Lion, Southbridge. (PE 47)

Browne, Archdeacon Simon
* Son of **Browne** of Balliol and Sussex, grandson of **Octavius Manton**, and brother of **Dorothea Browne Harcourt**, Dowager Duchess of Towers. He lives in London. (LAAA 59)

Browne
* Of Sussex, father of **Simon** and of **Dorothea Browne Harcourt**, Dowager Duchess of Towers. He was at Balliol in Jowett's time; a good Latinist but only took a Second. He and five others put a piglet dressed in the nightgown of the Mitre's barmaid in the Master's wastepaper basket. They were sent down, but term ended in a week anyway. (LAAA 59)

Browning, Dr.
* **Daphne Stonor** was his secretary, but he died. (BL 39)

Brownscu, Gradko ("Gogo")
* Husband of **Madame Brownscu**; Mixo-Lydian refugee. They bring embroideries for sale to **Mrs. (Amy) Birkett's** sherry party. (CBI 40)

* They arrange an exhibition of Slavo-Lydian atrocities in Winter Overcotes. (GU 43)

* With **Mrs. (Maud) Perry**, they attend Bobbin Day at the Hosiers' Girls' Foundation School at Harefield Park. (TH 44)

* They quarrel over the postwar policy of exterminating all Slavo-Lydians. (MB 45)

* They are now at Bathwater Cold in the Cotswolds, running a school for peasant weaving and folk dancing, but

turn up for the Barsetshire Archaeological in hopes of an embassy job for him from **Gradka Bonescu**, the Mixo-Lydian Ambassador. She refuses, as he was already dismissed from one embassy job for dishonesty. (DD 51)

❖ They sell items in aid of Mixo-Lydian miners at the Greshamsbury New Town Bring and Buy. (CQ 58)

Brownscu, Madame
❖ Wife of **Gogo Brownscu**; Mixo-Lydian refugee. They bring embroideries for sale to **Mrs. (Amy) Birkett's** sherry party. She also brings a crêche to the Southbridge Christmas Treat. (CBI 40)

❖ They arrange an exhibition of Slavo-Lydian atrocities in Winter Overcotes. (GU 43)

❖ With **Mrs. (Maud) Perry**, they attend Bobbin Day at the Hosiers' Girls' Foundation School at Harefield park. (TH 44)

❖ They quarrel over the postwar policy of exterminating all Slavo-Lydians. (MB 45)

❖ They are now at Bathwater Cold in the Cotswolds, running a school for peasant weaving and folk dancing. They attend the Barsetshire Archaeological and fail to get an embassy job for Gogo from **Gradka Bonescu**, the Mixo-Lydian Ambassador. (DD 51)

❖ They sell items in aid of Mixo-Lydian miners at the Greshambury New Town Bring and Buy. (CQ 58)

Buckley, Tom
❖ Of Baroona Station, Australia. Fined for not voting in the Federal Election, but the money for his fine (and a few

drinks afterward) is put up by **Mr. Wickham, Jim Brentwood** of Garoopna, and a fellow named **Troubridge**. (HRt 52)

Budge, Councillor

❖ Of the Gas Works. After **Sam Adams'** address to his election committee, he takes reporters from the *Barchester Chronicle* and the *Barchester Free Press* out to the Mitre and gets them drunk. (PBO 46)

❖ Attends the wedding of **Anne Fielding** and **Robin Dale**. (LAR 48)

❖ Wanted some land along the river for the Gas Works, but was pre-empted by Sam Adams, who bought it for his dairy herd on **Lucy Marling's** advice. (OBH 49)

❖ His wife calls him "Pops" or "Father" because they have five children, all married with young families. Three years ago they vacationed at the Aberdeathly Hydro, playing bridge and fishing with a **Mr. and Mrs. Clamp** from Southport, until they actually reeled a fish in. He attends **Eric Swan's** lecture at the Barchester Central Library. (HRt 52)

Bunce

❖ Cowman to the **Mertons** at Northbridge Manor; son of **Old Bunce** and **Mrs. Bunce**, brother of **Effie**, **Ruby**, and one other girl. (PE 47)

❖ Once misnamed **Pucken**. (WDIM 54)

Bunce, Effie

❖ Daughter of **Old Bunce** and **Mrs. Bunce**, sister of **Ruby** and one other girl. She "does for" **Miss Pemberton**. (SH 37)

* She is regularly beaten by her father. (NR 41)

* Now a stout Land Girl, delivering milk for Old Masters' dairy. Wins a goat cart at the Cottage Hospital Raffle. (MB 45)

* Now has one baby and another on the way, fathered either by **Young Hibberd** or **Syd Fitchett**. She plans to have both children christened together. (PE 47)

* She is now going out with a Hogglestock man. (OBH 49)

* Pregnant again, so she can't be in the June Coronation show. Nonetheless, she and Ruby are to play Elizabeth I's maids of honor in the Coronation pageant. They were once ward maids at Barchester General, and they now beat their father instead of his beating them. Their cousin Sid is **Mrs. Dunsford's** gardener and runs the Wolf Cubs. (WDIM 54)

* Now working for **Miss Heath** and **Miss Ward** at Punshions. Her fourth and latest child, the result of a day trip to the coast, is a boy named **Hovis** (from Hovis House, where she sometimes worked for Mrs. Dunsford and **Barbara Dunsford**.) (NTL 56)

* One of her or Ruby's children of shame has gotten a scholarship. (ADA 57)

* All the children of shame did well at school, married, got good jobs, and now send their lawful children to the grannies of shame for the holidays. (LAAA 59)

Bunce, George
* Regimental ne'er-do-well of the Barsetshires, he cheats at cards better than any man in the division. (OBH 49)

Bunce, Hovis

❖ Fourth child of shame of **Effie Bunce**, the result of a day trip to the coast. He was named for Hovis House, where his mother sometimes worked for **Mrs. Dunsford** and **Barbara**. (NTL 56)

Bunce, Mrs.

❖ Wife of **Old Bunce**, mother of three daughters, including **Effie** and **Ruby**. (SH 37)

❖ Beats her husband on Saturday nights, and he beats the girls. (NR 41)

❖ Wicked and foul-mouthed. (MB 45)

❖ Their son is **Bunce**, the cowman to the **Mertons**. (PE 47)

❖ Never married Old Bunce, which is why she bullies him and he can't beat her. (WDIM 54)

❖ Now beaten by Mr. Bunce. One of her grandchildren of shame has gotten a scholarship. (ADA 57)

❖ Died before Old Bunce did. (LAAA 59)

Bunce, Old

❖ Ferryman at Northbridge, deaf and heedless; husband of **Mrs. Bunce** and father of three daughters, including **Effie** and **Ruby**. (SH 37)

❖ He drinks at the Ferryman's Arms, and predicts the war. (CBI 40)

❖ His wife beats him, and he beats the girls. (NR 41)

❖ Wicked and foul-mouthed. (MB 45)

❖ Their son is **Bunce**, the cowman to the **Mertons**. (PE 47)

❖ His niece is **Mrs. Hicks** of Northbridge, née Bessie Bunce. (JC 53)

❖ Never married Mrs. Bunce, which is why she bullies him and he can't beat her. Now the girls beat him as well. He is past the ferry work, and the boat has rotted away. (WDIM 54)

❖ Now he beats Mrs. Bunce, but not the girls, as they'd beat him. One of his grandchildren of shame has gotten a scholarship. (ADA 57)

❖ Died soon after Mrs. Bunce. (LAAA 59)

Bunce, Old Miss
❖ Invalid at Rising Cottage Hospital, fond of peppermint drops. Friend of **Old Mrs. Grubb**. (TSAT 61)

Bunce, Ruby
❖ Daughter of **Old Bunce** and **Mrs. Bunce**, sister of **Effie** and one other girl. (SH 37)

❖ She and her sister are regularly beaten by her father. She comes to oblige the **Villars** at Northbridge Rectory. (NR 41)

❖ Now working for the **Mertons** at Northbridge Manor. Like her sister Effie, she has increased the county's population without benefit of clergy, and is about to again. Nonetheless, they are to play Elizabeth I's maids of honor in the Coronation pageant. They were once ward maids at Barchester General, and they now beat their father. Their cousin Sid is **Mrs. Dunstan's** gardener and runs the Wolf Cubs. (WDIM 54)

* One of her or Effie's children of shame has gotten a scholarship. (ADA 57)

* All the children of shame did well at school, married, got good jobs, and now send their lawful children to the grannies of shame for the holidays. (LAAA 59)

Bunce, Young
* Sixty-three years old, takes over as sexton when **Hibberd** gets the flu. (NR 41)

Bungay
* Head of firm of publishers in Paternoster Row, merged with Bacon in 1887. Along with **Mr. Hobb**, tries to lure **Mrs. (Hermione) Rivers** from **Mr. Johns'** firm. (PT 38)

* Has translating rights of state-published books from Mixo-Lydia. (LAR 48)

Bunting, Miss Maud
* Also known to her many pupils as "Bunny." At the start of the war, comes to Marling Hall to help **Mrs. (Amabel) Marling**, for whose brothers and nephews she was governess. Also worked for the **Marquess of Bolton**, Lord Lundy, and was companion of the **Dowager Marchioness of Hartletop**. Her sister is the widow of a clergyman and has a daughter who is a deaconess at Wolverhampton. (MH 42)

* She goes to Hallbury to be governess to **Anne Fielding**. Helps **Gradka (Bonescu)** with her exams. **David Leslie** was her favorite pupil. She has a stroke, dies, and is buried at Rushwater. (MB 45)

* There is a memorial to her in Rushwater church. (PBO 46)

* After Gradka passed her exams, she named the college she headed in Mixo-Lydia "the Bunting College." (DD 51)

* Gradka is in England to defend a Mixo-Lydian graduate of Bunting College from being fired by Frances Harvey, and to set up a memorial to Miss Bunting. She joins **Sam Adams'** Syndicate to buy **Wiple** Terrace, and sets up her "tabloid" to Miss Bunting there. (TSAT 61)

Burden
* Head waiter, the White Hart, Barchester. (LAR 48)

* His feet distress him, but they'll last out his time. (ADA 57)

* Though he has a Leg, he wouldn't let them X-ray it in the hospital. (TSAT 61)

Butters
* Boy at Southbridge School. He collides with another boy, **Johnson,** during a power failure, and has an eyebrow laid open, so that **Edward** has to rush them both to the doctor. (HR 33)

Camargou, Reynault

* Subject of a biography by **Mr. (Harold) Downing**, which is published by **Adrian Coates**. (NR 41)

Cameron, Mr. Alister

* Architect, junior partner to **Mr. (Jack) Middleton** for ten years; he has rooms in the Middle Temple, London. His father had been in the 23rd, **Colonel Stonor's** regiment, but his parents died when he was at school. He went to Oxford, then into an architect's office. He gets engaged first to **Daphne Stonor**, but afterward to her stepmother **Lilian Stonor**. (BL 39)

* Married to Lilian. (MH 42)

* They still live in one of the Inns of Court. (TSAT 61)

Campo, Cash

* Leader of the band, Cash Campo and his Symposium Boys. Their hit: "I'm All of a Muddle When We Cuddle, Cuddle, Cuddle." (TB 39)

* They have been in New York ever since the war. Their latest is "Kiss, Kiss, Kiss, and You'll Never Do Amiss." (PBO 46)

* Still in New York, and likely to stay there until the dollar and the pound are on better terms. (PE 47)

* Their new hot number: "The Boy from the Ships, He Sips from Her Lips." (CC 50)

Capes, the Earl and Lady Alice
* Of Capes Castle. He is a cousin of **Lady Norton** and a reluctant host to **Mr. Holt**; the latter was invited by Lady Alice, who mainly lives in the South of France. (WS 34)

le Capet, Jehan
* Pen name of **Eugene Duval**, French Romantic poet and Satanist. He published one very slim volume, *Belphégor*, then died young of absinthe. His other work was destroyed by his mistress **Nini le Poumon** (whose real name was **Angele Potin**). Other mistresses include **Mimi la Salope, Jehanne de Valois**, and a fourth one who ran away with an old *commis voyageur*. He is the object of **Hilary Grant's** interest and scholarship. (TB 39)

* Hilary's work on him, *A Diabolist at the Restoration*, is published. (MH 42)

* Hilary's growing eminence as an archaeologist wins belated recognition for his earlier work on le Capet. (HRt 52)

Captain of Hockey, the
* At the Hosiers' Girls' Foundation School. Plays Touchstone in their production of *As You Like It*. (TH 44)

Captain of Rowing, the: *See* Featherstonehaugh.

Carmichael, Miss

❖ Head of St. Bathos (Church of England) School. Takes her pupils to the Southbridge Christmas Treat. (CBI 40)

Carruthers

❖ Former under secretary for India and friend of **Alured, Lord Bond**, at his club. He washes his paintings with soap and water. (BL 39)

Carson, Mr.

❖ Vicar of Nutfield, with low-church opinions. He is afraid of his housekeeper, but then marries a nice widow from the Midlands who stands no nonsense from servants. (TB 39)

❖ His church is "a tin tabernacle," which is why his service is so austere. (PE 47)

Carter

❖ Chauffeur to the **Bartons**, Mellings. (PT 38)

Carter, Angela

❖ Second child of **Everard Carter** and **Kate Keith** Carter. Two years old. Her older brother is **Bobbie** and her new little brother **Philip**. (GU 43)

❖ There is another new little brother **Noel**; his permanence is uncertain. (MB 45)

❖ The children go to the seaside in Devonshire, to stay with Everard's mother. (PE 47)

❖ She is top of her form at school. (NTL 56)

❖ Now an older teenager. (LAAA 59)

Carter, Bobbie

* Eldest child of **Everard Carter** and **Kate Keith** Carter. Named Robert Philip, with **Philip Winter** as his godfather. (CBI 40)

* Four years old. His next sister is **Angela**, and his new little brother **Philip**. (GU 43)

* There is another new little brother **Noel**; his permanence is uncertain. (MB 45)

* The children go to the seaside in Devonshire, to stay with Everard's mother. (PE 47)

* Now in public school, with a scholarship. (JC 53)

* Going to Oxford in the autumn. (LAAA 59)

Carter, Mr. Everard

* History master and housemaster, Southbridge School. Was not at Oxford. The late husband of **Lady Sibyl Carter** (whose name is later specified as **Archdeacon Tom Carter**) was his great-uncle. He becomes engaged to **Kate Keith**. (SH 37)

* Their wedding. (TB 39)

* He was at Cambridge, and now becomes senior housemaster. Their son **Bobbie** (Robert Philip; **Philip Winter** is his godfather) is one year old. (CBI 40)

* Bobbie is four, **Angela** is two, and **Philip** is "very little indeed." (GU 43)

* He is openly designated as the next headmaster when **Mr. (Bill) Birkett** retires. Their new baby is **Noel**, named after **Mr. (Noel) Merton**, but *see* his entry. (MB 45)

* Before coming to Southbridge he had read law, until he found he couldn't afford it. He was 29 when he married. He advises **Robin Dale** on his career. (PBO 46)

* He is appointed headmaster, and has written a book on Lord Eldon. They take the children to Devonshire and leave them with his mother for the summer. (PE 47)

* They go to London with the children for the Coronation. Along with Kate's brother **Colin Keith**, they buy a vacation house in Devonshire. (WDIM 54)

* Through Archdeacon Tom Carter, he is a kind of cousin to **Richard A. Carter**. (NTL 56)

* Thinking of retiring and leasing the **Villars'** old house in Northbridge. (CQ 58)

* Now retired, at the Old Rectory, Northbridge. (LAAA 59)

Carter, (Mrs.) Kate: *See* **Keith, Kate**.

Carter, Noel
* Disappearing fourth child of **Everard Carter** and **Kate Keith** Carter. His elder siblings are **Bobbie, Angela,** and **Philip**. Just born, and named for **Noel Merton**. (MB 45)

* Now not named among the Keith children. (PE 47)

* The Keiths are referred to as having both three and four children. (OBH 49)

* Only three children from here on. (CC 50)

Carter, Philip
* Third child of **Everard Carter** and **Kate Keith** Carter, with elder siblings **Bobbie** and **Angela**. Born quite recently. (GU 43)

* They have a new little brother **Noel**; his permanence is uncertain. (MB 45)

* The children go to the seaside in Devonshire, to stay with Everard's mother. (PE 47)

* Thirteen years old; good at books, but great at sports. (NTL 56)

* At Southbridge School. (LAAA 59)

Carter, the Honourable Mrs. Richard

* Wife of **Richard A. Carter** and (at first the eldest, later the youngest) child of **Lord Crosse**, who rents the Old Manor House from the **Hallidays** for them. They have a three-year-old boy and a baby girl. Her older siblings are a married sister in London and **John-Arthur Crosse**. (NTL 56)

Carter, Richard A., Esq.

* Presumably a lawyer; husband of the daughter of **Lord Crosse**, who rents the Old Manor House from the **Hallidays** for them. They have a three-year-old boy and a baby girl. He is known as Dick, or Paterson; his wife even calls him "Tommy" at one point. He was once under **Sir Robert Graham** at the War Office; was also in Italy during the last year of the war, and picked up a bug that puzzled both Italian and English doctors. His family was Anglo-Indian, and they lived in South Kensington. His great-uncle was the late **Archdeacon Tom Carter**, which makes him sort of a cousin of **Everard Carter**. Another great-uncle had a family, unlike Great-Uncle Tom. (NTL 56)

Carter, Lady Sibyl
* Neighbor of **Mrs. (Helen) Keith**, whose **Uncle Oswald** knew the family in India. Her father was governor of a province. She is the widow of an archdeacon. (SH 37)

* She and the **Archdeacon** (whose name is now given as **Tom Carter**) had no family. (NTL 56)

Carter, Tom
* Father of **Mrs. (Mary) Grantly**. A hard-working land-owner in Omnium country, he died of a chill and pneumonia after hunting, soon after her marriage. (OBH 49)

Carter, Archdeacon Tom
* Egyptologist, husband of **Lady Sibyl Carter** (but no first name given). Great-uncle of **Everard Carter**. (SH 37)

* He and Lady Sibyl had no family. He is also great-uncle of **Richard A. Carter**, which makes him and Everard sort of cousins. (NTL 56)

Carton, Miss
* Replaced **Miss Cowshay** in the costing department of **Sam Adams'** Hogglestock Rolling Mills when she moved to their Pomfret Towers office. (ADA 57)

Carton, Mr. Sidney
* Oxford don, nearer sixty than fifty, who lives at Assaye House, Harefield, out of term. He was named for the Dickens character, and has a sister, plus a mother at Bognor who is eighty and still gardens. A friend of **Charles Fanshawe**, he writes a book on **Fluvius Minucius**, which he dedicates to **Canon Horbury**. He also grows to admire the Canon's granddaughter, **Miss (Madeleine) Sparling**; they plan to marry when she retires. (TH 44)

* His mother lives at Enitharmon, Blake Close, Bognor Regis, and has Miss Sparling there for the holidays. (MB 45)

* His edition of Fluvius Minucius is now out. (PBO 46)

* Now specified as being at Paul's College. He corresponds with **Eric Swan** over **Scriptor Ignotus**. (HRt 52)

Carton, Mrs. Sidney: *See* **Sparling, Miss Madeleine**.

Carver: Mr. (William) Marling's misnomer for **Geoffrey Harvey** (*q.v.*)

Catt
* Also known as "Puss-in-Boots"; bootmaker to **Lord Stoke**. *See also* **Cutt**. (TSAT 61)

Caxton
* Carpenter for the **Hallidays**, Hatch House. Married, no children. His father was one of **Lord Pomfret's** gamekeepers. His cousin Fred at Nutfield grew one-half inch with fever at age twenty-four. He plays the church organ. (PBO 46)

* He has been at Hatch House for forty-three years; his wife is rising seventy but still has all her teeth. (ESR 55)

* He can do any job, even electric, and is the church sexton. He makes **Mr. (Leonard) Halliday's** coffin. (NTL 56)

Caxton, Mrs.
* Housekeeper for the **Earl and Lady Pomfret**, Pomfret Towers. (PT 38)

Chaffinch

❖ Gardener to **Admiral Palliser**, Hallbury House. (MB 45)

Champion, Private

❖ In the office billeted on the **Villars**, Northbridge. Previously a male nurse for dipsomaniacs and epileptics, he helps with the flu outbreak. (NR 41)

Chapman, Bert

❖ Illegitimate child of **Mrs. Chapman**, the **Villars'** cook; his father, **Bob Chapman**, ran away before the wedding. He meets his father because they both turn out to be mess waiters in the same regiment in the Merchant Navy. (NR 41)

❖ He is a poor piece of work; though reported missing and presumed dead in the Far East during the war, he actually went off with a native girl and is probably the father of several families now. He still sends his mother a card every Christmas. (WDIM 54)

Chapman, Bob

❖ Intended husband of **Mrs. Chapman**, the **Villars'** cook, but ran away before the wedding. He meets his son, **Bert**, when they both turn out to be mess waiters in the same regiment in the Merchant Navy. (NR 41)

Chapman, Mrs. (by courtesy)

❖ Cook to the **Villars**, Northbridge. Her intended, **Bob Chapman**, ran away before they were married; the resulting son, **Bert**, is now a mess waiter in the Merchant Navy, and visits her on his leave. She is aunt of **Effie Bunce**, and her kitchen slave is **Edie Pover**. She walks out with **Corporal Jackson** to the Congregational Chapel, but once she hears that Bob is alive and in the same regiment as Bert, she allows Edie to become engaged to Corporal Jackson. (NR 41)

❖ Bert sends his mother a card from the Far East every Christmas. (WDIM 54)

❖ She has retired on her old age pension. (CQ 58)

Charles
❖ Nursery footman to **Lady Emily Leslie's** children in Cadogan Square. He sang comic songs, played the jew's harp, and pretended to fall downstairs after carrying the children up. (ESR 55)

Charles, Old
❖ Uncle of **Mrs. (Fred) Belton**, presumably his mother's brother, since in her dotage she used to mistake her son for his uncle Charlie. He had a wig and drank a bottle of port every night till he died. In his will, he left **Charles Belton** a hundred pounds. (LAR 48)

Chauffeur to the Gissings
❖ An ex-corporal in the Barsetshires, going into munitions. (CBI 40)

Chiendent, Mlle.
❖ French mistress at the Barchester High School; she teaches **Lavinia Merton**. (LAAA 59)

Chiffinch, Nurse ("Chiffy")
❖ Monthly (maternity) nurse to **Sibyl Knox** Coates and baby **Laura**. She shares a flat with her pals "Wardy" (see **Nurse Ward**) and "Heathy" (see **Nurse Heath**). (DH 34)

❖ Nurses **Julian Rivers** through the flu, and returns for Sibyl's second baby. (PT 38)

❖ She cares for **Mrs. (Helen) Keith** after her husband's death. (CBI 40)

❖ She nurses **Mr. (Henry) Leslie** at Holdings. (MH 42)

❖ She nurses **Elsa Belton** through the flu. (TH 44)

❖ As Sister Chiffinch, she heads the New Town, Hallbury, Cottage Hospital after **Sister Poulter**. She, Wardy, and Heathy want to run a small nursing home for the wealthy after the war. (MB 45)

❖ She keeps an eye on the failing **Dr. Dale**. (PBO 46)

❖ She is now about to retire from Harefield Cottage Hospital. She and Matron **Poppy Dudley** were trained by the strict **Matron at Knight's**. Her nephew spent the war in the Barsetshire regiment's quartermaster's office at Falmouth. She serves as monthly nurse to **Anne Fielding** Dale's twins and a **Mrs. Harris'** triplets, as well as to the premature girl of Lady Tadpole (née **Hermione Bingham**). Also nurses the **Marquis of Hartletop** through shingles, and **Mrs. (Priscilla) Dale** through her final days. (CC 50)

❖ Monthly nurse to **Lucy Marling** Adams and baby **Amabel Rose**. (DD 51)

❖ Monthly nurse to **Jessica Dean** and baby **Sarah Siddons Clover**. She was at school with **Mrs. (Poppy) Turner**. (WDIM 54)

❖ She is now living at Punshions with Miss Heath (but not Miss Ward?). (ADA 57)

* She is sharing the cottage with both Wardy and Heathy, and sees **Admiral and Mrs. Phelps** through to their deaths. (CQ 58)

* She had been monthly nurse for **Sally Wicklow** Foster, now Lady Pomfret, and her first child **Ludovic, Lord Mellings**; now also for **Edith Graham** Harcourt. (LAAA 59)

* Monthly nurse for **Susan Dean** Belton and her baby boy. (TSAT 61)

Chives

* Jobbing gardener for **Wiple** Terrace, and later for **Colonel Crofts**. A former corporal of the Barsetshires. (PE 47)

* Sexton as well as gardener at Southbridge (but see **Bateman**). (LAAA 59)

Choyce, Mr. Herbert, M.A.

* Vicar of Hatch End Church, which living he got through his old friend **Leonard Halliday**, who has it in his gift alternately with **the Bishop**. He had previously served a poor Liverpool parish. He obliges Mr. Halliday by speeding up the service. (PBO 46)

* An inventor of semi-ingenious items, who was at school with Mr. Halliday. He took a First in *Literae Humaniores*, and takes **Giles Foster** for coaching at Christmas. His father, an invalid, had wintered in Florence, where he met and disliked **Major Foster**. He does a six-year memorial service for **Lady Emily Leslie. Sir Robert Graham** will be his churchwarden after Mr. Halliday retires. (ESR 55)

* He used to deal with his tough Liverpool parishioners by knocking one or two of the liveliest out; as a parting gift, they gave him (stolen) silverware, and he still keeps open house for boys visiting from there. His deaf old aunt dies and leaves him a considerable sum; he and **Miss Merriman** become engaged. (NTL 56)

* Married to Miss Merriman at Easter. (ADA 57)

Choyce, Mrs.: *See* **Merriman, Miss**.

Clamp, Mr. and Mrs.
* A couple from Southport who vacation at the Aberdeathly Hydro along with **Councillor Budge** of the Gas Works and his wife. (HRt 52)

Clara, the Honourable: *See* **Bronson-Hewbury, the Honourable Clara.**

Clifford, Mr.
* Headmaster of the infants' school, Northbridge. (NR 41)

* An ardent pacifist, he plays the Saxon chief of the village in the Northbridge Pageant of History for the Coronation. (WDIM 54)

Clover, Aubrey
* Playwright, actor, and chameleon. His real name is **Caleb Lover**, which when signed "C. Lover," looked like "Clover." His mother is the widow of a bank manager in **Miss Hampton's** father's parish; she is

religious and doesn't approve of the theatre. He used to sing in the church choir, and his old nurse still lives with him, in a flat in London. He was hit in the stomach with shrapnel while trying to rescue men at Dunkirk (where he met **Mr. Wickham**), and thus could not enlist, so he went back on stage and entertained the troops. His leading lady is **Jessica Dean**, and their specialty is the "triangle play": *Three For a Letter*; *Hic, Haec, Hoc*; *Attitude to Life*; and *Out Goes She*. He puts on the latter for the Red Cross Fete, featuring Jessica, **Francis Brandon**, and **Peggy Arbuthnot**. (PE 47)

* His mother has arthritis. His latest play is *Home Is Best*. When the **Bishop's Wife** is rude to him at the Perpetual Curates' Benefit Fund Charity Matinee, he extemporizes a song, "I took my husband's gaiters off and put them on myself." (LAR 48)

* His mother died last winter. His latest hit is *If Turnips Were Watches*, and he marries Jessica Dean on a Thursday. (OBH 49)

* He does a two-man show with **Denis Stonor** while Jessica is pregnant, and his new play is *In for an Inch*. After the baby, **Sarah Siddons**, is born, they go to America for the autumn and winter. When the baby and Nannie want a breath of country air, they go to his mother, who seems to be alive again, and is known to **Isabel Dale** as **Mrs. Audrey Lover**. (CC 50)

* New play: *He Pulled Out a Plum*. (HRt 52)

* They extend their London flat into a duplex so that Sarah Siddons can have plenty of nursery room. Jessica is preg-

nant again, and if it is a boy they will name it for **Henry** Irving and Henry Kemble. After the birth, expected in October, they will go to America for the winter. His latest play: *Fly Away My Heart*. He agrees to do a sketch from *Two-Step for Three* for **Lydia Merton's** Northbridge Coronation show, and also involves **Ludovic, Lord Mellings**, in the production. (WDIM 54)

❖ They now have children, though no mention of whether the new one was a boy. His new comedy is *Pigs in Clover*. (ESR 55)

❖ He is thinking of doing a musical version of Shaw's *You Never Can Tell*. (TSAT 61)

Clover, Henry Irving/Henry Kemble
❖ Names chosen for the imminent second child of **Jessica Dean** and **Aubrey Clover**, if it's a boy; due in October. His older sister is **Sarah Siddons Clover**. (WDIM 54)

❖ They now have children, but nothing said as to name. (ESR 55)

Clover, Sarah Siddons
❖ Eldest child of **Jessica Dean** and **Aubrey Clover**; born in the coulisses, whatever they are. She and her Nannie stay with her grandmother, **Mrs. Audrey Lover**. (CC 50)

❖ "A dramatic little person, like her mother"; she is to be bridesmaid at the wedding of **Ludovic Foster, Lord Mellings**, and **Lavinia Merton**. (TSAT 61)

Cloves, Mr.
❖ Guest at **Pomfret** Towers; only a shooting man and of no interest. (PT 38)

Coates, Adrian

* Young publisher of **Mrs. (Laura) Morland's** books; many hints that his family is Jewish. While at Oxford, he wrote and had published a book of poetry, *The Golden Dust-Bin*, of which he is now rightly ashamed. He proposes to Mrs. Morland in a maudlin state, but is briskly refused and goes on to get engaged to **Sibyl Knox**. (HR 33)

* Married, with a baby, **Laura**. He takes **Tony Morland** and **Robert Wesendonck** out rowing. (DH 34)

* They are having a second baby. (PT 38)

* The second child's name is **Richard**. (TB 39)

* Now there are three children; they all evacuate to Mrs. Morland's house. (CBI 40)

* He employs **Mr. Holden**. (NR 41)

* He is interested in **Oliver Marling's** book on **Bohun**. (CC 50)

* He has urgent business in America and cancels his talk for the Barchester Central Library. (HRt 52)

* He has taken Mr. Holden as a partner. (JC 53)

Coates, Laura

* First child of **Adrian Coates** and **Sibyl Knox** Coates. (DH 34)

Coates, (Mrs.) Sibyl: *See* **Knox, Sibyl**.

Coates, Richard

* Unnamed second child of **Adrian Coates** and **Sibyl Knox** Coates. (PT 38)

* Now named. (TB 39)

Cobbold, Mr. and Mrs.
* Bailiff of Gatherum Castle, and wife. He is very sound on cows, so **Lucy Marling** Adams and **Emmy Graham** go to tea at their house rather than staying at the **Pallisers'** Conservative Do. (CC 50)

* He doesn't do bulls quite as well. (DD 51)

Codman, Hake
* Stars with **Glamora Tudor** in *Moslem Love*. (JC 53)

Collerton, Mrs. Commodore
* Object of **Tubby Fewling's** youthful affections, but she was twice his age, with a large family, and they were posted to Australia a few weeks later anyway. (JC 53)

Concord, Sherman
* Along with **Lee Sum(p)ter**, a beau of **Edith Graham** on her visit to the States. (ADA 57)

Conque, Amélie
* French lady's maid to **Lady Emily Leslie** at Rushwater; sometimes called "Conk." (WS 34)

* She and Lady Emily are now at the **Grahams'** house, Holdings. (MH 42)

* Her mangy poodle is named de Gaulle. (LAR 48)

* When Lady Emily dies, she is left a hundred pounds a year for life. She plans to go to **Mrs. Baker** at Folkestone, where she always took her holidays (and with whom she always quarreled), though **Emmy Graham** wants her as house-

keeper when she sets up at **Mr. Macpherson's** old house. (OBH 49)

* She is quarreling with her landlady (presumably Mrs. Baker), and visiting Rushwater once a year. Once, after the war, she returned to her home in Vache-en-Étable, but there was a family feud over a field of mangolds to be divided among eighteen legatees. (ESR 55)

* She apparently also visits Holdings once a year, but this year she goes to France to quarrel with her relations over the inheritance of a field of beetroot (which is pretty much the same as mangolds). (NTL 56)

Cook
* To the **Brandons**, Stories. She reads tea leaves. (TB 39)

* She only came to Stories after **Mr. Brandon's** death, not as early as **Rose** and **Nurse (Miss Vance)**. Her mother's aunt was third housemaid to the **Pallisers** at Gatherum Castle and went out with the second footman until he got one of the kitchenmaids into trouble and married her, so she took against men and rose to be head housemaid with six under her. (CC 50)

Cook
* Everyone in Barsetshire apparently has the same Cook. She is rather superstitious, reads tea leaves, and often has a Leg.

"Copper"
* A friend of **Charles Belton** who has a motorbike and works as ground crew at the aerodome. His actual name is Bobby, from Rickmansworth. (TH 44)

Cowman, Hilda

✦ Attended Fairlawns School with **Miss (Cicely) Holly** and **Mrs. (Molly) Watson**; she was a pal of the latter, but got a job in a factory and then looked down on her for being married. (MB 45)

Cowshay, Miss

✦ Former clerk in the cashier's office of Pilchard's Stores, at the desk marked G to M. She is now in the Regional Commissioner's Office, working with **Oliver Marling** and **John Leslie; David Leslie** is her "beau ideel." (MH 42)

✦ She now works for **Sam Adams** in the "casting department," Hogglestock Rolling Mills; likely a typo. (LAR 48)

✦ Now in the costing department. (OBH 49)

✦ Second-in-command of the costing department. She has a brother Bob, who has a son. When she was at the Regional Commissioner's Office in Barchester, she was in charge of the teleprinter. (CC 50)

✦ She has moved to become secretary of the Hogglestock Rolling Mills Office at Pomfret Towers, leaving the costing department to a **Miss Carton**. (ADA 57)

✦ She has become secretary to **Giles Foster, Lord Pomfret**. (LAAA 59)

Cox, Mrs.

✦ Landlady to **Mrs. (Joyce Perry) Smith**, and aunt of **Millie Poulter**. (MH 42)

✦ She sometimes obliges as cook for the **Marlings** as well as keeping lodgings. She is a cousin of the postmistress who keeps the Shop. (CC 50)

* Landlady to **Miss Hobb**. (HRt 52)

Coxon, Geoff

* Son of **Mr. Coxon** the garage owner. Eighteen years old, going into the Navy, and walking out with **Marigold Smith**. (LAR 48)

* His mother's name is **Ruth**. He and Marigold get engaged; he has a nice car. (DD 51)

Coxon, Miss

* A pretty girl from Northbridge, who did V.A.D. and served under **Matron** at Barchester General during the war. **Corporal Hoggett** scared her with plasticine scars on his face in the plastic surgery ward. (DD 51)

Coxon, Mr.

* Owner of the garage. His taxi breaks down. (GU 43)

* Husband of **Mrs. (Ruth) Coxon**, father of **Geoff**. (LAR 48)

Coxon, Mrs. Ruth

* Wife of **Mr. Coxon** the garage owner, and mother of **Geoff**. No first name as yet. (LAR 48)

* Her first name is given. When Geoff gets engaged to **Marigold Smith**, she gives her a Mizpah brooch. (DD 51)

Crackman, Bert

* Nephew of **Sidney Crackman**, who also works for the Railroad; he is in the driver's cab of the *Gatherum Castle*, but won't even polish her name plate. (LAR 48)

Crackman, Sidney

* Guard on Our Railway Line, with thirty years' service. (GU 43)

✤ His nephew **Bert Crackman** is in the driver's cab of the *Gatherum Castle*. (LAR 48)

Crammer
✤ Former gardener to the **Warings**, Beliers Priory; he leaves to help on his father's farm. (LAR 48)

Crawford of Lazarus
✤ **Master of Lazarus** College, Oxford (*see* also; he is often given no proper name, and later metamorphoses into **Lord Skinner**). Leftist; as the former headmaster of Southbridge School, he hired the young, communistic **Philip Winter**. (SH 37)

✤ He preceded **Mr. (Bill) Birkett** as headmaster. When he came to Lazarus, his leftist leanings drove **Simnet** to leave his position as scout there. His students do Modern Greats, and he maneuvers to get them moved out to St. Swithin's so that the Institute for Ideological Interference can be billeted at Lazarus. (CBI 40)

Crawley, Grace
✤ Eldest, fair-haired granddaughter of **Dean Josiah and Mrs. Crawley**; their eldest son, a clergyman, is presumably her father; her mother is a mild invalid. Her younger sister (by a year) is **Jane**; both are over twenty-one, have jobs, and the Dean's secretary, a young clergyman, is in love with both. Her brother, presumably younger, is a farmer out Chaldicotes way. She gets engaged to **John-Arthur Crosse** on the same night that Jane gets engaged to **George Halliday**, and they are married in a double ceremony in the Cathedral. (ADA 57)

Crawley, Jane

* Dark-haired granddaughter of **Dean Josiah and Mrs. Crawley**; their eldest son, a clergyman, is presumably her father; her mother is a mild invalid. Her elder sister (by a year) is **Grace**; both are over twenty-one, have jobs, and the Dean's secretary, a young clergyman, is in love with both. She left school before her exams and did hens at her brother's, who does mixed farming over Chaldicotes way. She gets engaged to **George Halliday** on the same night that Grace gets engaged to **Mr. (John-Arthur) Crosse**, and they are married in a double ceremony in the Cathedral. (ADA 57)

* They are farming at Hatch House, and have a new baby, **Martin Halliday** (after **Martin Leslie**). Their piglets win a silver medal at the High Rising Agricultural. (TSAT 61)

Crawley, Dr. Josiah (the Dean)

* Dean of Barchester cathedral, husband of **Mrs. Crawley**. They have many children, including one set of twins. They have **Mr. Johns** for a visit. (PT 38)

* He visits Finland. (TB 39)

* He was in Finland for six days for a conference. He was named for his grandfather (*cf.* Trollope), and was at Oxford with **Mr. Birkett**; he marries **Rose Birkett** to **John Fairweather**. Their youngest child **Octavia** (now engaged to his secretary **Tommy Needham**) was indeed an eighth child, though two of them were boys and one died quite young. (CBI 40)

* **Miss Pemberton** visits briefly, but he and Octavia have the flu and Mrs. Crawley is getting it, so she has to leave. (NR 41)

❖ Their two sons are in the Church, two daughters married clergymen, and Octavia is engaged to one. (GU 43)

❖ He did a lecture cruise of the Northern capitals with his wife and three of his daughters. He and his wife attend Robbin Day ceremonies at the Hosiers' Girls' Foundation School. (TH 44)

❖ He has personally christened all seventeen of their grand-children. Their third girl's second boy is going to the Southbridge Junior School soon; see, possibly, **Tertia Crawley** Beckett. Three of their grandsons have been demobilized and can't get jobs. **Susan Dean** lives with them during the week. (PE 47)

❖ He delivers the Congleton Divinity Lectures at Oxbridge, and marries **Anne Fielding** to **Robin Dale**. One son-in-law is a wealthy archdeacon, and there are almost twenty grandchildren. (LAR 48)

❖ He christens Robin and Anne Fielding Dale's twins. (CC 50)

❖ He finally publishes *A Foreigner in Finland*, about his trip to Scandinavia in 1938. (DD 51)

❖ Now all eight children are alive: six daughters, and two sons with wives and children who are advancing rapidly in their University and schoolmastering careers (but *see* above, CBI 40 and GU 43, and below, WDIM 54). Their daughter **Secunda's** husband is editor of a small church magazine, and **Tertia** is the wife of the **Rev. Anselm Beckett**. He also has Australian cousins doing very well in wool. (HRt 52)

❖ Their eldest son's cure of souls is in a mining district. (WDIM 54)

❖ **Grace** and **Jane Crawley** are presumably this eldest son's daughters, as Grace is his eldest granddaughter (of eight granddaughters in total); their brother is a mixed farmer. Grace and Jane are married in a double wedding in the Cathedral. He and Mr. Bostock also officiate at the wedding of **Miss Merriman** and **Mr. (Herbert) Choyce**. (ADA 57)

❖ He is seventy years old. Another one of the grandchildren, an undergraduate, sings "My Lesbia Hath a Beaming Eye" on a Hellenic cruise with **Miss Hampton, Miss Bent**, and **the Bishop**. The youngest grandson, **Septimus Arabin Crawley**, is still at school. (CQ 58)

❖ They have about sixty children, grandchildren, and great-grandchildren. (TSAT 61)

Crawley, Mrs.

❖ Wife of **Dean (Josiah) Crawley**. They have many children, including one set of twins. They have **Mr. Johns** for a visit. (PT 38)

❖ Their youngest child **Octavia** is engaged to **Tommy Needham**; she was indeed an eighth child, though two of them were boys and one died quite young. (CI 40)

❖ **Miss Pemberton** visits, but the Dean and Octavia have the flu and Mrs. Crawley is getting it, so she has to leave. (NR 41)

❖ Their two sons are in the Church, two daughters married clergymen, and Octavia is engaged to one. (GU 43)

❖ She and three of their daughters went along when the Dean did a lecture cruise of the Northern capitals. She and he attend Bobbin Day ceremonies at the Hosiers' Girls' Foundation School. (TH 44)

❖ She is the eighth child of a country vicarage herself. (PBO 46)

❖ **Susan Dean** lives with them during the week. They currently have seventeen grandchildren. Their third girl's second boy is going to the Southbridge Junior School soon; see, possibly, **Tertia Crawley** Beckett. Three of their grandsons have been demobilized and can't get jobs. (PE 47)

❖ One son-in-law is a wealthy archdeacon, and there are almost twenty grandchildren. (LAR 48)

❖ Now all eight children are alive: six daughters, and two sons with wives and children who are advancing rapidly in their University and schoolmastering careers (but *see* above, CBI 40 and GU 43, and below, WDIM 54). Their daughter **Secunda's** husband is editor of a small church magazine, and **Tertia** is the wife of the **Rev. Anselm Beckett**. (HRt 52)

❖ Their eldest son's cure of souls is in a mining district. (WDIM 54)

❖ She is sort of a cousin of **Lord Crosse**. (NTL 56)

❖ **Grace** and **Jane Crawley** are presumably their eldest son's daughters, as Grace is her eldest granddaughter (of eight granddaughters in total); their brother, presumably younger, is a farmer out Chaldicotes way. Grace and Jane are married in a double wedding in the Cathedral. (ADA 57)

* Another one of the grandchildren, an undergraduate, sings "My Lesbia Hath a Beaming eye" on a Hellenic cruise with **Miss Hampton, Miss Bent,** and **the Bishop**. The youngest grandson, **Septimus Arabin Crawley,** is still at school. (CQ 58)

* They have about sixty children, grandchildren, and great-grandchildren. (TSAT 61)

Crawley, Octavia

* Eighth and youngest child of **Dean Josiah and Mrs. Crawley**. She nurses at Barchester General Hospital, is engaged to **Tommy Needham**, and is a bridesmaid for **Rose Birkett**. (CBI 40)

* She is now at the Cottage Hospital, and keen on Caesareans. (MH 42)

* She wants to train for facial surgery or difficult baby cases. (GU 43)

* She and Tommy are recently married and expect their first baby in summer. She is doing wonders with the Moral Welfare Committee in Lambton and Worsted. (TH 44)

* Their first baby is a boy. (MB 45)

* She and her son visit her parents. (PBO 46)

* Their two elder children are of nursery-school age. (LAR 48)

* She now has four of the eight children she means to have. (DD 51)

* Pregnant again, she is the power behind **Lady Glencora Palliser** Waring's presidency of the Lambton Women's Institute. (HRt 52)

❖ She is expecting their seventh baby any minute, but it turns out to be twins (a boy and a girl), thus achieving the desired eight finally, and in the nick of time. (TSAT 61)

Crawley, Secunda

❖ Presumably the second daughter of **Dean (Josiah) and Mrs. Crawley**; wife of the editor of a small church magazine. (HRt 52)

Crawley, Septimus Arabin

❖ The youngest grandson of **Dean (Josiah) and Mrs. Crawley**, presumably a son's child, and in that family, perhaps even a seventh child. He is still at school. (CQ 58)

Crawley, Tertia

❖ Daughter of **Dean (Josiah) and Mrs. Crawley**, wife of the **Reverend Anselm Beckett**. (HRt 52)

❖ If her name is truly indicative, she was the Crawley's third girl whose second boy is going to the Southbridge Junior School soon. (PE 47)

Cripps, Mrs.

❖ Charwoman for **Noel Merton's** chambers in London. (GU 43)

Crofts, Lieutenant-Colonel the Reverend Francis Edward

❖ Known as Colonel Crofts, addressed as Edward. Born in India, he served in the artillery there for many years. His family had been there for four generations before him, and his two sons are also in the Indian army. They have their own children in India and their own country homes in England, as both inherited money from an uncle and married well. He has been a widower for twelve years;

on his retirement, he was ordained and became Vicar of Southbridge. His army batman **Bateman** accompanies him as general factotum. He gets engaged to **Miss Effie Arbuthnot**. (PE 47)

Crofts, Mrs. Colonel: *See* Arbuthnot, Miss Effie.

Crosse, Enid, Lady

❖ Unnamed wife of **Lord Cross** (spelled this way in this book alone) and mother of one daughter, then **John Arthur Cross**, and then another daughter. She has been dead for about twelve years. (ESR 55)

❖ Her name is given; she came of West Barsetshire stock. Her younger daughter is **Mrs. Richard A. Carter**; the elder daughter lives in London with her family. (NTL 56)

Crosse, Mr. John-Arthur

❖ In this book only, "John Arthur Cross"; a pleasant, thirty-ish bachelor, manager of the bank branch at the **Hallidays'** Old Manor House, Hatch End; he lives upstairs, but is to leave when the branch moves. He will be promoted and go to London. His father is **Lord Cross**, a well-off director of the bank; his mother, **Lady Cross**, has been dead for about twelve years. "Done for" by **Dorothy** Vidler (or Panter). He was a second lieutenant in France in '44. Both he and **George Halliday** are fond of **Edith Graham**. (ESR 55)

❖ His younger sister is **Mrs. Richard A. Carter**; his older sister lives in London with her family. He was at Winchester and New College. (NTL 56)

❖ He gets engaged to **Grace Crawley** and they are married in the Cathedral along with her sister **Jane** and **George Halliday**. (ADA 57)

Crosse, Lord (John Morton, Third Baron Crosse)

❖ In this book only, spelled "Cross"; of Cross Hall in East Barsetshire. **Lady Cross** has been dead for about twelve years. He has one son, **John Arthur**, and two daughters, one younger than John, both married with children. He is a well-off director of the bank John works for. (ESR 55)

❖ His wife, **Enid, Lady Crosse**, came of West Barsetshire stock; he is sort of a cousin of **Mrs. Crawley**. He has a long lease on the Old Manor House that John-Arthur used to live in, and gives it over to his daughter (at first the elder, later the younger) **Mrs. Richard A. Carter** and her husband and family. The elder daughter lives in London with her family. He proposes to **Mrs. (Laura) Morland**, but is turned down. (NTL 56)

Crowder, Miss

❖ Of Glycerine Cottage (named by her in error for *les Glycines*), which she shares with **Miss Hopgood** (*"chere amie"*). She is typically English in thinking herself spiritually French. They go to the Riviera every year, where they stay at the Pension **Ramsden** in Menton. (NR 41)

❖ She and Miss Hopgood organize the children's performance for the Coronation festivities, and she plays Elizabeth I. (WDIM 54)

Crump

❖ Builder from over Allington way; good at old houses. He works on The Cedars for **Oliver Marling**. (DD 51)

Cruncher, Old

❖ Of Hacker's Corner. Former head cowman at Rushwater under **Mr. (Henry) Leslie**. He has been dying for fifteen

months, and sends for **Martin Leslie**, then drinks a quart
of cider and feels better. (PBO 46)

✦ As a boy, he heard that the Frenchies were licked by the
Prooshans. (LAR 48)

Cumberboard, General ("Pinky")
✦ Friend of **Peggy Arbuthnot**, now in business. (PE 47)

Curwen
✦ Chauffeur to **the Brandons**. He can express disapproval
with his neck alone. (TB 39)

✦ He has returned from the aero-engine works to his cottage,
his contemptuous wife, and Mrs. Brandon's car. (PE 47)

✦ He has left to go into the garage business. (CC 50)

Cutsam, Constant
✦ The new American husband of **Evie Merivale**. (MB 45)

Cutt
✦ Of Saville Row; tailor to **Lord Stoke**. See also **Catt**.
(TSAT 61)

Dahlia, Miss
* ❖ Of the Maison Tozier, Barchester's best beauty parlor, which is owned by a cousin of **Mr. Tozer** the caterer. (JC 53)

Dale, Christopher
* ❖ Uncle of **Isabel Dale**; he grows Canadian wheat at Allington. (CC 50)

Dale, Dr.
* ❖ Rector of St. Hall Friars (*see* **Saint Aella**), Hallbury. An eighty-two-year-old widower with one son, **Robin**. Late in life, he married a woman thirty years younger than he, who then died when Robin was five or six. He is vice president of the Barsetshire Archaeological Society, and has them to the Rectory to look for Roman brickwork in the well. He writes on the classics as well as on Haggai, and teaches Latin to **Anne Fielding**. He encourages Robin to go back to Southbridge School to teach. (MB 45)

* His great-aunt was **Lily Dale** of Allington (*cf.* Trollope).
  He blesses Robin and Anne on their engagement, then
  dies. (PBO 46)

* He died only two years ago, but *see* above. (CC 50)

Dale, Dora Maud

* One of the twin daughters (the other is **Roberta Fielding**)
  of **Robin** and **Anne Fielding Dale**; named for her
  mother's mother and for **Miss Bunting**. (CC 50)

* Dora and Roberta are now four. (WDIM 54)

* They have a little brother. (ADA 57)

Dale, Isabel

* Assistant to **Eleanor Grantly** at the Red Cross Library.
  She lives with her mother at Allington. Her people are
  cousins of **Robin Dale**. (OBH 49)

* Twenty-nine years old; her home is the Great House,
  Allington, where her mother, **Mrs. (Priscilla) Dale**, still
  lives. Her father, the grandson of the patent-medicine
  heiress (*cf.* Trollope), died ten years ago, before the war.
  Her mother has all her own and her husband's family
  money for life, and keeps Isabel in line by throwing heart
  attacks; she also wouldn't allow Isabel to marry **John**, her
  fiancé, who was with the Barsetshires and was killed fighting in Italy. Isabel is writing about him for his friends. Her
  uncle is **Christopher Dale** at Allington. Her (mild) secret
  is that she writes thrillers under the anagrammatic pseudonym **Lisa Bedale**; her detective is Gerry Marston (*Aconite
  at Night*). Due to disagreements, she leaves the Red Cross
  Library when **Sally (Wicklow), Lady Pomfret**, does. She

goes to help with **Lucy Marling's** wedding, and stays on. She is godmother to **Roberta Fielding Dale**, and helps **Jeff Palliser, Lord Silverbridge**, with the regimental history of the Barsetshires that he is trying to write. Her mother finally has a real illness and dies, leaving Isabel a fortune. Isabel then gets a proposal from **Mr. Wickham** (declined with thanks), an almost-proposal from **Oliver Marling**, and finally accepts Jeff Palliser. (CC 50)

❖ Now married and the Countess of Silverbridge. They rent the Lodge at Silverbridge from **Cecil Waring**. She expects a baby in November, to be named after Jeff's brother **Lord Gerald Palliser**. (DD 51)

❖ **Gerald Palliser**, future Duke of Omnium, is born. (HRt 52)

❖ They have another boy. (JC 53)

❖ She is pregnant again. (ESR 55)

❖ Their son, presumably Gerald, is six or seven years old. (LAAA 59)

Dale, Lily

❖ Of Allington (*cf.* Trollope). She lived on the romance of her broken love affair until she was well over eighty, and was great-aunt (or something) to **Robin Dale**. (MB 45)

❖ Now she is great-aunt to Robin's father **Dr. Dale**. (PBO 46)

❖ Also great-aunt of **Miss Eleanor Grantly**. (LAR 48)

Dale, Mrs. Priscilla

❖ Of the Great House, Allington. Her family were Greshams, from Loamshire. For all the following *cf.* Trollope:

her grandfather Gresham had the Scatcherd fortune, and
the family also has the money left to Mary Thorne, niece of
Dr. Thorne and later Mrs. Frank Gresham. Priscilla's
husband was the grandson (or his grandfather married the
niece) of the patent-medicine heiress, and died ten years
ago, leaving everything to her for life. Her daughter is
Isabel Dale, whom she wouldn't allow to marry and has
kept in line by throwing heart attacks. She finally does die
and leaves Isabel a fortune, though the Great House and its
estates go to **Robin Dale**. (CC 50)

Dale, Roberta Fielding

❖ One of the twin daughters (the other is **Dora Maud**) of
  Robin and **Anne Fielding Dale**; named for her mother's
  father. Her godmother is **Isabel Dale**. (CC 50)

❖ Dora and Roberta are now four. (WDIM 54)

❖ They have a little brother. (ADA 57)

Dale, Robin

❖ Only son of **Dr. Dale** and his wife, who died when Robin
  was five or six. He was at Southbridge School as an upper
  boy, then returned as the junior classical master; when war
  broke out he went into the Barsetshire Yeomanry. He was
  commissioned, and fought in Africa and Sicily, but his foot
  was shattered at Anzio and had to be amputated. Now, at
  twenty-six, he is back at home tutoring six boys, including
  Frank Gresham. He gets his old job at Southbridge back,
  and has an Understanding with **Anne Fielding**. (MB 45)

❖ Now twenty-seven, he is teaching at Southbridge, and is
  designated to become housemaster of the junior house. He

is engaged to Anne Fielding, and his father blesses them, then dies. (PBO 46)

❖ He is assistant master at Southbridge, and will get his House after **Mr. (Bill) Birkett** retires. (PE 47)

❖ He marries Anne. (LAR 48)

❖ They expect a baby in spring. (OBH 49)

❖ They have twin girls, **Roberta Fielding** and **Dora Maud** (named for her parents and Miss Bunting). His mother had a fortune, which he inherited. He also inherits the Great House at Allington and its estates when **Mrs. (Priscilla) Dale** dies. (CC 50)

❖ Dora and Roberta are now four. He is thinking of starting his own prep school for boys. (WDIM 54)

❖ They have a little boy. (ADA 57)

❖ They and their growing family have moved to Allington and started a very successful pre-preparatory school for boys. (TSAT 61)

Damper, the Reverend J. J.

❖ Nineteenth-century headmaster of Southbridge School and author of *Perambulations in Palestine*. In 1854, he wrote the school song, or *Carmen Southbridgense*. (SH 37)

❖ Headmaster 1850–1868, he retired to an honorary canonry of Barchester, which he held in a state of mild imbecility for the next ten years. The Great East Window in the school chapel is in his memory. (CBI 40)

❖ Headmaster 1849–1856, but *see* above. The *Carmen* is set to an old German chorale. (PE 47)

Danby, Mr.

* Vicar of Southbridge. His two aunts live in **Wiple** Terrace. (CBI 40)

Dandridge, Amber

* Student at Barchester High School, refused swimming colors by **Miss Pettinger** because she cheeked **Miss Moore** in the bookroom. (SH 37)

Davies, Dr.

* Woman physician filling in in Lambton while the regular doctor is in the Middle East. (GU 43)

Dean, Betty

* Sixth child of **Frank** and **Rachel Dean**, now eighteen years old. Her elder siblings are (in rough order by age) **Laurence, Helen, Gerald**, and **the Twins**, younger are **Susan, Robin**, and **Jessica**. She has a Classics scholarship to Oxford, and is rather an intellectual snob. She steps in to play Phaedra in **Mrs. (Louise) Palmer's** production of *Hippolytus*. (AF 36)

* She took a First in Greats and went to graduate school at Bryn Mawr. Her name is occasionally spelled "Deane." She is engaged to **Woolcott Jefferson van Dryven** of New York. (BL 39)

* She works with the American Red Cross. (GU 43)

* She is her husband's right-hand man in reorganizing the peanut export trade. They have three children. (PE 47)

* They live in New York. She visits during the Marling Red Cross Fete. (LAR 48)

* They are almost millionaires, and have a place on Long Island and a ranch in Texas as well as the New York penthouse. (WDIM 54)

* They are now multimillionaires. (LAAA 59)

Dean, Mr. Frank
* Husband of **Rachel Dean** and father of (in rough order by age) **Laurence, Helen, Gerald, the Twins, Betty, Susan, Robin**, and **Jessica**. He is an engineer, runs his own firm, and gives **Richard Tebben** a job to thank him for saving Jessica from a bull. (AF 36)

* They now have a house near Winter Overcotes; at sixty-eight, he is retired and in the Observer Corps. (GU 43)

* With Susan's marriage to **Freddy Belton**, the County (including, unfortunately, **Lady Norton**) begins to recognize them. (OBH 49)

* As a young engineer, he built railways in South America. (WDIM 54)

* There are two Dean grandsons at Southbridge School who use engine oil to slick down their hair. (CQ 58)

* He joins the Syndicate formed by **Sam Adams** to buy **Wiple** terrace away from **Lord Aberfordbury** and give it to Southbridge School. (TSAT 61)

Dean, Gerald
* Third child of **Frank** and **Rachel Dean**; his elder siblings (in rough order by age) are **Laurence** and **Helen**, younger are **the Twins, Betty, Susan, Robin**, and **Jessica**. He is now in India with his regiment. He played cricket for the Army. (AF 36)

* Still in India. (GU 43)

* He has one child. (PE 47)

* Still in the Army. (LAR 48)

Dean, Helen

* Second child of **Frank** and **Rachel Dean**, born a year after **Laurence**, who is her particular brother. Following them are (in rough order by age) **Gerald, the Twins, Betty, Susan, Robin**, and **Jessica**. She is a race driver, twenty-five years old. She plays Artemis in **Mrs. (Louise) Palmer's** production of *Hippolytus*, and gets engaged to **Charles Fanshawe**. (AF 36)

* They are married. (CBI 40)

* She is driving for the Wrens. (GU 43)

* She runs an important bit of motor transport. (TH 44)

* They have three children. The eldest, **Ray (for Rachel)**, at eight, is the oldest of the Dean grandchildren. (PE 47)

Dean, Jessica

* Ninth and youngest child of **Frank** and **Rachel Dean**. Her older siblings (in rough order by age) are **Laurence, Helen, Gerald, the Twins, Betty, Susan**, and **Robin**. She gets donkey rides and is saved from a bull by **Richard Tebben**. (AF 36)

* She is still at home, collecting salvage and studying jiu-jitsu. (GU 43)

* The only explanation for her theatrical inclinations is that her great-great-great-grandmother was frightened by Mrs. Siddons' Lady Macbeth. She went to the Royal Academy

of Dramatic Art, became **Aubrey Clover's** leading lady as Mrs. Carvel in *Attitude to Life*, and plays the idiot soubrette maid in the Red Cross Fete production of *Out Goes She*. (PE 47)

❖ **Oliver Marling** proposes, she declines. (LAR 48)

❖ She marries Aubrey Clover on a Thursday. (OBH 49)

❖ She is pregnant. After their baby **Sarah Siddons** is born, they go to America for the autumn and winter. Her dresser is **Mrs. Tropes**, and **Miss Mowbray** takes care of everything else. (CC 50)

❖ They extend their London flat into a duplex so that they can have plenty of nursery room. She is pregnant again, and if it is a boy they will name it for **Henry** Irving and/or Henry Kemble. After the birth, expected in October, they will go to America for the winter. (WDIM 54)

❖ They now have children, though no mention of whether the new one was a boy. (ESR 55)

Dean, Laurence
❖ Eldest child of **Frank** and **Rachel Dean**; his younger siblings are (in rough order by age) **Helen, Gerald, the Twins, Betty, Susan, Robin**, and **Jessica**. He is also expected to be heir to his mother's brother, **Mr. (Fred) Palmer**. He is twenty-seven years old and working in his father's firm. While playing the title role in **Mrs. (Louise) Palmer's** production of *Hippolytus*, he flirts with **Margaret Tebben**. He twists his ankle and can't go on stage, but gets engaged to Margaret as a result. (AF 36)

❖ He is in Scotland doing liaison with the Poles; Margaret and the babies (a boy and a girl) are with him. (GU 43)

* He is on a home job. (MB 45)

* They have four children. (PE 47)

* They live abroad. Their son at Beliers Priory School is **Young Dean**. (LAR 48)

* They now live in Worsted. (WDIM 54)

Dean, Mrs. Rachel (née Palmer)

* Wife of **Frank Dean** and mother of (in rough order by age) **Laurence, Helen, Gerald, the Twins, Betty, Susan, Robin**, and **Jessica**. She is the youngest sister of **Mr. (Fred) Palmer**, who has them stay in the Dower House, Worsted, for the summer. She is an enchantress of almost fifty, with a slight heart condition, and **Richard Tebben** is infatuated with her. (AF 36)

* They now have a house near Winter Overcotes; she runs the local Land Army. (GU 43)

* Her heart is now all right, but she still uses it as an excuse. (PE 47)

* She falls asleep on **Mr. (Sam) Adams'** couch at the Old Bank House garden party. With Susan's marriage to **Freddy Belton**, the County (including, unfortunately, **Lady Norton**) begins to recognize them. (OBH 49)

* When young, she traveled with her husband to South America, where the doctors think she got a germ that makes her sleepy. (WDIM 54)

* There are two Dean grandsons at Southbridge School who use engine oil to slick down their hair. (CQ 58)

Dean, Robin

* Eighth child of **Frank** and **Rachel Dean**; his elder siblings are (in rough order by age) **Laurence, Helen, Gerald, the Twins, Betty**, and **Susan**; the only younger one is **Jessica**. He is a school friend of **Tony Morland**. (AF 36)

* He graduated at the top of his O.C.T.U. (GU 43)

* He has twin children. (PE 47)

* He is learning farming, and the agricultural college places him at Rushwater with **Martin Leslie**. (LAR 48)

* He is still at Rushwater. (OBH 49)

Dean, Susan

* Seventh child of **Frank** and **Rachel Dean**; her elder siblings are (in rough order by age) **Laurence, Helen, Gerald, the Twins**, and **Betty**; younger are **Robin** and **Jessica**. Sixteen years old, she is good at math; **Richard Tebben** names his new car after her. (AF 36)

* She is working with prisoners of war at Oxford. (GU 43)

* As well as her work on that Red Cross P.O.W. education project, she works for the Barsetshire Red Cross Hospital Library and lives with **Dean** and **Mrs. Crawley** during the week. A capable twenty-seven, she runs the Red Cross Fete, nurses **Lydia Keith** Merton through the measles, and indulges **Colin Keith**. (PE 47)

* She is Red Cross Depot Librarian. She rejects Colin Keith's proposal, and accepts **Freddy Belton's**. (LAR 48)

* Now married, they live on the second floor of Arcot House with his parents. They expect a baby in August. (OBH 49)

D

* There is a very satisfactory baby. (CC 50)

* Their son is named **Frederick**, but is called Baby to avoid confusion. She is known as Mrs. Freddy in the village. They moved to Dowlah Cottage after **Mrs. Hoare** died. (DD 51)

* They now have a daughter as well. (HRt 52)

* They live at Harefield and have a third baby, a boy. (TSAT 61)

Dean Twins, the

* Sons of **Frank** and **Rachel Dean**; their elder siblings are (in rough order by age) **Laurence, Helen**, and **Gerald**; younger are **Betty, Susan, Robin**, and **Jessica**. They are both at sea. (AF 36)

* They are still at sea, in the same squadron. (GU 43)

* They are "rising rapidly and equally in the senior service," but are still unmarried. (LAR 48)

* They had been with the Mediterranean fleet. (OBH 49)

Dean, Young

* Son of **Margaret Tebben** Dean and **Laurence Dean**, at Beliers Priory School with his friends **Addison** and **Pickering**. He makes his nose bleed, and wins the cricket match. (LAR 48)

* He is in his last term, to go on to Southbridge School. (DD 51)

* Shaping nicely to become a classics scholar, at Public School. (JC 53)

Deanna
* ❖ Kitchenmaid to the **Leslies,** Rushwater. Named after the movie star; her aunt is the cook. She won't wear her glasses and drops a pot of tea on her own foot. (PBO 46)

* ❖ She is either chasing the boys or being chased. (DD 51)

* ❖ She has been walking out with **Ted Higden** at the radio shop for ten years. (TSAT 61)

de Baruelh, Peire
* ❖ Twelfth-century Provençal poet; his *Tenso* is edited by **Mr. (Harold) Downing.** (PE 47)

de Courcy, the Honourable Augustus
* ❖ Last representative of old Barum before it was disenfranchised as a rotten borough. His draped statue is in Barchester Cathedral. (CBI 40)

de Courcy, George
* ❖ Before **Agnes Graham (née Leslie)** was married, old **Lady de Courcy** came to dinner at Rushwater and was offended by **Lady Emily Leslie** asking if he was out of prison yet (something about money matters). (ESR 55)

* ❖ A lout, like all the de Courcy boys. He was a beau of **Lady Agnes Pomfret,** but one night he got drunk, fell, and was put in the caterer's van and delivered the next day at Ennismore Gardens, the house his family took for the season. (NTL 56)

de Courcy, the Honourable and Reverend George
* ❖ Former vicar of St. Ewold's, who protected it from the earlier stage of Neo-Gothic restoration. (HRt 52)

de Courcy, Lady

* Of the Villa Thermogène, Menton. **Tommy Greaves** is her nephew. (NR 41)

* Before **Agnes Graham** was married, old Lady de Courcy came to dinner at Rushwater and was offended by **Lady Emily Leslie** asking if **George de Courcy** was out of prison yet. (ESR 55)

* She invites **Mrs. Halliday** to Villa Thermogène for the winter. (ADA 57)

de Courcy, Old Lord

* **Lord Stoke's** godfather, ca. 1876. (NTL 56)

* His grandfather or great uncle was known as Lord de Curse-ye. (LAAA 59)

de Courcy, the Honourable Reginald

* Rector of St. Hall Friars (see **Saint Aella**), Hallbury, in the 1830s. He suppressed the special prayers for Guy Fawkes Day owing to a deplorable access of broadmindedness. (MB 45)

de Hogpen, Nicholas

* Painter of the murals discovered by **Professor Lancelot** in the Pomfret Madrigal church. (TB 39)

de Malacord, Galfridus

* Twelfth-century Bishop of Barchester who died of a fell disease; judging from his effigy in the church, he is the spitting image of the present **Bishop**. (HRt 52)

des Égouts, the Vidame

* Subject of **Professor Gawky's** *Gaily the Troubadour*, a historical novel in which he made his wife eat her lover's heart

(**Miss Pemberton** corrected this in her review: it was his liver and lungs). (NR 41)

de Valois, Jehanne: *See* **le Capet, Jehan**

Dingle, Mrs. Gladys
* Married sister of **Eileen** from the Red Lion. She chars for **Wiple** Terrace. Her husband **Mr. Dingle** is troublesome, so in return for babysitting the **Bissells'** niece **Edna**, Mrs. Bissell gets her books on curing alcoholism and on jiu-jitsu. She also takes care of three evacuees: **Greta, Gary,** and **Gable**. (CBI 40)

* She is widowed, but at the same time Mr. Dingle is alive and has a drop too much occasionally. She works for **Miss Hampton** and **Miss Bent** three days a week, and does laundry. Her sister-in-law lets furnished rooms, and the telephone operator is her niece. She is rather deaf. (PE 47)

* She is a widow again. (TSAT 61)

Dingle, Mr.
* Troublesome husband of **Mrs. (Gladys) Dingle**. (CBI 40)

* Though Mrs. Dingle is a widow, he is said to be alive and to have a drop too much occasionally. (PE 47)

* He's dead again. (TSAT 61)

Diothermic, Brother, of Saint Aella: *See* **Aelthwithric, Bishop of Barchester**.

Diplomatic, Man in the
* Guest at **Pomfret** Towers. Consults with **Sally Wicklow** on how to break Bazouki dogs of eating live chickens. (PT 38)

Dixon, Mrs.
* The witch at Starveacres. She gets five shillings every Michaelmas so that she won't magic the fox away. (PT 38)

Dodder, Lord
* A well-known law lord who mentions the possibility of a Coronation knighthood to **Noel Merton**. (WDIM 54)

Doker, Crab
* Plays Amnon to **Glamora Tudor's** Tamar in *Too Close for Love*, a Mammoth Scenario of King David's Court. (CC 50)

Don
* A thirty-two-year-old paymaster general in Gibraltar who has private means and three married sisters, one in whole-sale hardware; he gets engaged to **Peggie Merivale**. (MB 45)

Doppelgänger, Lincoln Fish
* Alumnus of Porter University, Porterville. He made a fortune in the war, and endowed a lecture in Provençal poetry at his college, which **Walden Concord Porter** invites **Mr. (Harold) Downing** to give. (WDIM 54)

Dorothy
* Village woman, a Vidler or Panter, at Hatch End, who "does for" Mr. **John Arthur Cross(e)** at the Old Manor House. She has two brothers, **Jim** and **Harry**; Jim's wife's nephew is **Harry Hubback**, who meets **Odeena Panter** at tea at her house. (ESR 55)

Dorothy: *See* **Simnet, Mrs. Dorothy**.

Dowling, Mr.: *See* **Downing, Mr. Harold.**

Downing, Mr. Harold

❖ Philologist and scholar of Provençal language and literature, about fifty-five. He lives with **Miss (Ianthe) Pemberton** at Punshions cottage, and collaborates with her on the *Biographical Dictionary of Provence*. He was in R.N.V.R. in the First World War, and was invalided out in 1916. **Adrian Coates** published his biography of **Reynault Camargou**. Though tempted by comfort and **Mrs. (Poppy) Turner**, he returns to the rigors of scholarship and Miss Pemberton. (NR 41)

❖ Appears as **"Mr. Dowling."** He edited a twelfth-century *Tenso* of **Peire de Baruelh**, which is included in the Red Cross Library's display of local authors. (PE 47)

❖ He and Miss Pemberton are invited to Lille by **M. Bontemps** to celebrate their completion and publication of the *Féau–Filhz* volume of the *Biographical Dictionary*. They also attend the Conservative Do at Gatherum, where he wants to ride **Packer's** Universal Royal Derby. (CC 50)

❖ Former tutor and fellow of his college. Though they have reached the volume *Mas–Moult*, Miss Pemberton, now ill, gives him up to Mrs. Turner, whom he will marry and take to America with him when he gives the **Lincoln Fish Doppelgänger** lectures for **Walden Concord Porter** at Porter University, Porterville, in October. (WDIM 54)

❖ Now married to Mrs. Turner; Miss Pemberton has died. (NTL 56)

❖ Miss Pemberton left him the royalties from her cookbook, about twelve pounds per year. His fame has grown, and

D

with his wife accompanying him, he lectures in Europe and America. His Aunt Alice had consumption as a girl, was cured by six months on the Riviera, then came back to England and died of scarlet fever the next year. (ADA 57)

Downing, Mrs.: *See* **Turner, Mrs. Poppy.**

Drake, Miss "Draky"
* One of the two teachers with six evacuees billeted on the **Keiths**, Northbridge Manor; her colleague is **Miss "Pots" Potter**. (CBI 40)

Driver, Miss
* Along with **Miss Feilding** or Fielding, runs a small nursery school billeted on **Mrs. (Lavinia) Brandon** at Stories. (CBI 40)

Dubois, M.
* French master at Southbridge School, despised by the boys. (HR 33)

Duchaux, Mlle.
* Former governess to **Geoffrey** and **Frances Harvey**; she also taught French to a nephew of **Mrs. (Amabel) Marling's** in the consular service. Her nephew is a Free French officer, **M. Jules Duval**, who visits her at the Harveys'. (MH 42)

Dudley, Miss Poppy
* **Matron of the Senior School, Southbridge**, in **Mr. Everard Carter's** House. Devoted to **Kate Keith** Carter, and chief scourge of the housemaid **Jessie**. Her married sister, **Mrs. Empson**, has a son operating the wireless in the merchant navy. (SH 37)

* The wireless operator is now her eldest nephew. (GU 43)

* Now named **George Empson,** he visits her and rewires Editha Cottage for **Peggy** and **Effie Arbuthnot.** (PE 47)

* She trained under the strict **Matron at Knight's** along with **Nurse Chiffinch,** who alone calls her Poppy. (CC 50)

Dull Girl in the Upper Fifth
* Of the Hosiers' Girls' Foundation School. Balletomane, prompter for the school play, *As You Like It.* (TH 44)

Dumbello, Lord
* Title of the little heir to the **Marquis of Hartletop**; **Rose Bingham Leslie** and her children visit him at Hartletop. (LAR 48)

* Hartletop Priory is let as a girls' school. (CC 50)

* He is still in the nursery. (DD 51)

* He has just gone to pre-prep school, and wants to marry **Justinia Lufton** when he's ten. The family is living in the second-best dower house, and had to make room by sending the family papers to the Barchester Central Library. (HRt 52)

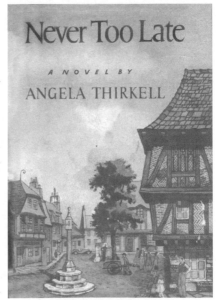

Never Too Late

A NOVEL BY

ANGELA THIRKELL

Dumka
* Maid to the **Richard Carters** at the Old Manor House. Her

father's late sister (who when alive was "schwenk, a peeg which is becomm dead and eaten of fat flies") was the cousin of the late mother of **Gradka Bonescu**, the Mixo-Lydian Ambassador, who got Dumka this job. She is Letter-maiden (Bachelor of Letters) of Bunting College, University of Mixo-Lydia, where she learned English. When **Cook** objects to her use of garlic, she retaliates with loud Mixo-Lydian songs and lets the milk boil over, so Mr. Carter calls Mixo-Lydian House and three large officials come in a car and remove her. (NTL 56)

❖ She is back, as Mrs. Carter's maid. (ADA 57)

Dunsford, Barbara

❖ Daughter of the late General and **Mrs. Dunsford**, of Hovis House. (NR 41)

❖ She volunteers as a bookbinder for the Red Cross Library. (PE 47)

❖ She and her mother help run the Northbridge Coronation festivities. (WDIM 54)

❖ An only child; her father has been dead a long time. While her mother has **Mrs. (Eleanor) Halliday** to visit at Hovis House, she goes off to the Pension **Ramsden** at Menton on the Riviera, where she acquires a Slave Friend named **Bronwen** ("Wendy" to her "Friendy"). (ADA 57)

❖ She is now permanently at the Pension Ramsden. (LAAA 59)

Dunsford, Mrs.

❖ Of Hovis House; widow of a general, with a daughter **Barbara**. They have working parties three days a week. Her

Aunt Louisa was a Mutiny baby, dyed brown and rescued from the Siege of Lucknow by a faithful ayah. (NR 41)

❖ She sometimes lets the first floor of her house, with service. (PE 47)

❖ She and Barbara help run the Northbridge Coronation festivities. (WDIM 54)

❖ She is nearer seventy than sixty, her husband has been dead a long time, and Barbara is an only child. She is a relation of **Mrs. (Eleanor) Halliday,** with whom she went to school; their grandmothers were sisters, and there was almost a romance between her mother and Mrs. Halliday's father. Mrs. Halliday's mother is Mrs. Dunsford's Aunt Sophy, who used to visit Hovis House and who died in the room Mrs. Dunsford gives Mrs. Halliday when she has her to stay. (ADA 57)

Dupont, M.

❖ French master, a stickler for punctuality; the young **John-Arthur Crosse** called him "Dupont de l'Heure" (*cf.* Dupont de l'Eure). (NTL 56)

Dusta, Nukkle

❖ Native trooper at Suhk Behar, whom **Colonel Crofts** knew in 1921. He had a horrible squint and a very large family. He later became a saint, and all his children went into the Indian civil service. (PE 47)

Dutton, Lieutenant

❖ A young don of leftist-intellectual leanings, billeted on the **Villars.** He enjoys asking "Socratic" questions and is eventually returned to the depot. (NR 41)

Duval, Eugene: *See* **le Capet, Jehan**.

Duvals, the
* Mme. Duval, her daughter Mlle. Marie-Claire Duval, and her daughter-in-law Mme. Henri Duval are Free French invited for Christmas by **Miss Crowder** and **Miss Hopgood**. But they despise England, and leave to stay with another daughter-in-law and five other relations near Wimbledon. (NR 41)

Duval, M. Jules
* Free French officer, nephew of **Mlle. Duchaux**, whom he visits at the **Harveys'**. (MH 42)

Duval, Mlle.
* French mistress at Barchester High School. (SH 37)

M. Duval or **Durand:** *See* **Boulle, Prof. Pierre**

Edie: *See* **Pover, Alice Edith.**

Edna

❖ Feeble-minded niece of a niece of **Mr.** and **Mrs. Bissell.**
She lives with them, and has fits. **Mrs. Dingle** babysits her.
(CBI 40)

❖ Now described as a great-niece, she is in the Ada Clotworthy Mental Institution. (PE 47)

Edward

❖ Enlisted at sixteen "for company"; after World War I
became "factotum and friend of all mankind" at Southbridge School. (HR 33)

❖ Repairs shoes and radios, helps **Tony Morland.** (DH 34)

❖ Only he understands the dampers in the school gymna-
sium. (CBI 40)

❖ He's a genius at housepainting. (PE 47)

* He came into **Everard Carter's** house under **Simnet**, and succeeds him as butler when Mr. Carter becomes Headmaster. (CC 50)

* He umpires the school cricket match. (NTL 56)

Edwards, Miss
* Secretary to **Lady Bond**, away caring for her sick mother. (BL 39)

Eightieth Son of the Head Chief of Mngangaland, the: *See* **Head Chief of Mngangaland, the Eightieth Son of the.**

Eileen
* Barmaid of the Red Lion, Southbridge (**Mr. Brown**, prop.). A blonde with a swanlike bust. Her married sister is **Mrs. (Gladys) Dingle**. (CBI 40)

* Her hair is increasingly gold, and she is walking out with **Bateman**. (PE 47)

* She had been keeping company with **Simnet** for some years, but threw him over for Bateman, meanwhile setting Simnet up to marry her sister **Florrie**. The implication is that she marries Bateman, but he is misidentified as **Jackson**. (CC 50)

* She is still unmarried and still at the Red Lion, though after walking out with Bateman for six years, she has agreed to marry him and leave the pub next year. (JC 53)

* She is married, but still working at the Red Lion. (NTL 56)

❖ Her hair is now red-gold, and she has been cook to **Colonel (Edward)** and **Mrs. Crofts** for some years. (CQ 58)

❖ Due to increased business, she still helps out in the Saloon of the Red Lion on her evening off. (TSAT 61)

Ellangowan, Lady Catriona

❖ Cousin of **Christopher Hornby**, who proposed to her once; she married Lord Ellangowan (presumably another relation), but they remained friends. She gives a party to celebrate Christopher's engagement to **Elsa Belton**. (TH 44)

❖ Their keeper **Angus** amused **Ludovic, Lord Mellings**, when the **Pomfrets** visited during shooting season. (OBH 49)

❖ She and Elsa are now firm friends. (DD 51)

Ellangowan-Hornby, Mrs. Admiral

❖ Daughter of a Scotch peer and late resident of the **Beltons'** Arcot House. She had a stroke two years before, then died, leaving her nephew **Christopher Hornby** a fortune and the lease to Arcot House, which he sublets back to the Beltons. (TH 44)

Elliman, Lily: *See* **Arbuthnot, Mrs. Colonel**.

Elphin, Marigold ("Boodle")

❖ According to the **Duchess of Omnium**, Lady Gwendoline Elphin's second girl's name was Marigold, but everyone called her Boodle. *See* also **Marigold Smith**. (DD 51)

Empson, George ("Sparks")

* Nameless second son of **Mrs. Empson**, the married sister of **Miss Dudley, Matron of the Senior School, South-bridge**. He is on the wireless in the merchant navy. (SH 37)

* He has been torpedoed twice and is about to join his third ship. (CBI 40)

* He is now the eldest nephew. He was at sea when his father died. The last time he was torpedoed, he was in a boat for five days before being picked up. (GU 43)

* His first name is now given. He was Sparks on the *Gridiron* in the Mediterranean; served under **Captain (Freddy) Belton**; and raced jerboas with **Mr. Shergold**. He is now wireless operator on the newest and largest Atlantic liner, and on his holiday rewires Editha on **Wiple** Terrace for **Peggy** and **Effie Arbuthnot**. (PE 47)

* His wife darns exquisitely, and his son was christened Marconi Sparks Empson. (CC 50)

Empson, Mrs.

* Married sister of **Miss Dudley, Matron of the Senior School, Southbridge**. Her second son is on the wireless in the merchant navy. (SH 37)

* He is now the eldest son, and was at sea when his father died. (GU 43)

Esme

* Married sister of **Wheeler** the Second Housemaid at Pomfret Towers. She fills in as a housemaid during the flu epidemic. (PT 38)

Ethel
* Parlourmaid to the **Middletons**, Lavering. (BL 39)

Ethel
* Upper housemaid to the **Brandons**, Stories. (TB 39)

* She only came to Stories when the children were older, so she was snubbed by both **Nurse** (Miss Vance) and **Rose**. (PE 47)

Evans, Mr.
* Production manager for **Sam Adams'** Hogglestock Rolling Mills. (LAR 48)

* In cahoots with **Miss Pickthorn**. (CC 50)

Everleen
* Under-nurse to **Mrs. Bill Marling**. (MH 42)

* She comes from an orphanage. (CC 50)

Ewold, Saint
* Cut down the Druids' oak grove on Bolder's Knob, where no tree has grown since. (PBO 46)

* According to **Everard Carter's** nurse, he lived in a forest hut and played cards with the Devil on Sunday nights. (CQ 58)

Fair Girl from the Lower Sixth
 * At the Hosiers' Girls' Foundation School. Plays Celia in *As You Like It*. (TH 44)

Fairfax-Raven
 * Friend of **John Villars** in the R.A.F. who hurt his foot parachuting. He invites John to his parents' place in Devonshire for the hunting. (NR 41)

Fairweather, A.L.
 * Seven- or eight-year-old boy who boxes against **J.W. Swift-Hetherington** in a match at Southbridge School. (HR 33)

Fairweather, Amy
 * Second child of **Rose Birkett** Fairweather and **John Fairweather**. (GU 43)

 * Supposed to be a boy. (CQ 58)

Fairweather, Edith: *See* **Keith, Mrs. Edith.**

Fairweather, Geoff

❖ First known as **Fairweather Senior**, Captain of Boxing at Southbridge School. He breaks Tony Morland's window while chasing a wasp. He fails his exams, can't go on to the upper school. (DH 34)

❖ Both he and his brother, **Fairweather Junior (John)** went on to Rugby; their elder sister is **Edith (Mrs. Robert Keith)**. He is on leave from his Army regiment in Burma; he and John take **Rose Birkett** for a ride in their sports car. (SH 37)

❖ Both parents are dead. He is in the Barsetshire regiment, doing a staff course at Camberley. He is best man at John's wedding to Rose Birkett and, after chasing off **Fritz Gissing**, becomes engaged to **Geraldine Birkett**. (CBI 40)

❖ He has been all through Libya, and he and Geraldine have a son, **John**. (GU 43)

❖ He is a full colonel, and they now have a good nanny for John. (PBO 46)

❖ They now have two babies but can't get any help. "The Fairweather granny," who was delightful but spoilt the grandchildren, died last year and left a nice sum to Geoff and John; however, she is supposed to have already died (*see* above, CBI 40). (PE 47)

Fairweather, Henry

❖ Eldest son of **Rose Birkett** Fairweather and **John Fairweather**. (GU 43)

❖ At school. (JC 53)

Fairweather, John

+ Younger brother of **Geoff Fairweather**, first known as **Fairweather Junior**. From Southbridge Junior School, both he and his brother went on to Rugby; their elder sister is **Edith (Mrs. Robert Keith)**. He is in the Navy, just home from his first cruise; he and Geoff take **Rose Birkett** for a ride in their sports car. (SH 37)

+ Both parents are dead. Though here John is supposed to have been the boy in a Southbridge School boxing match portrayed in *High Rising*, that was **A.L. Fairweather**, who would now be only fourteen or fifteen years old. John, however, is a Lieutenant, appointed Naval Attaché to Las Palombas in South America. He has been left a very nice fortune by his Aunt Emma, and he marries Rose Birkett. He takes her to South America, and their baby is due in August. (CBI 40)

+ He was at sea for eighteen months after South America; now with Rose on a two-year job in Washington. Their children are **Henry** and **Amy**; there is another due in June. (GU 43)

+ He is now a captain, on a mission in Portugal; they have had their third child. (MB 45)

+ After being naval attaché in Lisbon, he and the family come back to England, to a flat in Lowndes Square. (PBO 46)

+ "The Fairweather granny," who was delightful but spoilt the grandchildren, died last year and left a nice sum to John and Geoff; however, she is supposed to have already died (*see* above, CBI 40). Their fourth child, who is named Mary (not, as Rose wanted, Glamora), is born. (PE 47)

❖ He is now at the Admiralty. (CC 50)

❖ He and Rose stayed with the **Luftons** shortly before Lord Lufton's death, and John gave a talk to the Framley Sea Scouts. (HRt 52)

❖ He was a midshipman on a ship where **Tubby Fewling** was an officer; he now has every medal, order, and distinction. They are renting the **Umblebys'** house at Greshamsbury. "The boys" are at school, the two youngest (now both girls) at home with a nanny. (JC 53)

❖ He is still at the Admiralty. (ADA 57)

❖ Their first child was born in 1940, the last in 1946; despite the names above (Henry, Amy, ?, and Mary), the two youngest are girls, "the two elder are probably boys." (CQ 58)

Fairweather, John
  ❖ Eldest son of **Geraldine Birkett** Fairweather and **Geoff Fairweather**. (GU 43)

Fairweather Junior: *See* **Fairweather, John**.

Fairweather, (Mrs.) Rose: *See* **Birkett, Rose**.

Fairweather, Mary
  ❖ Fourth (and last) child of **Rose Birkett** Fairweather and **John Fairweather**. Her mother had wanted to call her Glamora, presumably after **Glamora Tudor**. (PE 47)

  ❖ At home, along with the (nameless girl) third child and a nanny. (JC 53)

Fairweather Senior: *See* **Fairweather, Geoff.**

Fanshawe, Charles

❖ Dean of Paul's College, close friend and distant relation of **Frank** and **Rachel Dean** (his aunt married into Frank Dean's family, and he is about Rachel's age). Author of *Platonic Liberalism* and mountaineer, he was tutor to **Winifred Tebben**. He becomes engaged to **Helen Dean**. (AF 36)

❖ He attends **Rose Birkett's** wedding. He would rather take the train than be driven by his wife. (CBI 40)

❖ He is seconded to the censor's office for special work. (GU 43)

❖ His secret code name is X47. (TH 44)

❖ They have three children. The eldest, **Ray (for Rachel)**, at eight, is the oldest of the Dean grandchildren. (PE 47)

❖ He was **Tom Grantly's** tutor at Oxford. (OBH 49)

❖ He was **Eric Swan's** tutor. His small book on Tibullus was published by Oxbridge University Press. (HRt 52)

Fanshawe, (Mrs.) Helen: *See* **Dean, Helen.**

Fanshawe, Rachel ("Ray")

❖ The eldest of **Charles** and **Helen Dean Fanshawe's** three children. At eight, she is the oldest of the Dean grandchildren. (PE 47)

Faraday-Home, Miss

❖ **The Screaming Girl**, a guest at **Pomfret** Towers. She loses two puff-billiards puffers squirting **Peter** and **Micky** in the bath; waltzes with **Mr. Johns**; and has a bet with Peter (or

Micky) about the chances for Monday. They all use the letters from a game for a paper chase. (PT 38)

Farker, Derrick
* Evacuee child; he, **Derrick Pumper**, and their cousin **Ron** are boarded by **Mrs. (Poppy) Turner** at the Hollies, Northbridge. (NR 41)

Farquhar, Gerry
* Of the Barsetshires, now headed to the Far East. He made fifty-nine not out in the cricket match against Southbridge School. (OBH 49)

Featherstonehaugh
* The **Captain of Rowing**, Southbridge School. Weighs twelve stone and is in love with **Matron**. Leaves school to join the Nigerian police. (SH 37)

* While coming home on leave at the outbreak of war, he was killed when the *Lancashire* was torpedoed. (CRI 40)

* His name is first on the Southbridge School Roll of Honour. (PBO 46)

Feeder, Mr.
* Master at Southbridge School, a bachelor, living in Louisa, **Wiple** Terrace. After the **Arbuthnots** leave, he takes Editha for his **Mother** to live in. (PE 47)

* His father was a great drinker; he plays the radio too loud, against **Mr. Traill's** gramophone. (CC 50)

* He went to Switzerland on holiday and broke his ankle skiing. (JC 53)

* Wiple Terrace is saved, and their leases are extended indefinitely. (TSAT 61)

F

Feeder, Mrs. (Mr. Feeder's Mother)

❖ **Mr. Feeder** gets Editha in **Wiple** Terrace for her to live in. (PE 47)

❖ Every year she takes three old family servants with her to Belgium, then sends them home after a night and is able to spend their monetary allotment for foreign travel as well as her own. (OBH 49)

❖ Her husband was a great drinker, and she is no slouch herself. (CC 50)

❖ She broke her wrist last winter, but sent her son on his planned holiday to Switzerland anyway, where he broke his ankle skiing. (JC 53)

❖ Her late husband called her "Little One." (CQ 58)

❖ In celebration of the rescue of Wiple Terrace and the indefinite extension of their leases, she goes to Monte Carlo, gambles heavily and wins. (TSAT 61)

Feilding, Miss

❖ Along with **Miss Driver**, runs a small nursery school billeted on **Mrs. (Lavinia) Brandon** at Stories. Initially spelled "Fielding." (CBI 40)

❖ Still at Stories with three of the more delicate babies, but then they move to Sussex, near Chanctonbury Ring. (PE 47)

Ferdinand, Isabella

❖ A dramatic girl at the Hosiers' Girls' Foundation School, with a crush on **Charles Belton**. Plays Rosalind in *As You Like It*. (TH 44)

❖ Her aunt is a friend of Jane Gresham. (MB 45)

Ferguson

❖ Chauffeur to the **Bonds**, Staple Park. (BL 39)

Ferris, Mr.

❖ A very young assistant master at Southbridge School. His father was a country doctor. He becomes engaged, but his fiancée is not very prepossessing. (HR 33)

❖ Now **Tony Morland's** housemaster (known as "Ferrett"), at war with **Matron**. (DH 34)

❖ He was once cheeked by **John Fairweather**, long ago. He became one of H. M. Inspectors of Secondary Schools, and the right place for him, too. (CBI 40)

Fewling, Father George ("Tubby")

❖ Formerly a commander of the Royal Navy, now of the higher persuasion of the Church of England. Appointed priest-in-charge of St. Sycorax, Northbridge, lodging with **Mrs. Hicks**. He does boy scouts, air wardens, astronomy with **Miss Hopgood's Aunt**, and is pursued by the **Misses Talbot**. (NR 41)

❖ His service was in World War I. (PE 47)

❖ He comforts **Isabel Dale** on the death of her fiancé **John**, which happened some time before. (CC 50)

❖ He had been on the China station, and in the *Scrapiron* when **Admiral Phelps** was her commander. He is left some money by an old uncle and aunt, and is appointed rector of Greshamsbury Church and honorary canon of Barchester. He wrote an article for the *Church Times* on St. Paul's

qualifications for the Royal Navy. His real first name is given for the first time. He is about to propose to **Margot Phelps**, but she gets engaged to **Mr. (Donald) MacFadyen** before he can say anything. (JC 53)

✤ He is an honorary Doctor of Divinity. (ADA 57)

✤ His father was in business at Plymouth, which is why he went to sea, and his mother, a clergyman's daughter, died when he was small. He takes in Admiral Phelps after **Mrs. Phelps** dies; then the Admiral goes downhill and dies too. He is appointed a full canon of Barchester, and will move to Acacia House in the Close. He gets engaged to the now-widowed Margot MacFadyen. (CQ 58)

✤ They are married, and he is less high than before. He has written a book about The Church at Sea. (LAAA 59)

Fielding, Miss: *See* **Feilding, Miss.**

Fielding, Anne
  ✤ Only daughter of **Sir Robert** and **Lady Dora Fielding**, just seventeen and of delicate health. She went to Barchester High School but the damp didn't agree with her; now she stays at Hall's End, Hallbury, under **Miss Bunting's** tutelage (their cook-housekeeper is **Gradka**), while her parents live in Barchester. She has an understanding with **Robin Dale**. (MB 45)

  ✤ At nearly nineteen, she is doing domestic economy and is slightly smitten with **David Leslie**, but becomes engaged to Robin. (PBO 46)

  ✤ She marries Robin Dale. (LAR 48)

✦ She is expecting a baby in spring. (OBH 49)

✦ She has twin girls, **Roberta Fielding** and **Dora Maud** (named for her parents and for Miss Bunting). (CC 50)

✦ They also have a little boy. (ADA 57)

✦ They and their growing family have moved to Allington and started a very successful pre-preparatory school for boys. (TSAT 61)

Fielding, Lady Dora
✦ Wife of **Sir Robert Fielding** and mother of **Anne**. They live at Number Seventeen, the Close, Barchester, and have a house at Hall's End, Hallbury. (MB 45)

✦ She is about forty-five, born and raised in the Close, now busy organizing war work. (PBO 46)

✦ She lends her piano for the Red Cross Fete. (PE 47)

✦ Anne marries **Robin Dale**. (LAR 48)

✦ She is godmother to **Dora Maud Dale**, one of Anne's twins. (CC 50)

✦ **The Bishop's Wife** forces them to have **Geoffrey** and **Frances Harvey** to stay. (WDIM 54)

Fielding, Sir Robert
✦ Husband of **Lady Dora Fielding** and father of **Anne**. He is Chancellor of the diocese of Barchester, aged not quite sixty. They live at Number Seventeen, the Close, Barchester, and have a house at Hall's End, Hallbury. (MB 45)

* He gardens and is a Governor of Southbridge School. He stands as a Conservative candidate for the seat of Barchester, but loses to **Sam Adams**. (PBO 46)

* Anne marries **Robin Dale**. (LAR 48)

* He refuses to stand for Parliament again. (CC 50)

* **The Bishop's Wife** forces them to have **Geoffrey** and **Frances Harvey** to stay. (WDIM 54)

* He is soon to retire. (CQ 58)

* He joins the Syndicate formed by **Sam Adams** to buy **Wiple** terrace away from **Lord Aberfordbury** and give it to Southbridge School. (TSAT 61)

Fillgrave, Sir Abel
* Surgeon at Barchester General. (CBI 40)

* He visits Beliers Priory Convalescent Home and operates on **Private Jenks**. (GU 43)

Fillgrave, Young
* Dentist in Barchester. (NR 41)

Finch
* Odd man for the **Pomfrets**, Pomfret Towers. His father was an under-gardener, his uncle a poacher. He is late with the ladies' shoes because of having to clean **Julian Rivers'** brushes. (PT 38)

* His uncle is **Old Finch**. (WDIM 54)

* Still doing boots and knives at Pomfret Towers. (LAAA 59)

Finch, Old

❖ Uncle of **Finch** and worst poacher in the county. Has been keeping a pig in the wash house and bees upstairs in his cottage for fifty years or so. (WDIM 54)

Finlay

❖ Squint-eyed boy at Coppin's School under **Mr. Villars**. He stole the toffee that **Mr. Holden's** uncle (or cousin) **"Merrylegs" Holden** kept in his desk. (NR 41)

Fitchett

❖ Son of **Fitchett the Grocer**; apprenticed to **Trowel** the builder. He works on the air-raid shelter. (NR 41)

❖ Probably the young **Syd Fitchett** whom **Mrs. Bunce** caught her daughter **Effie** with in the St. Sycorax air-raid shelter. (PE 47)

Fitchett the Grocer

❖ Also the Coals. Father of young **Fitchett**. (NR 41)

Fitzgorman, Dobby

❖ A Liberal, suspected of shooting foxes. He was engaged to **Lady Elaine Harcourt**, but he broke his neck. (ADA 57)

❖ The neck was broken in a steeplechase. (LAAA 59)

Fletcher, Eva

❖ Currently obliging the **Silverbridges** as cook at the Lodge. Her niece is **Gloria Fletcher**. (DD 51)

Fletcher, Gloria

❖ Currently obliging the **Silverbridges** as parlourmaid at the Lodge. Her aunt is **Eva Fletcher**. (DD 51)

Flo, Young

❖ Younger sister to **Mr. Knox's Annie**, disapproved of by both her sister and **Stoker**. Adenoidal and half-witted. She occasionally obliges for **Mrs. (Laura) Morland** at High Rising. Her aunt is **Mrs. Mallow**, housekeeper to **Dr. Ford**. (HR 33)

❖ Annie's brother (and so hers, also) is Lord Stokes' **Albert**. (DH 34)

Florrie: *See* Simnet, Mrs. Florrie.

Floyd, Miss

❖ Maths mistress at Barchester High School. **Grace Grantly** has a crush on her. (OBH 49)

Fluvius Minucius

❖ An unknown Latin poet of the fourth century. Manuscripts of his work are in Vienna, Lyons, Trèves, and Uppsala (though the latter wouldn't allow **Miss Sparling** a copy). Other scholars who have worked on him are **Canon Horbury**, **Mr. Carton**, and **Mr. Oriel**. (TH 44)

❖ Mr. Carton's edition is now out. (PBO 46)

❖ There is a newly discovered manuscript. (CC 50)

❖ **Eric Swan**, who has written a book on him, discerns a possible influence from **Scriptor Ignotus** of Aterra. (HRt 52)

Follanbee, Buck

❖ Stars in *Love in a Bath*, the true story of Marat and Charlotte Corday, with **Glamora Tudor**. (NTL 56)

Footman, the Young
* At **Pomfret** Towers. Receives **Guy** and **Alice Barton** and **Roddy** and **Sally Wicklow**. Also witnesses Roddy's removal of **Julian Rivers** from the running board of the car. (PT 38)

Ford, Dr. James
* Physician (with or, preferably, without fee) to **Mrs. Todd**. His housekeeper is **Mrs. Mallow**. He proposes to **Anne Todd**, but she refuses. (HR 33)

* He keeps **Tony Morland** in line. He proposes to **Sylvia Gould**, and she accepts. (DH 34)

* He is physician to **Miss (Amelia) Brandon**. (TB 39)

* Sylvia Gould broke off their engagement. He lectures on subtropical diseases to convalescent soldiers. (GU 43)

* He is treating **Anne Fielding**. (MB 45)

* He treats **Cecil Waring** at Barchester General. (DD 51)

* His old great-aunt was a kind of Wedgwood. (NTL 56)

* He proposes again to Sylvia Gould, who accepts. (TSAT 61)

Fortescue, Mrs. C. Augustus ("Fifi")
* Only child and heiress of **Bunyan, First Baron Alberfylde**; of The Cedars, Muswell Hill, which on her death is bought by **Sir Ogilvy Hibberd**. (BL 39)

Fosbery, Captain
* A flirting partner of **Peggy Arbuthnot** at Umbrella in India. (PE 47)

Foster

* Parlourmaid to the **Villars**, Northbridge Rectory. (NR 41)

* Faithful though rather tyrannical. (PE 47)

* Still keeping up standards. (WDIM 54)

Foster, Lady Agnes

* Ephemeral fourth child of **Sally Wicklow** Foster and **Gillie Foster, Lord** and **Lady Pomfret**. (PE 47)

Foster, Dolly

* A Victorian beauty, no first name given; wife of **Lord Mickleham** and mother of **Miss Starter**. (HRt 52)

* Now it is old Lord Mickleham's son (Miss Starter's brother) who married the heiress Dolly Foster. (LAAA 59)

Foster, Lady Emily

* Second child of **Sally Wicklow** and **Gillie Foster, Lord** and **Lady Pomfret**; younger sister of **Ludovic, Lord Mellings**, and older sister of **the Honourable Giles**. Three years old. (TH 44)

* Now about twelve. (JC 53)

* Fourteen, and cow-minded. (WDIM 54)

* She and Ludovic go to Switzerland for Christmas. (ESR 55)

* She is a weekly boarder at Barchester High School. (LAAA 59)

* Girl of Honour at Barchester High School. Interested in market gardening, she plans to summer in France and Holland and then go to horticultural college. She will be a

bridesmaid for Ludovic's wedding to **Lavinia Merton**. (TSAT 61)

Foster, the Honourable Giles

❖ Third child of **Sally Wicklow** Foster and **Gillie Foster**, **Lord** and **Lady Pomfret**; younger brother of **Ludovic, Lord Mellings**, and **Lady Emily**. Six months old. (TH 44)

❖ He gets a pony named Pillicock. (OBH 49)

❖ Eleven, in last year of prep school, he is popular, a natural athlete and rider. (WDIM 54)

❖ He has to go to **Mr. (Herbert) Choyce** for coaching in classics instead of spending Christmas in Switzerland with his brother and sister. (ESR 55)

❖ Still at school. (LAAA 59)

❖ At sixteen or seventeen, he is helping to run the pony club, and will leave school to go as a trainee to a pony breeding stables in the New Forest. (TSAT 61)

Foster, Gillie

❖ Son of **Major Foster**, brought up abroad by an aunt, who is now dead. Slightly delicate, he lives in London and works for art dealers. His father dies, leaving him as heir of **Giles, Seventh Earl of Pomfret**. **Miss Merriman** develops a regard for him, and he gets engaged to **Sally Wicklow**. (PT 38)

❖ Now married, they take Lord Pomfret on a cruise. (TB 39)

❖ Their baby, Giles (later Ludovic) is six months old. They vacation at Cap Martin. (BL 39)

* At Lord Pomfret's death, he becomes the **Eighth Earl of Pomfret**. He and Sally have two sons (but *see* below). (CBI 40)

* Their children are **Ludovic, Lord Mellings**, age four-and-a-half; **Lady Emily**, three; and the **Honourable Giles**, six months. In his capacity as Lord Lieutenant, they attend Bobbin Day at the Hosiers' Girls' Foundation School. (TH 44)

* They have a fourth child, **Lady Agnes**, who never appears again. (PE 47)

* Though he had been sick the past winter, he opens the Red Cross Fete and arranges that Winston Churchill be driven past the Conservative Rally, Staple Park. (LAR 48)

* The Conservatives have their eye on him. Miss Merriman returns to Pomfret Towers to help him. (OBH 49)

* The whole family goes to Cap Ferrat for the winter. (CC 50)

* They have a villa at Cap Ferrat, which they lend to **Charles** and **Clarissa Graham Belton** for their honeymoon. (HRt 52)

* He has an aunt in Smith Street, London, with whom they'll stay for the Coronation. He will lease the main part of Pomfret Towers to **Sam Adams**, who wants it for offices for his consortium with **Mr. (Donald) MacFadyen** and **Mr. Pilward**. (WDIM 54)

* The offices are now installed. (ADA 57)

* He was an only child. (LAAA 59)

Foster, Ludovic, Lord Mellings

* Eldest child of **Sally Wicklow** Foster and **Gillie Foster**, at first called Giles. Six months old. (BL 39)

* His father becomes Earl of Pomfret, which makes him Lord Mellings. There is said to be a second brother. (CBI 40)

* He is three. (MH 42)

* Now given his proper name, he has a younger sister, **Lady Emily**, and then a younger brother, **the Honourable Giles**. He is four-and-a-half years old. (TH 44)

* He is at day school in Nutfield, and will go to Southbridge School when he's eight. (MB 45)

* He is about six. (PE 47)

* He is delicate and afraid of horses; he is to go to prep school in the autumn. (OBH 49)

* Now fifteen; he hated his prep school, but likes Eton. Though destined for the Guards, he sings well, so **Aubrey Clover** and **Jessica Dean** line him up to perform (incognito) as the young lead in *Two-Step for Three* for the Coronation festivities. (WDIM 54)

* He is seventeen (a month younger than **Edith Graham**), and going to Sandhurst. He and Emily go to Switzerland for Christmas. (ESR 55)

* His full name is **Ludovic Neville Eustace Guido Foster, Viscount Mellings**. (NTL 56)

* Now nineteen and a little *older* than Edith Graham. (ADA 57)

* Still at Sandhurst. He is fond of **Lavinia Merton**. (LAAA 59)

* He is with the Brigade of Guards in West Germany. He gets engaged to Lavinia; they will have a flat in London while he is stationed there, and a house in Barsetshire. (TSAT 61)

Foster, Major
* Father of **Gillie Foster**; cousin and heir of **Giles, Seventh Earl of Pomfret**. A difficult, touchy man, who usually winters in South Africa. He dies and leaves Gillie the heir. (PT 38)

* He was a second cousin at that, an unloving father, and unkind to his wife. In his last row with Lord Pomfret at the Towers, he threw a volume of the *Peerage* out the window. (ESR 55)

* He used to live in Italy. (LAAA 59)

Foster, Miss
* Cousin of the **Sixth Earl of Pomfret**, she married the **Duke of Towers**, and their second daughter was **Dorothy "Dodo" Bingham**. There were no sons, so the title went to a nephew. (PBO 46)

Foster, Mrs.
* Of Hallbury. Her house is very small, and she has a sister at Torquay. (MB 45)

Fothergill, Mr.
* Agent to the **Duke of Omnium**. In 1937 he persuaded the Duke to make over two miles of land along the river Rising to the National Trust, to spite **Pattern and Son's** plans to put bungalows there. (MB 45)

Fothergill, Old Mrs.
* Cook (though mainly resting) for the **Hallidays,** Hatch House. (PBO 46)

* When **Caxton** came there forty-three years before, she was a scullery maid. (ESR 55)

* She has very bad feet. (NTL 56)

* She is widowed. (ADA 57)

Fred
* Carpenter at Marling Hall. He has a son, **Joe.** He repairs **Packer's** Royal Derby for the Red Cross Fete at Marling Hall. (LAR 48; but *see* MH 42, where **Mr. (William) Marling's** estate carpenter is **Mr. James Govern.**)

Freda
* The Major's daughter at Umbrella in India. **Henry Grantly** spent his time in the Far East avoiding her. (HRt 52)

Freeman
* Parlormaid to **Admiral Palliser,** Hallbury House. Sister of **Mr. Freeman.** (MB 45)

Freeman, Ernie
* The Bread, at Hallbury (drives the baker's van). (MB 45)

Freeman, Jennifer
* Spoilt only daughter of **Mr. and Mrs. Freeman.** Her mother sent her to Barchester High School as a boarder, and had her teeth straightened. (MB 45)

Freeman, Mr.
* Husband of **Mrs. Freeman,** father of **Jennifer,** and brother of **Freeman, Admiral Palliser's** parlormaid. He is a verger

in Hallbury, does the Home Guard, and reports local news to the *Barchester Chronicle*. His mother, **Old Mrs. Freeman**, is ninety, and his father had been an under-keeper at Pomfret Towers. (MB 45)

Freeman, Mrs.

* Wife of **Mr. Freeman**, mother of **Jennifer**. Previously shirked **Mrs. (Molly) Watson's** working parties, but soon saw the error of her ways. Sent Jennifer to Barchester High School as a boarder, and had her (Jennifer's) teeth straightened. (MB 45)

Freeman, Old Mrs.

* Ninety-year-old mother of **Mr. Freeman**; she cheers **Lord Stoke**, thinking he's the old Duke of Omnium. She is the sister of **Bill Wheeler** who used to clean the chimneys at Pomfret Towers, and her husband was an under-keeper there. (MB 45)

Froggy

* The poor younger son of an earl, boyfriend of **Lady Glencora Palliser**. He was killed in the war, at Arnhem. (CC 50)

Fyffe-Thompson, Professor

* Provençal expert, author of *Values and Virelais*. He is apt to go off on tangents. His brother's son passed the School Certificate at fourteen, and his sister Ivy was at school with **Mrs. (Poppy) Turner**. (NR 41)

Gable

❖ One of three evacuees living with **Mrs. (Gladys) Dingle**; the others are **Greta** and **Gary**. (CBI 40)

Gadson

❖ Piano tuner from Beechwood, about an eighth tone too high on C in alt. (WDIM 54)

Gale, Nurse ("Galey")

❖ Nurse to baby **Noel Winter**. (LAR 48)

❖ Nannie Gale to him and to his baby sister **Harriet**. (DD 51)

Garagou, Numa: *See* **Bontemps, M.**

Garcia, Senor

❖ Very rich Argentine breeder who buys the **Leslie** bulls from Rushwater practically before they're born. He also buys lots of English-style pictures. (NTL 56)

Gary
* One of three evacuees living with **Mrs. (Gladys) Dingle**; the others are **Greta** and **Gable**. (CBI 40)

Gaston
* **Jessica Dean's** London hairdresser. (LAR 48)

Gawky, Professor
* Female don, author of *Gaily the Troubadour*, a historical novel about the **Vidame des Égouts**, who made his wife eat her lover's heart (**Miss Ianthe Pemberton** corrected this in her review: it was the liver and lungs). She is a Communist and enemy of **Mr. (Harold) Downing**, and is disliked by **Walden Concord Porter**. (NR 41)

* She makes disparaging remarks about the *Biographical Dictionary of Provence* at a meeting of Friends of the Félibristes and in the *Félibriste Journal of Studies*. (WDIM 54)

George
* Convalescent soldier at Beliers Priory; he and a friend do cross-talk with **Mrs. (Laura) Morland** at her lecture. (GU 43)

George
* A bit soft, but had been at **Pilward's** Brewery and knows about casks. He and **Jim Snow** repair the **Phelpses'** rain barrel. (JC 53)

George, Old
* An old-age pensioner **Sister Chiffinch** found to do vegetable gardening for the Cottage Hospital. (MB 45)

Giacopini, Giacopone (detto "il Giacopinaccio")
* Possibly the child of **Cosimo di Strelsa** and the nun, **Violante**. His altarpieces haven't been seen since 1474. He

is the subject of a monograph by **Miss (Ianthe) Pember-ton**. (NR 41)

Gibbs, Mr. and Mrs.

❖ They are boarding an evacuee, **Ernie Wheeler**, but she doesn't know how to feed children (she lost her own). (NR 41)

Gissing, Fritz

❖ Conceited son of **Mr. (Oscar)** and **Mrs. (Gloria) Gissing**; the name was previously von Giesing, but the family was naturalized before World War I (as he is twenty-four, before he was born). They take **Harwood's** former cottage, Louisa, in **Wiple** Terrace; they drive a super Daimler-Rolls. He does *petit point*, and his book, *The Lion Turns Tail*, is with the Anti-Imperial Book Club. Though **Geraldine Birkett** is infatuated with him, he ignores her. The whole family leaves for America. (CBI 40)

❖ They are now called the **Warburys**, "a very unpleasant family connected with the films." (PE 47)

Gissing, Mrs. Gloria

❖ Wife of **Oscar Gissing** and mother of **Fritz**. The name was previously von Giesing, but the family was naturalized before World War I. They take **Harwood's** former cottage, Louisa, in **Wiple** Terrace. She paints, and wears very expensive clothes. They drive a super Daimler-Rolls. The whole family leaves for America. (CBI 40)

❖ They are now called the **Warburys**, "a very unpleasant family connected with the films." (PE 47)

Gissing, Mr. Oscar

❖ Husband of **Mrs. Gloria Gissing** and father of **Fritz**. The name was previously von Giesing, but the family was naturalized before World War I. They take **Harwood's** former cottage, Louisa, in **Wiple** Terrace. He worked in films in Munich, and now is something in the film industry (Dante-Technifilms). They drive a super Daimler-Rolls. The whole family leaves for America. (CBI 40)

❖ They are now called the **Warburys**, "a very unpleasant family connected with the films." (PE 47)

Glover, Molly: *See* Watson, Mrs. Molly.

Gobbett, Hash

❖ Actor co-starring with **Glamora Tudor** in *Burning Flesh*. (PBO 46)

❖ He plays Oliver Cromwell in *Mayflower Madness*, with a false forehead and a genuine grafted wart. He is supposed to be in love with Queen Henrietta Maria (played by Miss Tudor), and intends to sail on the *Mayflower*, but falls asleep during a reading by John Bunyan of *Pilgrim's Progress*. (PE 47)

❖ He was also in *Stiff Upper Lip* and *Where Next*. (LAR 48)

Goble

❖ The writer of the original plans for the **Beltons'** Harefield House was a Goble. (CQ 58)

Goble, Mr.

❖ Bailiff to the **Grahams**, Holdings. He raises their White Porkminster pig, Holdings Goliath. (LAR 48)

❖ His son is in the R.A.F. (DD 51)

❖ He is now raising Goliath's son, Holdings Blunderbore. His best sow took the Omnium cup at the Barsetshire Agricultural last year. (ESR 55)

❖ Holdings Goliath wins first prize at the Agricultural. (ADA 57)

Goble, Mrs.
❖ Postmistress at Edgewood, with a maid, **Sarah**. Her younger sister's boy over at Courcy is waiting for his call-up. (OBH 49)

❖ Her son, **Young Goble**, is now back and living at the post office. (HRt 52)

Goble, Young
❖ Son of **Mrs. Goble**, now back and living at the post office. Both he and **Henry Grantly** worked with the Kronk gun during the war. (HRt 52)

Goblin, Professor
❖ Russian astronomer. According to **Miss Hopgood's Aunt (Helen Hopgood)**, he tried to claim Porter Sidus as Goblin Sidus. (NR 41)

Godwin
❖ Porter, Hallbury Station. (MB 45)

Gorman, Jennifer
❖ Student at Barchester High School and friend of **Grace Grantly**, to whom her perm is a souce of endless interest. (OBH 49)

* Now Grace only exchanges threepenny Woolworth Christmas cards with her, and has secretly decided not to send one the next year. (DD 51)

* She is working as an assistant to **Madame Tomkins**. She still sees Grace (now Lady Lufton) occasionally. (LAAA 59)

Gould, Dora

* Fourth and youngest daughter of **Mr.** and **Mrs. Gould**; her elder sisters are **Ruth, Sylvia,** and **Rose**; the latter is her closest companion. She is twelve, and has an imaginary country named Dorland in competition with **Tony Morland**. (DH 34)

* Both she and Rose have jobs somewhere and do whatever it is they do competently. (LAAA 59)

* They must be well into their thirties. (TSAT 61)

Gould, Mr.

* Vicar of High Rising. Husband of **Mrs. Gould** and father of **Ruth, Sylvia, Rose,** and **Dora**. (DH 34)

* His service is very dull; he's got three girls (but *see* above) and the eldest is getting a bit long in the tooth. (NTL 56)

* He and his wife are elderly and dull. (TSAT 61)

Gould, Mrs.

* Wife of the vicar of High Rising, **Mr. Gould**, and mother of **Ruth, Sylvia, Rose,** and **Dora**. She, Rose, and Dora take **Laura** and **Tony Morland** to picnics at the Wishing Well and at Rushmere Pool. (DH 34)

* They've got three girls (but *see* above) and the eldest is getting a bit long in the tooth. (NTL 56)

* She heads the volunteer committee at the Rising Cottage Hospital.

* She and her husband are elderly and dull. (TSAT 61)

Gould, Rose
* Third daughter of **Mr. and Mrs. Gould**; her elder sisters are **Ruth** and **Sylvia**, the younger her close companion, **Dora**. She is fourteen. (DH 34)

* Both she and Dora have jobs somewhere and do whatever it is they do competently. (LAAA 59)

* They must be well into their thirties. (TSAT 61)

Gould, Ruth
* Eldest daughter of **Mr. and Mrs. Gould**; younger sisters **Sylvia**, **Rose**, and **Dora**. She runs a chicken farm with a friend near Southbridge. (DH 34)

* She may have been forgotten, as the Goulds are said to have only three girls. (NTL 56)

* Her partner is known as "The-Friend-That-I-Live-With." (TSAT 61)

Gould, Sylvia
* Second daughter of **Mr. and Mrs. Gould**; her elder sister is **Ruth**, the younger are **Rose** and **Dora**. She is twenty-three, games mistress at a large school for girls. She intended to go to a school in Switzerland, but becomes engaged to **Dr. Ford**. (DH 34)

* She broke off the engagement, probably wisely. (GU 43)

* She is still unmarried, now one of the secretaries for **Sam Adams'** offices at Pomfret Towers. She broke off the

engagement because she thought that Dr. Ford was only on the rebound from **Anne Todd**. The school in Switzerland was no fun; then there were a lot of jobs in other schools, and a secretarial course when she got too old for games. She did Red Cross work during the war. Finally, she turns down a proposal from the aged **Lord Stoke**, and accepts another from Dr. Ford. (TSAT 61)

Govern, Mr. James

❖ Estate carpenter to **Mr. (William) Marling** at Marling Hall. (MH 42)

❖ (But *see* LAR 48, where **Fred** has become carpenter at Marling Hall.)

Govern, Mr.

❖ Ironmonger and tinker in the High Street, Hallbury. (MB 45)

Gradka: though her surname is supposed to be impossible to say or memorize, *see* **Bonescu, Gradka**.

Graham, Lady Agnes (née Leslie)

❖ Wife of **Sir Robert Graham**, mother of **James**, **Emmy**, and **Clarissa**. Third child of **Mr. Henry** and **Lady Emily Leslie**. Of Holdings, though she often stays with her mother at Rushwater. Charming, muddled, but essentially practical, she deals with the unwanted visitor **Mr. Holt**. **Pierre Boulle** is infatuated with her, and rescues Emmy from the pond. (WS 34)

❖ The children now include **Robert** and **Edith**. (MH 42)

❖ In the list of her children who will be sad at **Miss Bunting's** death, there are (in this order) Emmy, James, Clarissa, **John**, Robert, and Edith. (MB 45)

* She loses her mother, Lady Emily. (OBH 49)

* She was married at twenty-one. (DD 51)

* She is fifteen years younger than her husband. (ESR 55)

* Arranges **Miss Merriman's** wedding, and serves as Matron of Honor. (ADA 57)

Graham, Clarissa

* Third child of **Lady Agnes** and **Sir Robert Graham**, younger sister of **James** and **Emmy**. Two-and-a-half years old. (WS 34)

* Now about nine, elder sister of **Robert** and **Edith**. (MH 42)

* Her brother **John** appears as the fourth child of the family. (MB 45)

* She will be fifteen on June nineteenth. She wants to go to boarding school, then on to Cambridge for engineering draughtsmanship. (PBO 46)

* She is eighteen, going to college on a math scholarship, and wants to be a draughtsman, perhaps for **Sam Adams'** office. She is difficult, but is managed by **Charles Belton**. (LAR 48)

* She is on half-term holiday, and very upset by the death of her grandmother, **Lady Emily Leslie**. (OBH 49)

* Still at college, she becomes informally engaged to Charles Belton. (CC 50)

* Graduated Cambridge in three years with a good Second in math and science; her **Professor Henbane** said that she

would have gotten a First if she had stayed the fourth year. She now doesn't want a career and is very dissatisfied and unpleasant, but Charles puts her in her place and they become formally engaged. (DD 51)

* She had a London Season but didn't enjoy it, and is once again being difficult. She marries Charles at Rushwater on New Year's Day, and they go to the **Pomfrets'** villa at Cap Ferrat for their honeymoon. (HRt 52)

* She is pregnant. (ESR 55)

* They have one child. (NTL 56)

* They have a fat little boy and an excellent small girl. (CQ 58)

Graham, Edith
* Fifth and last child of **Lady Agnes** and **Sir Robert Graham,** younger sister of **James, Emmy, Clarissa,** and **Robert.** No more than three years old, and can say "rice pudding." (MH 42)

* Now the sixth child, as **John** has appeared as the fourth. (MB 45)

* She can't read yet, but makes up rhymes. (PBO 46)

* Her couplets are recited at **Sam Adams'** garden party. (OBH 49)

* Now twelve. (CC 50)

* About sixteen, bumptious but still poetic. (WDIM 54)

* Nearly eighteen (one month older than **Ludovic Foster, Lord Mellings**), still at home, and interested in pigs. She

visits the **Hallidays** (where
she is fond of both **George
Halliday** and **John-Arthur
Crosse**) and goes to America
to visit **Rose Bingham Leslie**
(ESR 55)

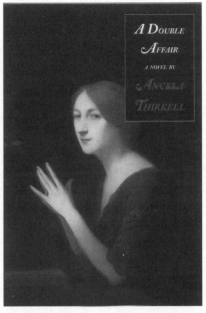

❖ Now barely eighteen and just
back from two or three
months in the U.S. She visits
Mrs. (Laura) Morland and
goes to Pomfret Towers to
study estate management
with **Roddy Wicklow**. (NTL
56)

❖ She is nineteen, and Lord
Mellings is a little *older* than she. She doesn't finish her
course, but goes back to visit **David Leslie** and Rose in
America, where her beaux include **Sherman Concord** and
Lee Sum(p)ter. She returns for Miss Merriman's wedding,
and now eighteen again, visits Rushwater. Her father and
mother go away, sending her to board with **Dean** and **Mrs.
Crawley** and finish her course. She falls in love with **Lord
William Harcourt**. (ADA 57)

❖ Married to Lord William, and pregnant; she engages
Sister Chiffinch, then gives birth to **Gwendolen Sally**,
named for Lord William's sister **Lady Gwendolen Harcourt** and for **Sally Wicklow** Foster, **Lady Pomfret**; the
godfather is **Robert Graham**. (LAAA 59)

❖ She is pregnant again. (TSAT 61)

Graham, Emmy

* Second child of **Lady Agnes** and **Sir Robert Graham**, younger sister of **James**, elder sister of **Clarissa**. Five years old, she falls in the pond in the kitchen garden and is rescued by **Pierre Boulle**. (WS 34)

* Further siblings: **Robert** and **Edith**. She is too old for dance class, and is left with a governess. (MH 42)

* Her brother **John** appears as the fourth child of the family, while she is named first. (MB 45)

* She is eighteen and a Land Girl, very cow-minded, at Rushwater for the summer. She wants to go to an agricultural college and to breed bulls. (PBO 46)

* Working at Rushwater with **Martin Leslie**. (LAR 48)

* Now twenty-odd, she mentors **Tom Grantly**, and well-nigh asks him to live with her and **Conque** in **Mr. MacPherson's** old house. (OBH 49)

* Engaged to Tom Grantly. (DD 51)

* Married. (HRt 52)

* They have a baby boy. (ESR 55)

* Her sister Edith refers to "all Emmy's children." (NTL 56)

* Her eldest child is **James** for his uncle, then several lusty brothers or sisters, and the youngest, **Agnes**, is a toddler. (TSAT 61)

Graham, Henry

* Name that **Mr. MacPherson** misuses for **John Graham**. (PBO 46)

❖ **Lady Agnes Graham** confirms that none of her sons is called after her father, **Mr. Henry Leslie**. (LAR 48)

Graham, James

❖ Eldest child of **Lady Agnes** and **Sir Robert Graham**, brother of **Emmy** and **Clarissa**. Seven years old, he holds a funeral for a thrush. (WS 34)

❖ Now at Eton. Further siblings: **Robert** and **Edith**. (MH 42)

❖ His brother **John** appears in the middle of the family while **Emmy** is listed as eldest. (MB 45)

❖ In **Mr. Manhole's** house at Eton, though he is presumably nineteen or twenty years old. He loves birds and has a reputation as an eccentric. (PBO 46)

❖ *Still* at Eton, though he is soon to begin military service in his father's old regiment. He was named for Sir Robert's father. (LAR 48)

❖ Now in the Army. (OBH 49)

❖ A guardsman, second lieutenant. (CC 50)

❖ Of the Graham sons, he was the only one to begin a military career in an O.C.T.U. before the peace. (DD 51)

❖ Now lieutenant. (HRt 52)

❖ Now a captain, though still referred to as Lieutenant Graham. (ESR 55)

❖ A captain, over twenty-five years old. (NTL 56)

❖ A major, and may soon be a colonel. (LAAA 59)

* Emmy's eldest son, **James Grantly**, is named after him. (TSAT 61)

Graham, John
* Inserted as the fourth child of **Lady Agnes** and **Sir Robert Graham**, younger brother of **Emmy**, **James**, and **Clarissa**, elder brother of **Robert** and **Edith**. (MB 45)

* He is at school. **Mr. MacPherson** misnames him **Henry**. (PBO 46)

* He is at Eton. (LAR 48)

* He is eager to join James in the Guards. (HRt 52)

* Now a professional soldier. (ESR 55)

* Over twenty-one and a second lieutenant, but James calls him the youngest son. (NTL 56)

* He is a full lieutenant. (ADA 57)

* Now a captain. (LAAA 59)

Graham, Robert
* Fourth child of **Lady Agnes** and **Sir Robert Graham**, younger brother of **James**, **Emmy**, and **Clarissa**, elder brother of **Edith**. Five years old. (MH 42)

* Now the fifth child, as **John** has appeared as the fourth. (MB 45)

* At **Mr. Manhole's** house, Eton. Comments on **Mr. Scatcherd's** "admiring picture." (PBO 46)

* He wants to be a poet. On half-term holiday, he is infatuated with baby **Eleanor Leslie**. (LAR 48)

❖ Still at school. (DD 51)

❖ He has a poem in the school magazine, and gets a scholar-ship. (HRt 52)

❖ Now a professional soldier. (ESR 55)

❖ James says that Robert is the next son after him, and John the youngest. (NTL 56)

❖ He is a second lieutenant. (ADA 57)

❖ Now a full lieutenant in the Guards, at St. James's Palace. He is godfather to his niece, **Gwendolen Sally Harcourt**. He adores both **Glamora Tudor** and **Franklin, Duchess of Towers**, and invites the latter, **Lee Sum(p)ter**, and **Lady Gwendolen Harcourt** up to London for a theater party as soon as **Bobby Skipper** repays him ten pounds. (LAAA 59)

Graham, Sir Robert

❖ (Generally absent) husband of **Lady Agnes Graham (née Leslie)**, father of **James**, **Emmy**, and **Clarissa**. Of Hold-ings, Little Misfit and the War Office, with the rank of colonel. His eldest sister is **Mrs. Preston**. He became engaged to Agnes after coffee was spilled on him. (WS 34)

❖ The children now include **Robert** and **Edith**. He is now Major-General Graham, C.B. He served on a military mission to Russia, and is to be made K.C.B. in the New Year's Honours List. (MH 42)

❖ Now a general. Related to Christopher Hornby's mother. (TH 44)

❖ Major-General again. **John** is inserted in the list of his children, somewhere in the middle. (MB 45)

* General again, and K.C.B. His family has been at Holdings since Waterloo. He covets **Mr. (Leonard) Halliday's** squirearchy, but hasn't been home much to exercise it since 1939. (PBO 46)

* His father's name was James. He can't get home to the Pig Breeder's Show; his bailiff **Mr. Goble** shows his Holdings Goliath. (LAR 48)

* He will soon retire and give up his directorships; the family will economize until he inherits from his Aunt Florence. He is so elusive because he hates to meet anyone he doesn't already know. (OBH 49)

* According to **Mrs. (Lucy) Belton,** if she hadn't been to the wedding she would never have believed in his existence. (DD 51)

* He is fifteen years older than his wife. He retires in a month, with K.C.M.G. and a great many other letters. His superior in the War Office is **General Platfield**. His nickname is Barking Bob, for being louder on parade than any other officer when he was a second lieutenant. He was at Saumur, so his French is perfect, as is his German, which is good for the missions he is constantly going on; but he can't learn Mixo-Lydian. His ancestor, **Robert Graham, Armiger**, was a contemporary of **Wm. Halliday, Gent.** His great-grandfather's illegitimate children were anagramatically named Ragham, and are now a plentiful, gypsy bunch in East Barsetshire. He finally enters in the last sentence. (ESR 55)

* He is still never at home, as he took on so many boards when he retired that he's always traveling, but he finally

really enters. He stands for County Council against **Sir Ogilvy Hibberd**. (NTL 56)

❖ He gives away the bride at the wedding of **Miss Merriman** and **Mr. (Herbert) Choyce**, and will take his wife along when he reorganizes the Mixo-Lydian army. (ADA 57)

❖ He couldn't be at Edith's baby's christening because he was abroad on a mission. (LAAA 59)

❖ He joins the Syndicate formed by **Sam Adams** to buy **Wiple** terrace away from **Lord Aberfordbury** and give it to Southbridge School. (TSAT 61)

Grant, (Mrs.) Delia: *See* **Brandon, Delia.**

Grant, Edward
❖ Husband of **Mrs. (Felicia) Grant**, father of **Hilary**. His mother was a **Miss Morton**, youngest sister of **Old Mrs. Brandon**, and his father was **Robert Grant** of the Barsetshire Regiment. (TB 39)

Grant, Felicia
❖ Second child of **Hilary** and **Delia Brandon** Grant. (PE 47)

Grant, Mrs. Felicia
❖ Widow of **Edward Grant**, mother of **Hilary**. She lives in Italy, where she adores the peasants in her dear Calabria. She comes to Barsetshire to visit Hilary, staying at the Cow and Sickle and then with **Lady Norton**. (TB 39)

❖ Despite the war, she will not leave Calabria, where she lodges with a chemist and part-time bandit named **Marco Aurelio** and his wife.

❖ She is writing a book on Calabrian folklore. (CBI 40)

G

* She is collecting folksongs in Calabria. (GU 43)

* She now lives almost entirely in Sicily. (OBH 49)

* She visits England. Back in Calabria, her landlord Aurelio has killed five men. (CC 50)

* **Eric Swan's** mother (the former **Flora Ramsay**) is a friend of hers, and visits Rome at Christmas. (HRt 52)

Grant, Freddie
* Eldest child of **Hilary** and **Delia Brandon** Grant. He has chicken pox and stays with his mother and his grandmother, **Mrs. (Lavinia) Brandon**, at stories. (GU 43)

Grant, Hilary
* Son of **Edward** and **Felicia Grant**, nephew (actually first cousin once removed, on his father's side) of **Miss (Amelia) Brandon**. He is twenty-three, at Oxford, reading Classics with **Mr. Miller** to prepare for the bar. He is writing about **Jehan le Capet**, and is infatuated with **Mrs. (Lavinia) Brandon** until **Delia Brandon** carves his name on a vegetable marrow. (TB 39)

* He is in intelligence and engaged to Delia Brandon. (CBI 40)

* They are married; he publishes *A Diabolist at the Restoration* about le Capet. He is in the Intelligence Corps for his Italian. (MH 42)

* He is in Washington; Delia and their little boy **Freddie** are at Stories. (GU 43)

* Their new baby is a girl. (TH 44)

* They are having another baby in August. (PBO 46)

❖ The latest baby is a girl named **Felicia**, but now they have only two babies. (PE 47)

❖ He has his excavating job, and they now have twins, "darling little boys." During their holidays, the boys will fly out and stay with their parents at the dig. His book for Oxbridge University Press on the pre-Grombolian pottery from the excavations near Chankly Bore will win him a seat in the *Académie des Inscriptions* and belated recognition of his work on le Capet. (HRt 52)

Grant, Captain Jerry
❖ Works with **Lucy Marling** at A.F.S. He is a bit cross at being out of the war because of a bad foot. He sends Lucy a Xmas card (his word, not ours). (MH 42)

Grant, Robert
❖ Of the Barsetshire Regiment. Father of **Edward** and grandfather of **Hilary Grant**. (TB 39)

Grantly, Agnes
❖ Youngest daughter of **Tom** and **Emmy Graham Grantly**. Her elder siblings are **James**, then several lusty brothers or sisters; she is a toddler. (TSAT 61)

Grantly, Commodore
❖ Brother of **Rector Septimus Grantly**, who was previously said to be an only child; at Portsmouth in 1915. (JC 53)

Grantly, Eleanor
❖ Daughter of a parson, granddaughter of a major, great-granddaughter of the Archdeacon at Plumstead, and great-niece of **Lily Dale** (*cf.* Trollope). She is secretary to **Susan Dean** at the Red Cross Library. (LAR 48)

✦ Second child of **Rector Septimus** and **Mrs. (Mary) Grantly**, sister of **Tom, Henry,** and **Grace**. The earlier genealogy now places her in her own father's generation. She was named after Mrs. Arabin, Archdeacon Grantly's sister-in-law (*cf.* Trollope). She has now become Red Cross Depot Librarian in succession to Susan Dean; her assistant is **Isabel Dale**. She visits an aunt in London, and **Sally, Lady Pomfret** has her to Pomfret Towers. She becomes slightly infatuated with **Gillie Foster, Lord Pomfret,** but then gets engaged to **Colin Keith**. (OBH 49)

✦ She is to be married after Christmas (after the Michaelmas Law Sitting). She stays on to break in the new secretary after both Lady Pomfret and Isabel Dale leave the Red Cross library. (CC 50)

✦ Now married, living in London, with a baby girl. (DD 51)

✦ They have bought a big house and consider getting a lodger, but decide they don't need to. She is pregnant again, due in April. (HRt 52)

✦ Their children are girls. (WDIM 54)

Grantly, (Mrs.) Emmy: *See* **Graham, Emmy.**

Grantly, Grace
✦ Fourth and youngest child of **Rector Septimus** and **Mrs. (Mary) Grantly,** sister of **Tom, Eleanor,** and **Henry**. She was nearly named Griselda for her father's great-aunt Grantly (who married Lord Dumbello who became Lord Hartletop, *cf.* Trollope); but became Grace after his grandmother. She is secretary of the Barchester High School Senior Debating Team, endlessly concerned with the perm

of her friend **Jennifer Gorman**, and gets six credits on her School Certificate. (OBH 49)

❖ She is named after the Grace Crawley who married the Archdeacon's son, Major Henry Grantly (*cf.* Trollope), and looks like her as well.

❖ Now she only exchanges Christmas cards with Jennifer Gorman, and has secretly decided not to send one next year. **Ludovic, Lord Lufton**, is attracted to her. (DD 51)

❖ Now twenty, working at the Barchester Central Library in the section on Barsetshire and Barchester history (specifically, the Hartletop Letters, *cf.* Trollope). Though **Eric Swan** falls in love with her, she gets engaged to Lord Lufton, and is to be married at her father's church. (HRt 52)

❖ She is married, pregnant, and living at Framley Court. (JC 53)

❖ They have two daughters. (CQ 58)

❖ She still sees Jennifer Gorman sometimes. (LAAA 59)

❖ Her brood is still increasing. (TSAT 61)

Grantly, Henry Arabin
❖ Third child of **Rector Septimus** and **Mrs. (Mary) Grantly**, brother of **Tom, Eleanor,** and **Grace.** He is named for his father's grandfather who married Miss Crawley (*cf.* Trollope). He is waiting for his military call-up, and finally is sent to the Far East. (OBH 49)

❖ He is occasionally called Harry as well as Henry, and is still in the service. (DD 51)

* He spent two years in the Far East, meanwhile avoiding **Freda**, the Major's daughter at Umbrella in India. He is now at home and studying to be a solicitor, articled to **Keith** and Keith. (HRt 52)

Grantly, James

* Eldest son of **Tom** and **Emmy Graham Grantly**, here not yet named. (ESR 55)

* Named for his mother's brother; then he has several lusty brothers or sisters, and the youngest, **Agnes**, is a toddler. (TSAT 61)

Grantly, Mrs. Mary (née Carter)

* Wife of **Rector Septimus Grantly**, and mother of **Tom, Eleanor, Henry**, and **Grace**. Her father was **Tom Carter**, who died soon after her marriage. Her Aunt Patience went to London as head almoner at St. Sinecure's. (OBH 49)

Grantly, Rector Septimus

* Husband of **Mrs. (Mary) Grantly**, and father of **Tom, Eleanor, Henry**, and **Grace**. Rector of St. Michael and All Angels church, Edgewood. Despite the name, he is an only child, the great-great-grandson of Bishop Grantly and of Warden Harding, via Archdeacon Grantly; great-grandson of Mr. Crawley, curate of Hogglestock, later of Barchester, whose daughter (his grandmother) married Major Henry Grantly, son of the Archdeacon (*cf.* Trollope). Now sixtyish and very handsome. (OBH 49)

* He was at Paul's, and is now a rural dean. He christens **Amabel Rose Adams**. (DD 51)

* **Octavia Crawley** Needham says that it was his great-grandfather who married **Dean (Josiah) Crawley's** mother's great-aunt. (HRt 52)

* Despite being an only child, he is said to have a brother, **Commodore Grantly**, who was at Portsmouth in 1915. (JC 53)

Grantly, Tom

* Eldest child of **Rector Septimus** and **Mrs. (Mary) Grantly**, brother of **Eleanor, Henry**, and **Grace**. Twenty-eight years old, a former major of the Barsetshires who served two years, up to D-Day. He was in Iceland with **Young Ted Pilward**. After demobilization, he went back to Oxford, where he got a Second in Greats. He works on the land for **Lucy Marling** and **Mr. Sam Adams**, mentored by **Emmy Graham**; she well-nigh asks him to live with her and **Conque** in **Mr. Macpherson's** old house. He plans to go to Rushwater and work on produce there. (OBH 49)

* Still twenty-eight, he is doing well at Rushwater but dissatisfied. He takes a job at the Red Tape and Sealing Wax office at Silverbridge, but **Geoffrey Harvey** turns against him and he resigns. He returns to Rushwater after a year, is gently rebuffed by **Lady Glencora Palliser**, and gets engaged to Emmy Graham. After some accountancy training, he will become agent to Rushwater. (DD 51)

* He is married to Emmy. (HRt 52)

* They have a baby boy. (ESR 55)

* **Edith Graham** refers to "all Emmy's children." (NTL 56)

* **Martin Leslie** is to take him in as a partner in Rushwater. (ADA 57)

* Their eldest child is **James** for his mother's brother, then there are several lusty brothers or sisters, and the youngest, **Agnes**, is a toddler. (TSAT 61)

Greaves, Crosby ("Bing"): *See* **Greaves, Lieutenant Tommy**.

Greaves, Lieutenant Tommy
* Billeted on the **Villars**, Northbridge Rectory. He would have been sent down from Oxford for excessive joviality had he not gone straight into the army. He is keen on old churches and things. His mother's elder sister is **Lady de Courcy**. He gets engaged to **Mrs. (Poppy) Turner's Other Niece**. (NR 41)

* They are married, he has become a stockbroker, and they live in an expensive flat with small rooms and a restaurant downstairs so she needn't cook. They have no children yet. Now he is misnamed **Crosby** (after an uncle) and nick-named **"Bing."** (WDIM 54)

Greens, the
* Some nice uninteresting people who rent the Laurels from the **Umblebys**, and sublet it to **John** and **Rose Birkett Fairweather**. (JC 53)

Gresham, Beatrice ("Batty"): *See* **Gresham, Jane**.

Gresham, Lieutenant Commander Francis
* Husband of **Jane Gresham**, father of **Frank**. He was on a battleship in the Far East, and has been missing for four years. His family is from Greshamsbury, and his grandfather Frank Gresham married a fortune (*cf.* Trollope). **Sam**

Adams finds out that he was seen on a jungle island two years before, and that he had fever but was still free. Finally, he is on his way back to England. (MB 45)

✤ He is well, with a shore job in Plymouth; he and Jane are there, but their permanent home is with **Admiral Palliser**. (PBO 46)

✤ He is a captain, now said to have spent several years as a P.O.W. in Japan. He is therefore at the Admiralty, and is not allowed much active service. They live at Greshamsbury House, in a wing leased from a quiet elderly couple of Greshams who live in London and abroad. They now have two little girls as well. (JC 53)

✤ The girls are **Jane** and **Mary**. Greshamsbury House has become a National Trust estate. (ADA 57)

✤ The elder girl, formerly Jane, is now **Beatrice**, nicknamed "Batty" by Frank. (CQ 58)

Gresham, Frank
✤ Son of **Lt. Commander Francis** and **Jane Gresham**; eight-and-a-half years old. He goes to **Robin Dale's** school and is friends with **Tom Watson**. His cousins at Greshamsbury (descendants of Squire Gresham, *cf.* Trollope) have measles, so he can't visit them. He throws a crucial bit of brick into the Hallbury Old Rectory well, which stymies the Barsetshire Archaeological. (MB 45)

✤ He is now at Southbridge School. (PBO 46)

✤ He now has two sisters. (JC 53)

✤ His sisters are **Jane** and **Mary**. (ADA 57)

* The elder girl, formerly Jane, is now **Beatrice**, nicknamed "Batty" by him. (CQ 58)

Gresham, Jane

* One of the two (unnamed) daughters of **Lt. Commander Francis** and **Jane Gresham**; their elder brother is **Frank Gresham**. (JC 53)

* The girls are **Jane** and **Mary**. (ADA 57)

* The elder girl, presumably Jane, is now **Beatrice**, nicknamed "Batty" by Frank. (CQ 58)

Gresham, Mrs. Jane (née Palliser)

* Wife of **Lt. Commander Francis Gresham**, mother of **Frank**, younger daughter of **Admiral Palliser**. Her husband has been missing for four years, and she and Frank are living with her father.

* She is befriended by **Sam Adams**, who finds out that her husband is alive and on his way back. (MB 45)

* She and her husband are living in Plymouth, but their permanent home is with Admiral Palliser. (PBO 46)

* She is godmother to **Dora Maud Dale**. (CC 50)

* Now living at Greshamsbury House, in a wing leased from a quiet elderly couple of Greshams who live in London and abroad. They now have two little girls as well. (JC 53)

* The girls are **Jane** and **Mary**. Greshamsbury House has become a National Trust estate. (ADA 57)

* The elder girl, formerly Jane, is now called **Beatrice**, nicknamed "Batty" by Frank. (CQ 58)

Gresham, Mary

* One of the two (unnamed) daughters of **Lt. Commander Francis** and **Jane Gresham**; their elder brother is **Frank Gresham**. (JC 53)

* The girls are **Jane** and **Mary**. (ADA 57)

Gresham, Mr.

* Conservative M.P. for East Barsetshire. Re-elected over the **son of Sir Ogilvy Hibberd (Lord Aberfordbury)**. (PBO 46)

* Permanent honorary chairman at the Conservative Rally and Pig Show, Staple Park. (LAR 48)

* A middle-aged bachelor, he is best man at **Sam Adams'** wedding. (CC 50)

* He stands, and is elected, again. (HRt 52)

* You can't understand him since he got his new teeth. He is the local Master of the Hounds. Having been in Parliament for almost fifty years, he has decided not to stand for election again. (NTL 56)

* He is best man for **Mr. (Herbert) Choyce's** wedding. (ADA 57)

Gresham, Mr.

* Of East Barsetshire; he has farmed all his life and his father's before him. Served as judge of the Barsetshire Agricultural last year, when he preferred Norfolk Nobbler pigs. (ESR 55)

Greta

* One of three evacuees living with **Mrs. (Gladys) Dingle**; the others are **Gary** and **Gable**. (CBI 40)

G

Grey, Una

+ "The Incubus," a neurotic but efficient young woman who gets secretarial jobs, falls in love with her employer, and tries to alienate all his other friends. After trying this with **Mr. and Mrs. Birkett** at Southbridge School, she moves on to **George Knox**; she is foiled by Mrs. Birkett and **Anne Todd**. Though she claims to be alone and friendless, she has a mother in County Cork. She is sent on to work for **Miss Hocking**. (HR 33)

+ She went as companion to **Old Mrs. Knox**. (DH 34)

+ After being companion to Mrs. Knox, she married a Navy man after great exertions. (TB 39)

Griffiths, Miss

+ Music mistress, Hosiers' Girls' Foundation School. (TH 44)

Grimier, M.

+ Schoolmaster, colleague of **Mr. (Sidney) Carton**. He cannot control small boys. He is writing a life of Gambetta. (TH 44)

Gristle, Mr.: Geraldine Birkett's misnomer for Mr. Bissell. (*q.v.*)

Grobury

+ Gardener at the Lodge, Silverbridge: "Grobury's my name, and Growberry's my nature." His father's uncle was a baker (a family business) and a principal creditor of Mr. Crawley, who was wrongly accused of stealing a cheque and whose daughter married Major Grantly (*cf.* Trollope). (DD 51)

Groom, Old
 * From the Omnium Arms. Helps out at the Hallbury Cottage Hospital Bring and Buy Sale. (MB 45)

Grubacker, The Reverend
 * Preacher at a church in Texas that the **van Dryvens** attend. (WDIM 54)

Grubb, Old Mrs.
 * Invalid at Rising Cottage Hospital. She has a mathematical mind, and would take it hard if **Old Miss Bunce's** twelve peppermint drops didn't match her ten barley sugars. (TSAT 61)

Gudgeon, Mr.
 * Butler at Rushwater House to the **Leslies**. He likes to sound the dinner gong, and sings "The Body in the Bag" for the annual concert in the racket court. (WS 34)
 * Now lives with his sister at Bovey Tracey. (PBO 46)

Guidone, Guido
 * Painter of a celebrated picture bought by **Woolcott Jefferson van Dryven** from the **Duke of Towers'** collection. (LAAA 59)

Gumm, Captain
 * Dentist at the Hush-Hush camp, Dower House. His father, a dentist, forced him into the business despite his wish to go into the Air Force. (GU 43)

Gunnarssen, Hjalmar
 * Playwright; his leading lady is **Selma Lundquist**. (LAR 48)

Hacker, Percy ("Hack")

* Student at Southbridge School, excellent at classics. He keeps a chameleon named Gibbon (formerly Greta Garbo; he also threatens to name it after **Philip Winter**). He sets a table on fire, floods the bath, and wins the Montgomery Open Scholarship to Lazarus College.

* On **Mr. Lorimer's** death, he writes Latin verse in his memory, and lines Gibbon's cage in black. (SH 37)

* He is in the Ministry of Information. (GU 43)

* M.A., senior classical tutor at Lazarus, winner of the Hertford and Craven prizes. (MB 45)

* Fellow of Lazarus and reader in Neo-Platonism and Aristotelian Ethics to the University of Oxford, the best classics scholar Southbridge ever produced. Now writing a book on Sophocles, he attends the School Speech Day and adds verses to the school *Carmen*; he still has Gibbon. (PE 47)

❖ Now professor of Latin at a famous university. (DD 51)

❖ Holds the chair of Latin at Redbrick University. (HRt 52)

❖ Presided at the opening of the new Southbridge School Library in 1958. (TSAT 61)

Hagenstolz, Fräulein
❖ Governess to the children of **Mr. Henry** and **Lady Emily Leslie**. Subject of **John Leslie's** couplet written on the wall of the Temple at Rushwater: "Ding, dong, bell / Fräulein goes to hell." (LAR 48)

❖ Now called Fräulein Hagestolz, she was governess to **Jeff Palliser**, but she used to hit his fingers with a ruler when he played scales wrong, so the Pallisers got rid of her. (DD 51)

Halliday, Mrs. Eleanor ("Ellie")
❖ Wife of **Mr. (Leonard) Halliday** and mother of **George** and **Sylvia**. Of Hatch House, Hatch End. (PBO 46)

❖ Her brother was missing, reported killed in World War I. Her mother's sister is deaf. (ESR 55)

❖ Her husband dies. (NTL 56)

❖ Though she visits Sylvia at Rushwater, she isn't getting along well with her or with George. Her mother lived at Northbridge at Hovis House, owned by **Mrs. Dunsford**, a relation of hers (her mother was Mrs. Dunsford's Aunt Sophy); she and Mrs. Dunsford were at school together, though she is a little younger. She goes to Mrs. Dunsford for a long visit, and then on to the Riviera, where **Lady de Courcy** invites her to stay on through the winter. (ADA 57)

❖ She now lives mainly in the South of France. (TSAT 61)

Halliday, George

❖ Eldest son of **Mr. Leonard** and **Mrs. (Eleanor) Halliday**, brother of **Sylvia**. Twenty-four years old, Captain of the Barsetshire Yeomanry, stationed in Italy. He comes home on leave. Before the army, he had gone to Southbridge School and then for a year at St. Jude's, where he climbed around the quad in a cape and tights. (PBO 46)

❖ Now thirtyish and running the farm for his father. Both he and **John Arthur Cross(e)** (whom he knew at Vache-en-Étable) are fond of **Edith Graham**, but they remain friends. (ESR 55)

❖ He also knew **Tony Morland** at Vache-en-Étable. His father dies, and he inherits and keeps running Hatch House and the farm. (NTL 56)

❖ He is improving the farm, which is paying its way. He is put up for County Council and gets engaged to **Jane Crawley**, whose sister **Grace** gets engaged to John-Arthur Crosse; they are all married in a double ceremony in the Cathedral. (ADA 57)

❖ They have a new baby, **Martin** (after **Martin Leslie**). Their piglets win a silver medal at the High Rising Agricultural. (TSAT 61)

Halliday, George

❖ Ancestor of **Mr. (Leonard) Halliday**; was in trouble after the battle of Bosworth. (ESR 55)

Halliday, Jane: *See* **Crawley, Jane**.

Halliday, Mr. Leonard

* Husband of **Mrs. (Eleanor) Halliday** and father of **George** and **Sylvia**. Of Hatch House, Hatch End. He descends from **Wm. Halliday, Gent.**; the family has been in the neighborhood since Domesday. Their Tudor stone house is now the bank. He has precedence as squire and churchwarden over **Sir Robert Graham** at Holdings. He was at Ypres. (PBO 46)

* He was at Paul's, Oxford. He had two spinster aunts, Jessie and Sylvia, who lived upstairs in the Old Manor House even after it became a bank; Sylvia outlived Jessie. He also had an ancestor, **George Halliday**, who was in trouble after the Battle of Bosworth. Now an invalid, he finally resigns as chuchwarden. (ESR 55)

* He is deaf and gently dotty. Though he never made the land over to George as he intended, he did insure against death duties. He dies. (NTL 56)

Halliday, Martin

* Son of **George** and **Jane Crawley Halliday**, of Hatch House. Named for his uncle, **Martin Leslie**. (TSAT 61)

Halliday, Sylvia

* Second child of **Mr. (Leonard)** and **Mrs. (Eleanor) Halliday**, sister of **George**. Twenty-two years old, a dancer, now with the WAAFs. Though she has a soft spot for **David Leslie**, she gets engaged to **Martin Leslie** at the birth of the Jersey's calf. (PBO 46)

* Their daughter **Eleanor** is a year old. (LAR 48)

* She is pregnant again, due in March. (OBH 49)

* She is godmother to **Roberta Fielding Dale**, daughter of **Robin** and **Anne Fielding Dale**. (CC 50)

* Her two children are Eleanor and **Georgy**, and she is pregnant again. (DD 51)

* Still pregnant; number three is to be called Leonard Martin or Emily. (ESR 55)

* She has been married for almost ten years, and is still pregnant. (NTL 56)

* She finally has three children, of whom Eleanor is about seven. She is again pregnant. (ADA 57)

Halliday, Wm., Gent.
* Ancestor of **Mr. (Leonard) Halliday**. He married a lady of property and built Hatch House in 1721. (PBO 46)

Hammer, Mr.
* Estate agent for **Wiple** Terrace. (CBI 40)

Hamonet, Mlle.
* French mistress at **Lavinia Brandon's** old school. (LAAA 59)

* She also taught at **Mrs. (Laura) Morland's** London day school. Her deadly enemy was **Fräulein Kessler**, due to the Franco-Prussian War. (TSAT 61)

Hamp
* Obliging owner of Hamp's Motor Haulage Ltd., a carrier company at Hatch End. (HRt 52)

Hamp, Miss
* Lame and much-respected keeper of the village shop at Pomfret Madrigal. Her aunt had twins at forty-four and buried them both. (HRt 52)

Hamp, Mr.

❖ Tailor at Worsted; does some alterations for **Lady Harriet Waring**. He was sent to Mutta Kundra in India in World War I, where he got sunstroke and was kicked in the head by a mule; as a result he has a prominent bump on his (bald) head, and has been sensitive to cold since 1915. His son, **Mr. Hamp**, is also a tailor, but is too busy to take over his father's business; his sister-in-law **Mrs. Hamp** runs the village shop in Lambton. (GU 43)

❖ He comes to Gatherum once a year to go through the **Duke of Omnium's** suits and repair them. (DD 51)

❖ His shop is in the same building as **Madame Tomkins'**, Barchester. (JC 53)

Hamp, Mr.

❖ Son of **Mr. Hamp** the tailor at Worsted. He is lame, in the Home Guard, and has a good job in The People's Tailoring Limited, so he can't take over his father's business. (GU 43)

Hamp, Mrs.

❖ Runs the village shop at Lambton. Her brother-in-law is **Mr. Hamp** the tailor at Worsted; her sister cleans at the Dower House. (GU 43)

Hampton, Miss

❖ Gentlemanly friend of **Miss Bent**, with whom she shares Adelina cottage, **Wiple** terrace, Southbridge. Her sensational novels include *Temptation at St. Anthony's*, and she supports four nephews: two in the Army, one in the Navy, and one in the consular service in Spain. She drove an ambulance in Mixo-Lydia in 1918. (CBI 40)

* She is in the Southbridge A.R.P., and confers with **Mrs. (Minnie) Paxon** of the Northbridge A.R.P.; she wants to use the shelters for release of inhibitions. (NR 41)

* She once wrote a book about an old lady and her house-keeper, but her new work is *Chariots of Desire*, about lorry-drivers. (MB 45)

* They give a farewell party for **Mr. and Mrs. Bissell** of the Hosiers' Boys' Foundation School. (PBO 46)

* She is now writing *A Gentle Girl and Boy*, about co-ed schools. Her father was a parson, and **Aubrey Clover's** family lived in his parish. She still returns to visit her aunt, who hasn't read any of her books. (PE 47)

* Her new book on agricultural life under present conditions (as absorbed on a tour of the Morgan ap Kerrig country) is called *Ways be Foul*. (OBH 49)

* Has just finished an exposure of Infidelity, to be called either *My Lesbia Has a Roving Eye* or *My Sister, My Spouse*. (CC 50)

* She educated her four nephews, and has recently taken Miss Bent to Mixo-Lydia to ski. Her new book on incest is *Crooked Insect*, and she is at work on *My Daughter Is My Son*. (JC 53)

* *Chariots of Desire* won the *Prix d'Immondices* in Paris. (NTL 56)

* She and Miss Bent set **the Bishop** straight about Lesbos on their Hellenic cruise. (CQ 58)

* She speaks against **Lord Aberfordbury's** plans for a post-card factory in Wiple Terrace. (TSAT 61)

Handiman, Lucius, Gent.

❖ In 1672, he planted several acorns brought back by him from Virginia; the lone survivor, a large blasted tree near the common, is called Hangman's Oak, somewhat after him. (BL 39)

Hands, Eliodora

❖ Co-stars with **Chat Huckaback** in *I Gonna Make You Love Me*, produced in New York and in London. (LAAA 59)

Harberton, Lord: *See* Humberton, Lord.

Harcourt, Dorothea (née Browne), Dowager Duchess of Towers

❖ As-yet-unnamed (but known as the Plunger) widow of the **Old Duke of Towers**, perhaps **Thomas Harcourt**; her children are **Lady Gwendolen** and **Lady Elaine Harcourt**, the current **Duke of Towers**, and **Lord William Harcourt**. She and the family used to live in Harcourt Abbey, but her husband fobbed it off onto a sporting syndicate before he died. (ADA 57)

❖ She squashed it whenever someone proposed to her daughters, so now they're spinsters. (CQ 58)

❖ She is now named fully, and known as "Dow." Their house is now known as The Towers, and none of the family has lived in it since the War. She, Lady Gwendolen, and Lady Elaine live in a house at the lower end of the village. She was the daughter of **Browne** of Balliol and Sussex, and her grandfather was **Octavius Manton**, who taught her some Latin; her brother **Simon Browne**, an Archdeacon, lives in London. (LAAA 59)

Harcourt, Duke of Towers (no first name given)
- ✤ Third? child of the **Old Duke (Thomas Harcourt?)** and
  Dowager Duchess of Towers; younger brother of **Lady
  Gwendolen** and **Lady Elaine Harcourt**, elder brother of
  Lord William Harcourt. Their home is Harcourt Abbey.
  His wife is an American; he is presently in poor straits,
  thanks to two lots of death duties close together. He sits in
  the Lords so that he can attend Royal Society meetings. An
  earlier, related branch of the family included a bad Duke in
  the Diplomatic and his wife Mary Seraskier (*cf.* Trollope);
  their only son died and she separated from him; when he
  died, the present, respectable branch of the family came in.
  (ADA 57)

- ✤ His wife's name is revealed as **Franklin**. Their home, now
  called The Towers, is now open to the public on certain
  days, and leased to Barchester magnates (like **Sam Adams**
  and **Old Pilward**) as a country club, with the stables let to
  the West Barsetshire Hunt. None of the family has lived
  there since the War. He, his Duchess, and their young
  children live in a house at the upper end of the village. He
  sells at auction in New York a celebrated **Guido Guidone**,
  a Primitive by **Pictor Ignotus**, an Etruscan statue, and the
  Très Jolies Heures of St. Panurge to **Woolcott Jefferson van
  Dryven**. (LAAA 59)

Harcourt, Lady Elaine
- ✤ Second? child of the **Old Duke (Thomas Harcourt?)** and
  Dowager Duchess of Towers; younger sister of **Lady
  Gwendolen Harcourt**, elder sister of **the Duke of Towers**
  and **Lord William Harcourt**. She was once engaged to
  Dobby Fitzgorman (a Liberal, suspected of shooting
  foxes) but he broke his neck. (ADA 57)

❖ Her mother the Dowager squashed any other proposals. (CQ 58)

❖ She, the Dowager, and Lady Gwendolen live in a house at the lower end of the village. Her aunt, Lady Fredegond, bred Arab ponies and smoked cheroots. She is nearly forty. She makes friends with the Duchess' cousin **Lee Sum(p)ter** and plans a visit to America. (LAAA 59)

Harcourt, Franklin, Duchess of Towers
❖ The as-yet-unnamed American wife of **Harcourt, the Duke of Towers**, of Harcourt Abbey. She races, and has some money. (ADA 57)

❖ She is named; their home, now The Towers, is now open to the public on certain days, and leased to Barchester magnates (like **Sam Adams** and **Old Pilward**), with the stables let to the West Barsetshire Hunt. None of the family has lived there since the war. She, the Duke, and their young children live in a house at the upper end of the village. She is of New England stock; her home town is Lumberville, and she is said to be from Virginia and to have a Southern voice. She was named for her mother's mother, who was a Franklin from Franklinsville, Georgia. Her brother has a ranch in Arizona, and her cousin is **Lee Sum(p)ter**. She arranged the **Cutsam van Pork** wedding in Baltimore. (LAAA 59)

Harcourt, Lady Gwendolen
❖ Eldest child of the **Old Duke (Thomas Harcourt?)** and **Dowager Duchess of Towers**; older sister of **Lady Elaine Harcourt, the Duke of Towers**, and **Lord William Harcourt**. A spinster, she has a passion for the celibate clergy. (ADA 57)

* Her mother the Dowager squashed any proposals. (CQ 58)

* She, the Dowager, and Lady Elaine live in a house at the lower end of the village. She is godmother to **Gwendolen Sally Harcourt**, daughter of Lord William and the former **Edith Graham**. Her aunt, Lady Fredegond, bred Arab ponies and smoked cheroots. She discreetly adores **Mr. (Caleb) Oriel**, vicar of Harefield, and occasionally drives herself over to hear him. They become engaged and are married in the Cathedral, with the reception at the **Jorams'** and honeymoon in Brighton, which she had visited at age seven. (LAAA 59)

Harcourt, Gwendolen Sally

* First child of **Lord William** and **Edith Graham Harcourt**; named for her father's sister **Lady Gwendolen Harcourt** and for **Sally, Lady Pomfret**; her godfather is **Robert Graham**. (LAAA 59)

(Harcourt), Thomas, Duke of Towers (the Old Duke?)

* Nameless nephew who inherited the title from the **Duke of Towers** who married a **Miss Foster** and whose second daughter was **Dorothy "Dodo" Bingham**. (PBO 46)

* The current Duke, known to **Rose Bingham** as Uncle Tom, is now impoverished. (LAR 48)

* This may be the "Old Duke of Towers" who was the husband of the **Dowager Duchess of Towers** (later identified as **Dorothea Harcourt, née Browne**). If so, he has now died, leaving his heir in poor straits thanks to two lots of death duties close together. The children are **Lady Gwendolen** and **Lady Elaine Harcourt**, the heir, the current **Duke of Towers**, and **Lord William Harcourt**. The

family used to live in Harcourt Abbey, but he fobbed it off onto a sporting syndicate before he died. An earlier, related branch of the family included a bad Duke in the Diplomatic and his wife Mary Seraskier (*cf.* Trollope); their only son died and she separated from him; when he died the present, respectable branch of the family came in. (ADA 57)

Harcourt, Lord William

❖ Fourth? child of the **Old Duke (Thomas Harcourt?)** and **Dowager Duchess of Towers**; younger brother of **Lady Gwendolen Harcourt, Lady Elaine Harcourt**, and **the Duke of Towers**. He was at **Dean Crawley's** old college at Oxford and is currently his chaplain, while also writing on his family history. He is interested in **Edith Graham**. (ADA 57)

❖ He and Edith are married, with one child, **Gwendolen Sally**. His brother has given them a living and a parsonage in the village. (LAAA 59)

Harcourt, Lady William: *See* Graham, Edith.

Hargreaves, Sir Featherly

❖ Well-known medical consultant; his daughter is engaged to **Dr. Robert Perry**. (LAR 48)

❖ Unfortunately, Dr. Perry's wife turns out to be **the Honourable Clara Bronson-Hewbury**. (HRt 52)

Hargreaves, Old Major

❖ Of "Chandernagore," Harefield. Brings croquet mallets for ice hockey on the **Beltons'** lake. (TH 44)

Harker, Mr.
* Curate to **Mr. Villars**, Northbridge. An uninteresting man. (NR 41)

Harris, Mrs.
* **Nurse Chiffinch** goes for the month to her and her triplets. (CC 50)

Harrison
* Teacher of the mixed fifth, Southbridge School. No scholar, but he knows boys. When he breaks his leg in the Lakes, **Colin Keith** replaces him. He returns the next term for the Junior Classical. (SH 37)

Harrison, Job
* Of Reservoir Cottage. One of his twins, Rezzervah, died at five days old. (MH 42)

Harry
* A Vidler or Panter, at Hatch End. He has a brother **Jim** and sister **Dorothy**; Jim's wife's nephew is **Harry Hubback**. (ESR 55)

Hart, Miss
* Schoolmistress at Northbridge. Organizes the children's performance at the Coronation entertainment. (WDIM 54)

Hartletop, the Dowager Marchioness of
* **Miss (Maud) Bunting** was once companion to her. (MH 42)

Hartletop, Lady (the Marchioness of)
* Wife of **the Marquis of Hartletop**, mother of **Lord Dumbello**. Hartletop Priory is let as a girls' school. According to

her, only **Nurse Chiffinch** can deal with the Marquis when he has shingles. (CC 50)

❖ Lord Dumbello is still in the nursery. (DD 51)

✦ They are living in the second-best dower house, and had to make room by sending the family papers to the Barchester Central Library. (HRt 52)

❖ Her daughter is a shadow of her. (ESR 55)

Hartletop, the Marquis of
❖ **Rose Bingham Leslie** and her children visit his heir, little **Lord Dumbello**, at Hartletop. (LAR 48)

❖ Husband of **Lady Hartletop**. Hartletop Priory is let as a girls' school. Only **Nurse Chiffinch** can deal with him when he has shingles. (CC 50)

❖ Lord Dumbello is still in the nursery. (DD 51)

❖ They are living in the second-best dower house, and had to make room by sending the family papers to the Barchester Central Library. (HRt 52)

Harvest, Joan: *See* **Stevenson, Joan**.

Harvest, Lionel
❖ Underling of **Joan Stevenson** at the BBC. He and his friend **Mr. Potter** try a conspiracy against her, which fails. He is a nephew of **Dodo Bingham**, who implies that he is gay but also tells Joan that he'll come into four thousand pounds a year when old General Harvest dies. Joan persuades him into a companionate marriage. (WS 34)

* After getting his inheritance, he retires and writes *Cast Me Abroad*, "a scathing exposure of Broadcasting House." (MH 42)

Harvey, Frances
* Elder sister of **Geoffrey Harvey**. She had a First in Economics, and is secretary to **Oliver Marling** at the Regional Commissioner's Office; he comes dangerously close to proposing to her. She and her brother lease the Red House from **Joyce Perry Smith** because it is "too off-white and Sloan Square." (MH 42)

* She is now in the Censorship office. (TH 44)

* In Athens, being an infernal nuisance at the Embassy. (PBO 46)

* Now happily engaged in persecuting underlings in a government department. (LAR 48)

* Secretary to **Sir Ogilvy Hibberd, Lord Aberfordbury**. (OBH 49)

* Now in the Ministry for General Interference, cutting its staff at Gatherum Castle. When she says that she is a socialist, she is snubbed by **Gradka Bonescu**, the Mixo-Lydian Ambassador. (CC 50)

* She is head of Efficiency and Purging via the General Interference Personnel Secret Seeding. She almost gets Oliver Marling to rent The Cedars to her, but is stymied by **Maria Lufton**. (DD 51)

* She argues with Geoffrey over their Uncle George's legacy. She has now become his younger sister. (WDIM 54)

* She is still at Gatherum. (ADA 57)

✦ In her personnel cuts for the Labour government, she fired a Mixo-Lydian clerk, and the present government won't accept her explanation of this. She is still a "friend" of Lord Aberfordbury, with a scheme to direct all married women near Gatherum to work in his proposed factory in **Wiple** terrace, Southbridge. She lectures on "How to Direct Our Mothers into Industry." (TSAT 61)

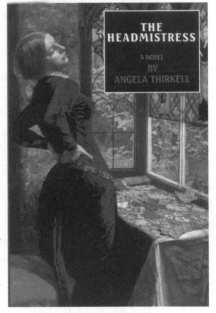

Harvey, Geoffrey

✦ Bombed out of London, he goes to work with his elder sister **Frances Harvey** and **Oliver Marling** at the Regional Commissioner's Office. He and Frances rent the Red House from **Joyce Perry Smith**. He is a cousin to **Eleanor Norton**, who is a cousin of **Mr. (William) Marling**, who keeps calling him **"Carver."** He admires the Russians, and writes poetry and a novel about Pico della Mirandola. (MH 42)

✦ He is back in London, sharing a flat with his friend Peter. (TH 44)

✦ His main work is with the Board of Red Tape and Sealing Wax. In the Pan-European Union for General Interference, he quarrels with **Miss Banks** and gets her fired. (LAR 48)

* He was always a Liberal, but joined the Labour party last year, for the influence. He had a run-in with **Sam Adams** around 1944, from which he came off the worse. (CC 50)

* The London office of Red Tape and Sealing Wax is being decentralized, so he organizes a branch at Silverbridge and gets **Tom Grantly** a job in it, though he turns against him soon after; he uses the Red Tape and Sealing Wax Secret Seeding to purge Undesireables from the office. He has been in the Civil Service since he left Cambridge, though he was at Lazarus, which is supposedly Oxford. He went to France with the Red Cross in 1939, but was back in a government job by 1940; he got some sort of B.E. (but nothing important) for his war work, as well as a French decoration of some kind for giving talks behind the Maginot Line. (DD 51)

* Their Uncle George left him and Frances a small legacy and two French snuffboxes, over which they quarrel. He has now become the elder of the two. (WDIM 54)

Harwood
* Cricket pro, Southbridge School. (SH 37)

* He lived in a cottage in **Wiple** Terrace, and only taught senior boys, but is now dead. (CBI 40)

Hastings, Mr.
* Best surgeon in the West; he removes shrapnel from **Cecil Waring** in an operation at the Barchester General Hospital. (DD 51)

Head, Miss
* Literature mistress, Hosiers' Girls' Foundation School. (TH 44)

❖ Since the end of the war, she is the very competent head-mistress of the new Preparatory School attached to the Barchester High School. (WDIM 54)

Head Chief of Mngangaland, the

❖ He is in England with a large retinue on V-J Day, to put his **eightieth son** (his favorite) into Balliol. He still keeps in touch with **Dr. Joram**, former **Bishop of Mngangaland**. (PBO 46)

❖ He had a new gramophone and two thousand records every year, and went through Gilbert and Sullivan three times a year. (CC 50)

❖ His eightieth son returned home after Balliol and ritually murdered him, becoming king. (NTL 56)

† The ritual slaughter was to the accompaniment of the Eton Boating Song. (TSAT 61)

Head Chief of Mngangaland, the Eightieth Son of the

❖ Favorite son of the **Head Chief of Mngangaland**, now in England to enter Balliol. **Dr. Joram**, former **Bishop of Mngangaland**, keeps in touch with events in his life. (PBO 46)

❖ He is reading P.P.E. (Politics, Philosophy, Economics). (PE 47)

❖ He is now at Lazarus College, and feels called to take orders and become a native bishop. (LAR 48)

❖ Since he spent his time reading Proust and Sartre and attending exhibitions of the Neo-Phallic Group, he has taken a Fourth in his Schools. (OBH 49)

* Now said to have finished Balliol with a good Second. He is reading law. He takes a house on the Coronation route and invites Bishop and Mrs. Joram (the former **Lavinia Brandon**). (WDIM 54)

* Now he took a Third at Balliol owing to his preoccupation with gambling. He then went home, ritually murdered his father, gave his seventy-nine brothers and sisters small government jobs, and is now king. (NTL 56)

* He seems to have returned to his student days; some time within the past year, he was at Oxford to be scared out of his wits when **Leslie Minor** walked around the outside of St. Jude's on the second floor, and he immediately summoned his father's **head witch doctor** by airplane. (CQ 58)

* He is said to have taken a Third in P.P.E., to have read some law, and then to have come home and ritually slaughtered his father and most of his relations to the accompaniment of the Eton Boating Song (he was fooled by bad friends at Lazarus). He made himself king, but now intends Mngangaland to be a republic, of which he will be elected president automatically. (TSAT 61)

Head Prefect, the
* Of the Hosiers' Girls' Foundation School. She wants to be a teacher, but has claustrophobia and acrophobia. She plays Jacques in *As You Like It*. (TH 44)

Head Witch Doctor of Mngangaland, the
* **Bishop Joram** used his services to help control his Mngangaland flock; he spent a year at Keble College, Oxford, before going into the family business. (CC 50)

* **The eightieth son of the Head Chief of Mngangaland** immediately summoned him by airplane when he was frightened by the appearance of **Leslie Minor**. (CQ 58)

Heath, Nurse ("Heathy")

* She shares a flat with her pals "Wardy" (**Nurse Ward**) and "Chiffy" (**Nurse Chiffinch**). (DH 34)

* The three want to run a small nursing home for the wealthy after the war. (MB 45)

* She nurses **Cecil Waring** at Beliers Priory, and once nursed **Mrs. (Hermione) Rivers**. (DD 51)

* She is looking for lodgings at Northbridge; she stays with **Mrs. (Poppy) Turner**, and nurses **Miss (Ianthe) Pemberton** at Punshions. (WDIM 54)

* Miss Pemberton died after a few months, and then she and Miss Ward took Punshions and renovated it for themselves. She has worked with Miss Ward since Knight's; at **Kate Keith** Carter's recommendation, they nurse **Mr. (Leonard) Halliday**. (NTL 56)

* Now living at Punshions with Nurse Chiffinch (but not Miss Ward?) (ADA 57)

* Sharing the cottage with both Wardy and Chiffy. (CQ 58)

Heathy: *See* Heath, Nurse.

Hedgebottom, Mr.

* Left-wing and antireligious head of the Hiram Road School; nonetheless, he takes his pupils to the Southbridge Christmas Treat. (CBI 40)

Heeling, Mrs.
> ✦ Cook to the **Palmers**; she is late with breakfast due to a toothache on the Day of Misfortunes. (AF 36)

Heinz, Hicky
> ✦ New American boy film star, who uses Smartikreem on his hair. (CQ 58)

Henbane, Professor
> ✦ At **Clarissa Graham's** college, Cambridge. She knows more about the Counter-Irritant of Constant Relations than anybody. (DD 51)

Henry, Mr.
> ✦ Youngish clerk in a Barchester lawyer's office (he talks about "we lawyers"), unfit for service due to bad eyes. He serves as secretary of the Barsetshire Archaeological Society in order to get away from his mother. (MB 45)

Herdman, Mrs.
> ✦ Wife of **Old Herdman**, Rushwater Farm. She is always cleaning. (PBO 46)

Herdman, Old
> ✦ Herdman to the **Leslies**, Rushwater Farm (though this is apparently his real name; his wife is **Mrs. Herdman**). He came to Rushwater as a boy in the year of Victoria's first Jubilee, and hasn't missed a calving since. He has lumbago. (PBO 46)
>
> ✦ He brings Rushwater Churchill to church to meet **Lady Emily Leslie**. (LAR 48)
>
> ✦ Rushwater Churchill tried to gore him in his stall, but he was saved by **Emmy Graham**. (OBH 49)

* His father was at Rushwater for eighty-five years. (DD 51)

* **Dr. Ford** treats his boils. (TSAT 61)

Hermon, Garstin
* Plays the villain in the film *Going for a Ride.* (TB39)

Hettie, Mr. Turpin's: *See* **Turpin, Hettie.**

Hibberd, Doris
* Daughter or granddaughter to **Old Hibberd;** maid to **Mrs. (Poppy) Turner.** (NR 41)

* She is now pregnant and going to be married; but when she returns to work for Mrs. Turner again, her boy is a Wolf Cub, in school. (WDIM 54)

* "A curious girl. She was never an unmarried mother."— **Mrs. Villars, Sylvia Halliday** Leslie thinks of hiring her as a cook. (ADA 57)

Hibberd, Sir Ogilvy
* Of Wopford in Loamshire. A Lloyd George knight, in shipping, from Goole. He is a Liberal and "not quite the sort we want"; **Dean (Josiah) Crawley** blackballed him for the Polyanthus. First he tried to buy Laverings, and when foiled by **Lord Bond,** bought "The Cedars," Muswell Hill, from the estate of **Mrs. C. Augustus Fortescue.** He then buys Pooker's Piece for a teashop/roadhouse and garage; **Lady Bond** begins to rally the county against it, but is forestalled by **Lord Pomfret,** who bullies Hibberd into selling the property for what he gave for it. (BL 39)

* As a Liberal M.P. and "trade expert," he gets free quarters at a London hotel and all the petrol he wants. (MB 45)

* He has been made a baron, **Lord Aberfordbury** ("it begins Aber or Inver"). His **son** is a lawyer and director of the National Rotochrome Polychrome Universal Picture Post Card Company. (PBO 46)

* His secretary is **Frances Harvey**. (LAR 48)

* He likes to preach leftist lay sermons, but when he tried it at Barchester Cathedral he was insulted by the choir. (HRt 52)

* Occasionally called "Lord Abbotsfordbury," his dog ran loose and was worrying sheep and killing hens until **Mr. Wickham** caught it. (JC 53)

* A gang broke into his house and stole all the whiskey. (ESR 55)

* In trying to get onto the West Barsetshire County Council (against **Sir Robert Graham**), he re-opens **the Bishop's** suggestion of building a chapel to the **Rev. Thomas Bohun**. (NTL 56)

* He is on a mission to promote good feeling between Mixo-Lydia and Slavo-Lydia. He is the plainest man in Barsetshire. (ADA 57)

* He was bested by **Mr. (Donald) MacFadyen** over a bit of land. (CQ 58)

* He was involved in a bad deal with the Mixo-Lydian government. He owns a hideous modern mansion, and ran his new 100 m.p.h. Cascara-Sagrada car into the sewage works outside Hogglestock. (LAAA 59)

* Via the new bursar of Paul's College, who has Labour leanings, he tries to buy **Wiple** Terrace to build a factory

for his son's unsuccessful National Rotochrome Polychrome Universal Picture Post Card Company. But he is ousted by a Syndicate led by **Sam Adams** and **Gradka Bonescu**, the Mixo-Lydian Ambassador. (TSAT 61)

Hibberd, Sir Ogilvy, the son of

❖ A lawyer and director of the National Rotochrome Polychrome Universal Picture Post Card Company, stands as a Labour candidate for East Barsetshire, but loses. (PBO 46)

❖ His large salary is insufficiently taxed, with the connivance of the Commissioners of Inland Revenue. (HRt 52)

❖ Despite the lack of success of his National Rotochrome Polychrome Universal Picture Post Card Company, his father tries to buy **Wiple** Terrace to build a factory for it. But he is ousted by a Syndicate led by **Sam Adams** and **Gradka Bonescu**, the Mixo-Lydian Ambassador. (TSAT 61)

Hibberd, Old

❖ Sexton and gardener to **Mr. (Gregory) Villars**, Northbridge Rectory. He wears a Newgate frill. **Young Hibberd** is his grandson, and **Doris Hibberd** his daughter or granddaughter. He gets the flu and can't dig **Old Mrs. Trouncer's** grave; he is nursed and bossed by a great-niece by marriage. (NR 41)

Hibberd, Young

❖ Grandson of **Old Hibberd**; he does the wiring for **Father "Tubby" Fewling's** Warden's Shelter. (NR 41)

❖ Now called the son of Old Hibberd; caught coming out of the bushes with **Effie Bunce** at Christmas. (PE 47)

Hicks, Mrs. Bessie (née Bunce)

❖ Landlady to **Father "Tubby" Fewling** and mother of **Mrs. (Verena) Villars'** head housemaid. Her niece **Ruby Bunce** goes in as temporary second housemaid when there is flu at the Villars'. (NR 41)

❖ She moves to Greshamsbury with Father Fewling, and is welcomed when it's found that her late husband's aunt was cousin of an old man whose grandfather had worked in the stables at Greshamsbury Park. Before she married, she was a housemaid at Gatherum Castle when **Lady Glencora Palliser** was little, and Hicks was temporary in the boot-room; they married and moved to his father's business in Northbridge, but Hicks died and she began to take in lodgers. Her uncle, probably **Old Bunce** the ferryman, is a bad lot; her one niece's daughter and young son go to church with her, and her other niece got married just in time; except for the marriage part, this could be **Effie** and **Ruby Bunce**. (JC 53)

❖ She goes to **Mr. Parkinson's** church in New Town because Father Fewling's service is too high. (CQ 58)

Hickson, Roger

❖ One-time butler to the **Sixth Earl** and **Lady Pomfret**, who formerly worked for **Lord** and **Lady Dumbello**; but he stayed only a short time. (WDIM 54)

Higden

❖ Old man on the estate, Rushwater. (DD 51)

Higden, Ted

❖ Works at the radio shop and walks out with **Deanna** from Rushwater. (TSAT 61)

Higgins: *See* **Hopkins, Sergeant Ted.**

Highmore, Mr. Henry Peel

❖ Priest-in-charge of St. Sycorax after Father Fewling leaves. An only son, his mother was the former **Florence Peel**; her theatrical bent passed to him, and he played Richard III in an O.U.D.S. performance at Lazarus. He repeats the role for the Northbridge Pageant of History, replacing **Mr. Hopper.** (WDIM 54)

❖ His great-uncle was a clergyman with five daughters who lived at Menton because it was cheaper; all the girls married Italians or French. (ADA 57)

Hipcock, Miss

❖ Head of **Heather Adams'** college, Cambridge. (PBO 46)

Hipkins, Major

❖ A flirting partner of **Peggy Arbuthnot** at Umbrella in India. (PE 47)

Hippersley, Miss

❖ Taught Upper Fifth literature class at the Barchester High School. (JC 53)

Hippocampus

❖ Nestorian bishop of Rhinoceros in Cappadocia in the sixth century; author of the *Pastoral Charges*, on which **Canon Thorne** was writing a commentary in his last years. (CC 50)

Hislop, Father

❖ The very high church rector of St. Oregon's at Nutfield. (NR 41)

Hoare, Mr.

* Old agent to **Giles, Lord Pomfret**, training **Roddy Wicklow** to take over his position. He resents **Gillie Foster's** existence as heir. (PT 38)

* He has died, leaving **Mrs. Hoare** a widow. He came in as under-agent for the Pomfret estates at age thirty. (TH 44)

Hoare, Mrs.

* Widow of **Mr. Hoare**, living in Dowlah Cottage, Harefield. Her daughter Gladys in Australia married a man who was part Dutch, and has four daughters, one just born. She has nursed, and been left odd legacies by, relations all over England: Aunts Fanny and Patience, Aunt Janet and her husband Uncle Harry; Uncle Joe and Uncle Andrew (brothers); Cousin Harriet; Uncle Beecham; and Cousin Sarah Hoare. (TH 44)

Hobb, Miss

* An ex-kennelmaid, hired to take care of **Maria Lufton** Marling's cocker spaniels while she has her baby; lodging with **Mrs. Cox** in the village. (HRt 52)

Hobb, Mr.

* A literary agent, very tall and large, well-dressed, bald, and depressing. He and his partner **Bungay** tried to lure **Mrs. (Hermione) Rivers** from **Mr. Johns**. (PT 38)

* He is now called Hobbs. (JC 53)

Hobson, Bert

* Under the pen name **Dhoidreagh O'Seianmhe**, writes a mystery play that is chosen to be performed in the Crypt of Barchester Cathedral for the Coronation festivities. It is

enacted in a shebeen (which **the Bishop** says is a cottage), and features Mrs. O'Gonnoreagh the Bad One, Pegeen the Prostitute, Mickeen the Murderer, Father Aloysius the Good One, and Himself from Below. (WDIM 54)

Hocking, Miss
* Runs a hostel for foreign students, and takes **Una Grey** as a secretary at the last minute. (HR 33)

Hodgkins, Father
* Roman Catholic priest, known to **Conque** as "Père Ossquince." (LAR 48)

Hodgkins, Joe
* Of the Barsetshires. A bridge shark; he sent some Marsala to **Mr. Wickham**. (CC 50)

Hoggett
* Waiter at the White Hart, under **Burden's** direction. (ADA 57)

Hoggett, Corporal
* In the plastic surgery ward of Barchester General Hospital, he scared **V.A.D. Coxon** with plasticine scars on his face. (DD 51)

Hoggett, Grace
* Niece of **Miss Hoggett**, named after Grace Crawley at Hogglestock who married Major Grantly (*cf.* Trollope). She is nurse to **Heather Adams** Pilward's baby. (DD 51)

Hoggett, Miss
* Housekeeper to **Sam Adams**. Of an old Hogglestock family; her father's father was a brickmaker, and his father was helped by Mr. Crawley, curate at Hogglestock and

Rector (Septimus) Grantly's great-grandfather (*cf.* Trollope). Her mother's half-brother is cousin to **Old Bodger** the rat-catcher. (OBH 49)

❖ Her staff consists of Annie and Eileen. (CC 50)

❖ She is now **Lucy Marling** Adams' ally and slave. Her niece is **Grace Hoggett,** her brother is second-in-command to **Mr. (Donald) MacFadyen** at Framley, and her nephew Giles is conductor of the Hogglestock Brass Band. (DD 51)

❖ She and her niece Ireen from Hogglestock help with **Mrs. (Laura) Morland's** birthday tea at the Old Bank House. (TSAT 61)

Holden
❖ Sexton of St. Mary's, Rushwater. (LAR 48)

Holden, "Merrylegs"
❖ Assistant Master at Coppin's School under **Mr. (Gregory) Villars,** and also **Mr. Holden's** uncle (or cousin). A boy, **Finlay,** stole the toffee that he kept in his desk. (NR 41)

Holden, Mr.
❖ Captain, billeted on the **Villars** at Northbridge Rectory. Thirty-three or thirty-five years old, and slightly infatuated with **Mrs. (Verena) Villars**. He has a mother, and a sister who has three children. Before the war, he worked for **Adrian Coates** in London, and he gets him to publish **Miss (Ianthe) Pemberton's** cookbook. He gets a bad case of flu, then gets the captaincy he already has and leaves for Sparrowhill Camp. (NR 41)

* He is now Adrian Coates' partner. (JC 53)

* He visits the Villars; he is married, with three children. (WDIM 54)

Holinshed, "Holly"

* A boy at Southbridge School, one of seven children of a clergyman who faints in the heat at the School sports. (SH 37)

* His father insists on conducting family prayers wherever he visits. He is perhaps now known as Young Holinshed; he is seventeen, and wants to enlist. (CBI 40)

Holly, Miss Cicely

* Secretary/Assistant to **Miss (Madeleine) Sparling**, headmistress of the Hosiers' Girls' Foundation School. (TH 44)

* Coaching **Heather Adams**; they are paying guests of **Mrs. Merivale**. She has five younger brothers, and is a first-class amateur billiards player. She went to Fairlawns School with **Mrs. (Molly) Watson**. (MB 45)

* She is now headmistress of the Hosiers' Girls' Foundation School, which is still at the **Beltons'** Harefield Park. (LAR 48)

Holman, Mr.

* Producer of "Holman's Phospho-Manuro" (in which his friend **Sam Adams** has a controlling interest) as well as "Washington's Vimphos" and "Corbett's Bono-Vitasang." (OBH 49)

* "Growalot" is added to the group. (DD 51)

Holroyd-Skinner

 * He rowed with **Mr. (Justin) Miller** and **Tommy Needham's** father from Oxford to Kingston in the summer term of 1911 or '12. He was killed in the early days of the First World War; his mother, in poor health, lives on the Riviera. (CBI 40)

Holt, Mr. C.W.

 * Though trained for the law, he lives as a professional guest and gardening specialist, visiting **Lord** and **Lady Capes** and **Lady Norton**. He descends on the **Leslies**, where he is covered with duckweed by **Emmy Graham**. On his next uninvited visit, he attends **Martin Leslie's** birthday dance, is carried off by **Dodo Bingham**, and is lined up for the BBC by **Joan Stevenson**. (WS 34)

 * The **Marquess of Bolton** wouldn't let his Marchioness invite him. (MB 45)

 * He is probably dead, as his books were sold at Sotheby's. **Mr. (Bill) Birkett** buys his complete set of **Mrs. (Laura) Morland's** books to give to **Dr. (Madeleine) Sparling** as a wedding present. (PE 47)

 * He is definitely dead. (LAR 48)

Honeyman, Mr.

 * Vicar of the *Église Protestant*, Menton, which **Miss Hopgood** and **Miss Crowder** attend when visiting the Pension **Ramsden**. (NR 41)

Hook, Miss

 * Holiday governess to the **Grahams**, Holdings; she reads Burns' poetry aloud. (ESR 55)

Hooker, the Reverend
❖ He visits Barchester General Hospital on Thursdays. (WDIM 54)

Hooper
❖ **Miss (Amelia) Brandon's** second chauffeur. He drives the party on a picnic to the wishing well, and is befriended by **Tony Morland**. (TB 39)

Hooper, Lieutenant
❖ A prig, with false teeth, billeted on the **Villars**, Northbridge Rectory. (NR 41)

❖ Now a captain, but still no gentleman. Billets the **Mertons** on the **Warings**. (GU 43)

❖ "The Hush-Hush man"; he tried to get his own billet at Beliers Priory but **General (Sir Harry) Waring** wouldn't have him. (MB 45)

Hooper, Miss
❖ An heiress from Somerset, daughter of **Squire Hooper** of Rumpton; first wife of **Old Lord Stoke** and mother of **Thomas, Lord Stoke**. (MH 42)

Hooper, Squire
❖ Of Rumpton, Somerset. Drove the last coach. Father of **Miss Hooper**, the heiress who married **Old Lord Stoke**. (MH 42)

Hopgood, Farmer
❖ Of Foxling-in-Henfold. He crossed a Jersey with a West Midland shorthorn; the resulting heifer has no stamina, as **Lord Bond** foretold. (BL 39)

Hopgood, Mrs. Helen (Miss Hopgood's Aunt)

❖ Of the Milky Way, Northbridge; her late husband, **Professor Hopgood**, was an astronomer and Head of the Matthews Porter Observatory in Texas, and she has a telescope for parachute spotting. She is known more by her relationship to **Miss Hopgood** than by her name. (NR 41)

❖ She was at school with **Miss Pettinger**, but married young and was trained by her husband to help him; he called her S.W., for Star Watcher, but her name is now given as Florrie. She is on the Joint Coronation Committee, Northbridge. (WDIM 54)

❖ She went back to Portersville for the opening of the so-called Matthew Porter Observatory's new buildings. (ADA 57)

Hopgood, Miss Miriam

❖ Shares Glycerine Cottage with **Miss Crowder**, "my friend with whom I live." They believe themselves to be spiritually French, and visit the Pension **Ramsden** at Menton on the Riviera every year. (NR 41)

❖ She is secretary of the Red Cross Library Committee, and takes illegible minutes. (PE 47)

❖ Her aunt is known better as **Miss Hopgood's Aunt** than as **Mrs. (or Helen) Hopgood** (*q.v.*). (NR 41)

❖ She organizes the children's performance for the Northbridge Coronation festivities. (WDIM 54)

❖ She claims to be the first to discover the Riviera, with a party from the Barchester Polytechnic after the First World War. (ADA 57)

Hopgood, Professor

❖ Late husband of **Miss Hopgood's Aunt**. He was Head of the Matthews Porter Observatory in Texas (funded by **Walden Concord Porter** of Portersville), with whose forty-foot Zollmer-Vollfuss telescope he discovered Porter Sidus in the constellation Algareb. (NR 41)

❖ He trained his young wife to help him, and called her S.W., for Star Watcher. (WDIM 54)

Hopkins, (Mrs.) Selina: *See* **Allen, Selina**.

Hopkins, Gwenda

❖ Attended Fairlawns School with **Miss (Cicely) Holly** and **Mrs. (Molly) Watson**. She married a man in the Indian Civil Service and has three daughters, all in the Forces. (MB 45)

Hopkins, Norma

❖ Land Girl on the **Warings'** Beliers Priory Farm. (GU 43)

Hopkins, Mr.

❖ Science master at the Hosiers' Boys' Foundation School. He was born in Glamorganshire and has a very good degree from Aberystwyth. Now over forty-five and limps, but claims to be a conscientious objector. He leaves the School (unregretted) at term's end for a good job at Monmouth, but is then interned as a fifth columnist. (CBI 40)

❖ He was locked up on suspicion of trafficking with the enemy, but is now standing as an Independent Communist for a by-election at Mewlinwillinwodd. (PE 47)

Hopkins, Sergeant Ted

❖ Sergeant in charge of the convalescent soldiers at the
  Warings' Beliers Priory. He was in the Cameroons in
  World War I; in the current war he served under **Colin
  Keith**, who helped him when his wife died. He was then
  hit by a lorry while doing a course in Middleshire (where he
  knew **Tony Morland** as a cadet), his injuries affected his
  eyes, and he is invalided out. He catches **Bill Morple**
  stealing. He is engaged to **Selina Allen,** and they will go
  to his greengrocery business in Northbridge, which his
  mother is currently running. (GU 43)

❖ He and Selina are married. His mother dies, and they leave
  the greengrocery to return to Beliers Priory, where he
  becomes the gardener and is occasionally called **Higgins**.
  (LAR 48)

❖ He is now said to have not gotten further than a training
  camp in the West Riding in World War I. (DD 51)

Hopkinson, Dame Monica

❖ She was a queen-policewoman in World War I, and now
  wears chauffeur's gaiters and lunches with old generals at
  the Carlton Grill. (PBO 46)

Hopper, Mr.

❖ The less popular of the two Northbridge cobblers. His son
  Jimmy broke his leg sliding on the ice in the flooded
  air-raid shelter. (NR 41)

❖ An avowed Communist and atheist. He was to play Rich-
  ard III in the Northbridge Pageant of History for the
  Coronation, but is replaced by **Mr. (Henry) Highmore**.
  (WDIM 54)

Hopper, Mr. ("Grasshopper")
✢ Science master at the Honourable **Giles Foster's** school. Was in the Navy during the War. (LAAA 59)

Horbury, Canon
✢ The late expert on ecclesiastical garments and on **Fluvius Minuclus**, whose manuscripts he hunted on bicycling holidays in Europe through libraries and monasteries in Vienna, Lyons, and Trèves. He lent his Slawkenbergius edition of Minucius (*cf. Tristram Shandy*) to **Mr. (Caleb) Oriel** in 1902. His daughter Madeleine's daughter was **Miss (Madeleine) Sparling**, whom he took in, made to get scholarships, and to whom he bequeathed his library. (TH 44)

Hornby, Catriona
✢ Eldest daughter of **Elsa Belton** Hornby and **Christopher Hornby**. (LAR 48)

Hornby, Christopher
✢ Of Aberdeathly, on Ben Gaunt, above Loch Gloom, ten miles from Inverdreary. A captain in the Royal Navy, forty years old, currently doing a temporary job at the Admiralty. His father was Admiral Hornby of the *H.M.S. Carraway*; his mother, who died when he was a year old, was related to **General Robert Graham**. He is nephew and heir of **Mrs. Ellangowan-Hornby**, who left him almost a fortune and the leasehold to the **Beltons'** Arcot House. He once proposed to his cousin, **Lady Catriona Ellangowan**, but is now engaged to **Elsa Belton**, who tries unsuccessfully to involve him in her father's finances; he dissuades her, and they are married by special license. (TH 44)

❖ He is now a rear-admiral, at sea. (MB 45)

❖ They have two children, **Catriona** and **Freddy**. He is an admiral, and will stand for Parliament in the next general election. (LAR 48)

❖ They have a third child. (DD 51)

❖ He is now Sir Christopher. (HRt 52)

Hornby, (Mrs.) Elsa: *See* **Belton, Elsa**.

Hornby, Freddy
❖ Second child of **Elsa Belton** Hornby and **Christopher Hornby**. (LAR 48)

Horne, Dr.
❖ Doctor to the **Leslie** children. (WS 34)

Horniman, Miss
❖ Sister of **Mr. Horniman**, with whom she lived in the Vicarage, Lambton. After his death, she stays there, deaf, half-blind, and gaga, until she dies. (GU 43)

Horniman, Miss
❖ Niece of **Mr.** and **Miss Horniman**, she presides at the latter's funeral. She was formerly maths mistress at Barchester High School, where she taught **Octavia Crawley**. (GU 43)

Horniman, Mr.
❖ Vicar of Lambton, brother of **Miss Horniman**. He died recently, leaving her alone in the Vicarage. (GU 43)

Horrabin, Old

✣ A man in Hull with a gap in his front teeth. He sends **Mr. Wickham** six dozen of champagne every year in memory of a night in Malta in 1942. (CC 50)

Horton

✣ Butler at Mellings, to **the Bartons**. (PT 38)

✣ **Mr. (Caleb) Oriel** presides at his funeral at Nutfield. (TH 44)

Horton, the Rev. Dunstan (the Vicar)

✣ Vicar of Southbridge, as yet with no last name. His **Aunt (Monica)** moves into the Vicarage with him. His grandfather married twice, with large families each time; he is the eldest grandson of the first marriage, while his aunt, who is five or six years his junior, is the youngest daughter of the second. He is appointed principal of **St. Aella's** Home for Stiffnecked Clergy, but he and his aunt stay on for a few days at the Red Lion to show approval for his successor, **Colonel Crofts**. (PE 47)

✣ He now has a last name. He does locum while Colonel Crofts is away for two weeks. (JC 53)

Horton, Monica (the Vicar's Aunt)

✣ Aunt of **Dunstan Horton, the Vicar** of Southbridge, as yet with no last name. She moves from Editha Cottage, **Wiple** Terrace, into the Vicarage with him. Her father married twice, with large families each time; she is the youngest daughter of the second marriage, while her nephew, at five or six years her senior, is the eldest grandson of the first. She goes with him to **St. Aella's** Home for Stiffnecked Clergy, but they stay on for a few days at the Red Lion to show approval for his successor, **Colonel Crofts**. She sees colors psychologically. (PE 47)

* She now has a last name. (JC 53)

Hosskiss, Croke
* Stars with **Glamora Tudor** in both *Love and Lust* (about New York gangsters) and *The Ladies' Man* (about Casanova). (OBH 49)

Hubback
* Uncle of the **Hallidays' Miss Hubback**. He is too short, and makes a bad emergency pallbearer. (NTL 56)

Hubback, Agnes ("Aggie")
* Great-niece of **Mrs. Hubback** at the Shop, now working as parlormaid (on approval) for the **Grahams** at Holdings. (ESR 55)

Hubback, Betty
* Wins a vase for **Lord Stoke** at the Holdings Bring & Buy Sale. (PBO 46)

Hubback, Harry
* Carpenter at the Housing Estate, walking out with **Odeena Panter**, whom he meets for tea at his aunt's house; she is married to **Jim** (Vidler or Panter). (ESR 55)

Hubback, Miss
* Household help to the **Hallidays**, Hatch House. Her mother, **Mrs. Hubback**, keeps the Shop at Hatch End, and her sister is **Mrs. Panter**, wife of the carter. Her uncle is the village baker, who knows things like when Easter and the Armistice will occur, so he won't open. (PBO 46)

* She is now said to be a cousin of the Shop's Mrs. Hubback. (ESR 55)

* Her uncle is the short-statured **Hubback**, and her much-younger sister is another (unnamed) **Miss Hubback**. (NTL 56)

* The Shop's Mrs. Hubback is again her mother. (ADA 57)

Hubback, Miss

* Unnamed nurse to the Honourable **Mrs. Richard Carter**; but she is the much younger sister of **Mrs. Panter**, the carter's wife, who was a Hubback; thus she must also be sister to the **Hallidays' Miss Hubback**, and her mother must be **Mrs. Hubback** of the Shop. She was formerly under-nurse to **Francis** and **Peggy Arbuthnot Brandon's** children. (NTL 56)

Hubback, Mr. and Mrs.

* Landlord and -lady of the Bridge Inn. He does a little poaching, and she serves "cold tea" before hours. (PE 47)

Hubback, Mrs.

* Keeper of the Shop, Hatch End. Mother to **Miss Hubback**, the **Hallidays'** household help, and to **Mrs. Panter**, wife of the carter. Her own invalid half-witted mother lives upstairs. Her cousin is **Geo. Panter** of the Mellings Arms. (PBO 46)

* "When people want to die they never do, like Old Mrs. Hubback."—**Emmy Graham**. (OBH 49)

* Now said to be cousin of the Halliday's Miss Hubback. Her grandmother was a witch, who spoke pure Barset. Her great-niece is **Aggie Hubback**. (ESR 55)

* Apparently has a much-younger daughter, an (unnamed)
  Miss Hubback who is nurse to **Mrs. Richard Carter**.
  (NTL 56)

* Again mother to the Hallidays' Miss Hubback. She is
  ninety-one years old, and her grandson-in-law is the local
  postman. (ADA 57)

Hubback, Young Mrs.
* She has a little girl who is rather spastic. (ESR 55)

Huckaback, Chat
* Co-stars with **Eliodora Hands** in *I Gonna Make You Love
  Me*, produced in New York and in London. (LAAA 59)

Humberton (or Harberton), Lord
* As Lord Humberton, **Lord Platfield's** eldest son, married
  Phoebe Rivers, but can't stand her mother. They live in
  Shropshire. (CBI 40)

* Now Lord Harberton, with one child, in Shropshire;
  though **Lady Griselda Palliser** ran after Lord Humberton
  before he married Miss Rivers. (MH 42)

* "That nice Lord Harberton down in Shropshire." (HRt 52)

* Again, Lord Humberton's father is General Platfield,
  which makes it Humberton 3, Harberton 2. (ESR 55)

Humble, Ellen
* Granddaughter of **William Humble**, now working for
  Miss (Madeleine) Sparling, headmistress of the Hosiers'
  Girls' Foundation School at Harefield. She has anemia, but
  her mother makes her throw any medicine that **Dr. Mor-
  gan** gives her down the sink. Her nephew has been stoning

the **Beltons'** chestnut tree; she takes the bells from his reins to make Touchstone's bauble for the School production of *As You Like It*. (TH 44)

❖ She is now serving **Miss (Cicely) Holly**, new headmistress of the School. She has an Aunt Sarah, whose baby **Points** is her third child out of wedlock; *see*, perhaps, **Mrs. Humble**. Her other aunt is **Miss Faithful Humble**. (LAR 48)

❖ She is niece to **S. Wheeler** at **Mrs. Belton's**. She is now working for a nice family as under-nurse, and is recommended as nanny for the twin daughters of **Robin** and **Anne Fielding Dale**. (CC 50)

❖ After being nanny to the Dale twins, she went to one other place and gave great satisfaction; now becomes nanny to the baby girl of **Edith Graham** Harcourt. (LAAA 59)

Humble, Miss Faithful
❖ She keeps a twopenny library as a branch of a small tobacconist's shop. (TH 44)

❖ **Ellen Humble** is her niece. (LAR 48)

Humble, Mr. J.
❖ Proprietor of the General Supply Store, Harefield. (TH 44)

Humble, Mrs.
❖ Lives down near the Three Tuns. Her husband is away in the Forces, but she has her second baby. (TH 44)

❖ **Ellen Humble** has an Aunt Sarah, whose baby **Points** is her third child out of wedlock; there is some resemblance. (LAR 48)

Humble, William

⁕ Cowman to the **Beltons**, Harefield Park. His granddaughter is **Ellen Humble**. He sells milk illegally, and is an expert on Harefield lake and its ice. (TH 44)

⁕ Now he is general factotum; too old to cut the rushes in the lake, he helps others do so. At the Barsetshire Archaeological, he takes children out on the lake in his boat, at threepence a time. His mother was a Wheeler; when young, he traded in arrowheads on the Downs, but now he trades in archaic-sounding folksongs ("Young Job Potter's a Gormed Young Fool"). (DD 51)

⁕ His son is **Young Humble**. (HRt 52)

Humble, Young

⁕ Son of **William Humble** and darts champion of West Barsetshire. (HRt 52)

Hunter, Mrs.

⁕ A refugee from London who is asked to **Mrs. (Maud) Perry's** working party on approval. But she doesn't bring her own ration of milk or sugar for the tea, and is a rampant supporter of Slavo-Lydia against Mrs. Perry's Mixo-Lydia, so she is blackballed. She comes to the Mixo-Lydian Bring and Buy Sale; her Slavo-Lydian girl student tries to talk at **Sam Adams'** factory but is stymied. (TH 44)

Hurdles

⁕ The butcher at Harefield. (TH 44)

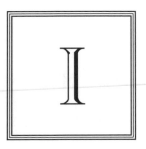

Icken

* Estate carpenter to the **Beltons, Harefield Park.** (TH 44)

Ignotus, Pictor: *See* **Pictor Ignotus.**

Ignotus, Scriptor: *See* **Scriptor Ignotus.**

Ivy

* Nursery maid to **Lady Agnes Graham's** children. At Rushwater, she skylarks in the pantry with **Walter** and cries over the death of a canary. (WS 34)

* She left Rushwater when all the boys went to school, and became nurse to a woman who hadn't heard from her husband in the Far East for four years. Recommended by the Grahams' **Nannie**, she becomes nurse to **Rose Bingham** Leslie's children. (PBO 46)

Jackson, Corporal Arthur Fishguard

* Billeted on the **Villars**, Northbridge Rectory, where he helps out in the kitchen and flatters **Mrs. Chapman**; she eventually allows him to get engaged to the kitchenmaid **Edie Pover**. (NR 41)

* He and **Private Moss** are working for **Philip Winter** at the Hush-Hush camp. (GU 43)

* Confused with Colonel Crofts' batman **Bateman**. (CC 50)

* He had been an electrician before the War; afterward he went back to it, and settled in Northbridge with Edie. They are happily married, and have no children. (CQ 58)

Jackson, Flight Commander

* "At the aerodrome, about the pig-swill." (**Lucy Marling**). (MH 42)

Jasper, Old: *See* **Margett, Jasper**.

James, Miss

* ❖ Secretary to **George Knox**. Her sister got sick and she had to leave; she was replaced by **Una Grey**. (HR 33)

Jenks, Private Tom

* ❖ Son of **Lord Pomfret's** head keeper, and a notable shot. He is convalescing from appendicitis at Beliers Priory and mistakenly shoots **Matron's** cat. He is **Mrs. Phipps'** sister's nephew, and can mend anything. He needs a serious operation, and is worked on by **Sir Abel Fillgrave**. He proposes to **Selina Allen**, but is turned down. (GU 43)

* ❖ He is now quite fit again, and engaged to a nice girl in the Land Army. (TH 44)

Jessie

* ❖ Head housemaid under **Matron (Miss Dudley)** at **Everard Carter's** house, Southbridge School. She is nearsighted but won't wear glasses, so is continually using the wrong color thread for her darning. (SH 37)

* ❖ Her brother does the milk rounds for **Abner Brown**. (CBI 40)

* ❖ In Matron's opinion, it's a good thing she ruined her eyes, because she won't be called up. Her cousin is manager of the laundry. (GU 43)

* ❖ Her position is given as under-housemaid. She gets a nasty cold. (PE 47)

* ❖ Again head housemaid; her cousin is the Northbridge policeman (this could be **P.C. Haig Brown**, but he lives at Southbridge). (CC 50)

J

Jessie (properly Jessica)

 ⁕ Named after **Jessica Dean**, as her mother had been kitchenmaid to **Mrs. (Rachel) Dean**. She is a cousin's niece of
the **Nurse** at **Pomfret** Towers. She had been kitchenmaid
to **Noel** and **Lydia Keith Merton**, then went on to **Lord
George** and **Lady Norton**, but that family was too stingy.
She is about to become an usherette at the Barchester
Odeon. (LAAA 59)

Jim

 ⁕ A Vidler or Panter, at Hatch End. Has a brother **Harry**
and sister **Dorothy**; his wife's nephew is **Harry Hubback**.
(ESR 55)

Jobson, Mr. and Mrs.

 ⁕ Of the Chemical Works; members of the London circle of
Mrs. and Mrs. Bissell. (CBI 40)

Joe

 ⁕ He and his wife **Vivien** are acquaintances of **Charles
Belton**. He is twenty-three; they have two babies and live
in two rooms in Chelsea. His only relative is a grandmother, he has no job, and he spent all his money on the
honeymoon. (LAR 48)

Joe

 ⁕ Son of **Fred**, the carpenter at Marling Hall. He helps to
repair **Packer's** Royal Derby for the Red Cross Fete at
Marling Hall. (LAR 48)

John

 ⁕ Fiancé of **Isabel Dale**; he was with the Barsetshires fighting in Italy and was killed. His father died of grief. Isabel is
writing about him for his friends. (CC 50)

John
* Cowman to the **Palmers**. (AF 36)

Johns, Mr.
* Partner in Johns and Fairfield, publishers of **George Knox**. His American wife gives dreadful literary parties. He tries, unsuccessfully, to lure **Mrs. (Laura) Morland** away from **Adrian Coates**. (HR 33)

* Publishes both **Mrs. (Hermione) Rivers'** and **Mrs. (Susan) Barton's** books. He visits Pomfret Towers for the weekend. Despite Mrs. Rivers' gyrations, he remains her publisher, and also gets **Lord Pomfret's** book, *A Landowner in Five Reigns*, which becomes an unexpected best-seller. (PT 38)

* They publish *My Burning Flesh* (translated from the Mixo-Lydian). (CBI 40)

* They publish **Effie Arbuthnot's** bird book (thanks to the influence of his cousin, **Mr. Wickham**) and **Colin Keith's** *Commentaries upon Lemon on Running Powers*. (PE 47)

* He visits **the Bishop**, and publishes **Philip Winter's** Latin grammar. (LAR 48)

* He is now "sort of an uncle" of Mr. Wickham. He publishes a nature series illustrated by Effie Arbuthnot Crofts, as well as the thrillers of **Lisa Bedale (Isabel Dale)**. **Jeffrey Palliser, Lord Silverbridge**, works for him. (CC 50)

* He is to publish **Margot Phelps'** book on gardens, hens, and goats. (JC 53)

Johnson
* Boy at Southbridge School who has hair fixative. He collides with another boy, **Butters**, during a power failure,

and gets a bleeding lip. **Edward** has to rush them both to the doctor. He later gets influenza. (HR 33)

✣ He did well at Oxford in Modern Greats, and is due to come back to Southbridge as a master in the Junior School. (CBI 40)

Jones
✣ Batman to **Captain George Halliday**. (PBO 46)

Joram, Bishop William (the Bishop of Mngangaland)
✣ Perhaps the unnamed Colonial Bishop who serves as locum to **Tompion** at Little Misfit. (CBI 40)

✣ Former bishop of Mngangaland in Africa, he rowed for his college. Having practised on the chiefs in Mngangaland in drinking 'Mpooka-'Mpooka, he drinks **Mrs. Valoroso** under the table. (MH 42)

✣ He has been in England for four or five years. He has a job in the Close that **Dean (Josiah) Crawley** found for him, and lodges with **Madame Tomkins**. He serves as locum to other clergymen (such as **Dr. Dale** and the Vicar of Rushwater) at odd times, and is thirty years younger than Dr. Dale (so around fifty-two). (MB 45)

✣ He helps out Dr. Dale occasionally. He still hears from the **Head Chief of Mngangaland**, who is in England with his **eightieth son**. (PBO 46)

✣ He is now a canon of Barchester; he has been in love with **Mrs. (Lavinia) Brandon** (as with every other nice woman) since the first year of the War. (PE 47)

✣ He tells the story of **the Bishop of Barchester's** socks. (LAR 48)

❖ In 1927, he quelled a revolt in Mngangaland by reciting book VI of the *Aeneid*. He moves into **Canon Thorne's** former house. (OBH 49)

❖ He used to control his Mngangaland flock via the **Head Witch Doctor of Mngangaland**, who had spent a year at Keble before going into the family business. He got back to England in 1941. The Archbishop confers a Lambeth degree (Doctor of Divinity) upon him, so he is now known as Dr. Joram; his first name is now given. His aunt has left him some money, with which he redid his new house, the Vinery. He becomes engaged to Mrs. Brandon. (CC 50)

❖ They are married, and have a month's holiday in France with a Count whom he met on vacation in Madagascar. (DD 51)

❖ **The Prime Minister of Mngangaland** sent him a leopard skin on his birthday. (HRt 52)

❖ The eightieth son of the Head Chief of Mngangaland takes a house on the Coronation route and invites him and his wife to stay. (WDIM 54)

❖ He and Mrs. Joram give a wedding reception for the **Oriels**. (LAAA 59)

Joram, Mrs.: *See* **Brandon, Mrs. Lavinia.**

Junior Master, the
❖ At Beliers Priory School. He was a captain (and so out-ranked the **Senior Master**) before the peace. (LAR 48)

❖ He, the Senior Master, and a party of others are going to Switzerland for the holidays. (HRt 52)

J

Katzenjammer, Fräulein

* German mistress at Barchester High School; she teaches **Lavinia Merton**. (LAAA 59)

Kedgeree, the Suffragan Bishop of: *See* **Suffragan Bishop of Kedgeree, the**.

Keith, Catherine

* Second child of **Robert** and **Edith Keith**; younger sister of **Henry**.

* She is under two years old. (SH 37)

* She gets another sibling. (CBI 40)

* The third child was a brother. She is now eighteen. (WDIM 54)

Keith, Colin

* Third child of **Henry** and **Helen Keith**; younger brother of **Robert** and **Kate**, older brother of **Lydia**. Hired by **Mr.**

(Bill) Birkett as junior classical master at Southbridge School. Goes on to read for the bar with **Noel Merton**, and visits Austria with him and **Philip Winter**. (SH 37)

* They visited Hungary as well. He is now in the Territorials, training gunners, and comes home for his father's funeral. (CBI 40)

* Now a staff captain. He visits Beliers Priory to say good-bye to Lydia before leaving for the front. (GU 43)

* He is thirty-four, out of the army, and back at the bar, in Noel Merton's chambers. He was formerly at Lazarus College. He has his first big infatuation, for **Peggy Arbuthnot**, but she discourages him. His book, *Commentaries upon Lemon on Running Powers*, is accepted by **Johns** and Fairfield. (PE 47)

* He half-heartedly proposes to **Susan Dean**; she ignores his hints. (LAR 48)

* His book is out and successful. He proposes to **Eleanor Grantly**, and is finally accepted. (OBH 49)

* They are to be married after Christmas (i.e., after the Michaelmas Law Sitting). (CC 50)

* They are married, living in London, with a baby girl. (DD 51)

* They have bought a big house and consider getting a lodger, but decide they don't need to. Eleanor is pregnant again, due in April. (HRt 52)

* Their children are girls. He and his brother-in-law **Everard Carter** buy a vacation house in Devonshire. (WDIM 54)

Keith, Mrs. Edith (née Fairweather)

* Wife of **Robert Keith**, mother of **Henry** and **Catherine**. She is the elder sister of **Geoff** and **John Fairweather** of Southbridge School. She was formerly captain of hockey, captain of cricket, and Girl of Honour at Barchester High School. (SH 37)

* They now have a third child. (CBI 40)

* They sell the Manor to **Noel** and **Lydia Keith Merton**, and buy the house Edith has always wanted at Nutfield. (GU 43)

* They live on the Hallbury side of Barchester. (PE 47)

* They have two boys and a girl, so the third must have been a boy. (WDIM 54)

Keith, (Mrs.) Eleanor: *See* Grantly, Eleanor.

Keith, Mrs. Helen

* Of Northbridge Manor. Wife of **Mr. (Henry) Keith**, mother of **Robert, Kate, Colin,** and **Lydia**. Her grandfather married three times, and her father was the youngest of the third family. The eldest of the first family was her **Uncle Oswald**, of whom she often speaks. Her Uncle Andrew was the youngest of the second family, and his second wife was a Miss Winter from Bermuda. Her Aunt **Marian (Mrs. Purvis)** was the third daughter of the second family; she produced **the Honourable Eleanor Purvis**, who is engaged to **the Honourable Mr. Norris**. (SH 37)

* She has a heart condition, and lets Lydia run the house. She runs sewing parties. For a while, they are billeted with

six child evacuees and two teachers, **Miss "Draky" Drake** and **Miss "Pots" Potter**. When her husband dies, she goes under **Nurse Chiffinch's** care. (CBI 40)

* The Manor is now full of typists for a business firm, while she is staying with her daughter Kate at Southbridge. (NR 42)

* She is happy with her sister, Kate, at Bournemouth, which suits her heart. (GU 43)

Keith, Mr. Henry
* Of Northbridge Manor. Husband of **Mrs. (Helen) Keith**, father of **Robert, Kate, Colin,** and **Lydia**. Senior partner of Keith and Keith, solicitors for the Cathedral, Barchester. (SH 37)

* For a while, they are billeted with six child evacuees and two teachers, **Miss "Draky" Drake** and **Miss "Pots" Potter**. He is hit by a lorry and dies. (CBI 40)

* He never managed the estate himself. (PE 47)

Keith, Henry
* Eldest child of **Robert** and **Edith Keith**; brother of **Catherine**. He is five years old. (SH 37)

* He gets another sibling. (CBI 40)

* The third child was a brother. (WDIM 54)

Keith, Kate
  * Second child of **Mr. (Henry)** and **Mrs. (Helen) Keith**; younger sister of **Robert**, older sister of **Colin** and **Lydia**. She does occasional secretary work for **Dean Crawley**, and becomes engaged to **Everard Carter**. (SH 37)

  * Their wedding. (TB 39)

  * Their son **Bobbie** (Robert Philip; **Philip Winter** is his godfather) is one year old. Everard becomes senior house-master. (CBI 40)

  * Bobbie is four, **Angela** is two, and **Philip** is "very little indeed." (GU 43)

  * Everard is designated as the next headmaster when **Mr. (Bill) Birkett** retires. Their new baby is **Noel**, after **Noel Merton**; but he disappears after this. (MB 45)

  * She was twenty-one when she married. (PBO 46)

  * Everard is appointed headmaster. A mumps scare at the House turns out to be an impacted wisdom tooth, but they take their children (as well as **Lavinia** and **Harry Merton**, because Lydia has measles) to Devonshire and leave them with his mother for the summer. (PE 47)

  * They are referred to as having both three and four children. (OBH 49)

  * Three children from here on. (CC 50)

  * They go to London with the children for the Coronation. Along with Kate's brother Colin, they buy a vacation house in Devonshire. (WDIM 54)

* Everard is thinking of retiring and leasing the **Villars'** old house in Northbridge. (CQ 58)

* They are now retired, at the Old Rectory, Northbridge. (LAAA 59)

Keith, Lydia

* Fourth child of **Mr. (Henry)** and **Mrs. (Helen) Keith**; younger sister of **Robert, Kate**, and **Colin**. Sixteen and at Barchester High School, where she played Ferdinand in *The Tempest*. An enthusiast of Shakespeare and Browning. (SH 37)

* She tears her dress while acting as bridesmaid for her sister Kate's wedding to **Everard Carter**. She rides **Packer's** roundabout with **Delia Brandon** and **Tony Morland**. (TB 39)

* She is about twenty-one, running her parent's house, and overworked. She is a bridesmaid for **Rose Birkett**. She marries **Noel Merton** before he goes to war. (CBI 40)

* She and Noel are in Scotland. (NR 41)

* She did a year on the land in Scotland, then hospital work in Yorkshire, where she was ill. She is now twenty-four, and she and Noel are billeted on the **Warings** at Beliers Priory, while she runs the Northbridge Manor estate for her brother Robert. She fixes things between **Leslie Waring** and **Philip Winter**. She and Noel buy the Manor from Robert, and she becomes pregnant. (GU 43)

* They are now settled at Northbridge Manor, and their daughter **Lavinia** is six months old. (TH 44)

* She is pregnant, due in January. (PBO 46)

* She has baby **Harry**, and has been married for seven years. She gets the measles from Lavinia, and Kate takes the children to Devonshire with their cousins. She also feels low due to Noel's flirtation with **Peggy Arbuthnot**; he gives her a bolt of purple silk in tacit apology. (PE 47)

* He formally apologizes. They have a third child, called **Kate**, in the perambulator. (OBH 49)

* Their third child is now **Jessica**, after Jessica Dean. She is chosen as President of the Joint Coronation Committee at Northbridge, and helps the **Pomfrets**, especially **Ludovic Foster, Lord Mellings**. She will become Lady Merton when Noel is knighted. (WDIM 54)

* The Mertons and Carters joke about marrying their children to their cousins. (LAAA 59)

* The third child's name is reconciled as **Kate Jessica**; Lavinia is engaged to Ludovic. (TSAT 61)

Keith, Robert

* Eldest child of **Mr. (Henry)** and **Mrs. (Helen) Keith**; older brother of **Kate, Colin**, and **Lydia**. His wife is **Edith Fairweather Keith**, and their children are **Henry** and **Catherine**. He is a solicitor, junior partner to his father in Keith and Keith. (SH 37)

* They now have a third child. His father dies. (CBI 40)

* He inherited Northbridge Manor on his father's death, but leased it to an insurance firm, while Lydia ran the estate. Now they sell the Manor to Lydia and **Noel Merton**, and buy the house Edith has always wanted at Nutfield. (GU 43)

* They live on the Hallbury side of Barchester. (PE 47)

* They have two boys and a girl, so the third was a boy. (WDIM 54)

Kessler, Fräulein
* German mistress at **Mrs. (Laura) Morland's** London day school. Due to the Franco-Prussian War, deadly enemy of **Mlle. Hamonet.** (TSAT 61)

King, the Honourable Henry
* A case of **Nurse Ward's**; he wouldn't allow his (mental) wife to go into a nursing home, and in the end he had to be certified. (NTL 56)

Kitson
* Housemaster of the Junior House, Southbridge School. Resigns when his uncle offers him a post in a good family business. (PBO 46)

Klawhammer, Klaus
* According to **Mrs. (Gloria) Gissing**, he is one of New York's brightest literary agents. (CBI 40)

Klobber, Mr.
* A London tailor, refugee from Vienna before 1914. He makes for **Sally (Wicklow), Lady Pomfret**, and for **Susan Dean.** (PE 47)

Knight, Mr.
* French master, Southbridge School. He taught **Tony Morland** the Romantics. (TB 39)

Knox, (Mrs.) Anne: *See* **Todd, Anne.**

Knox, Mr. George

* Long-winded biographer (published by **Johns** and Fairfield), of Low Rising; widower of Rhoda Knox, an invalid who died four years ago; their only child is **Sibyl**. His father was a well-off Irish merchant, his mother is **Old Mrs. Knox**. He is a friend and neighbor to **Mrs. (Laura) Morland**. When his usual secretary **Miss James** is unavailable, he hires **Una Grey** on a temporary basis to help with his book on Edward VI. She has a more permanent relationship in mind, but he escapes and gets engaged to **Anne Todd**. (HR 33)

* He has a book on Charles II, and took a First in Greats in 1903. While writing on the Abbots of Barchester, he visits Barchester cathedral with the Morlands, where **Tony Morland** and **Robert Wesendonck** drive him mad. (DH 34)

* He lectures on the Inquisition to the convalescent soldiers at Beliers Priory. (GU 43)

* He has a talking contest with **Mr. (Jack) Middleton** on the field of the Barsetshire Archaeological meeting. (MB 45)

* One of his former secretaries, the youngest daughter of a clergyman, is now in the Red Tape and Sealing Wax office, where she interviews Tony Morland. (PE 47)

* His new biography of Cardinal Wolsey is entitled *King's Bishop*. (CC 50)

* He was an only child. (NTL 56)

* He grew up in the big house in Rutland Gate, London. (TSAT 61)

Knox, Old Mrs.

* Formidable French mother of **George Knox**, grandmother of **Sibyl**. Her husband, now dead, was a merchant, and well off. She lives in Rutland Gate in London, and goes to Torquay for the summer. (HR 33)

* She takes **Una Grey** as a companion. (DH 34)

* Now long dead. George was an only child. She gave **Mrs. (Laura) Morland** a work table as a wedding present. (NTL 56)

* She was almost ninety when she died. (TSAT 61)

Knox, Sibyl

* Daughter of **George Knox**; her mother, Rhoda, has been dead for four years. Now twenty, she attempts to be a writer, but happily fails and becomes engaged to **Adrian Coates**. (HR 33)

* Now married, with an eight-week-old baby, **Laura Coates**; they visit her father. (DH 34)

* They are having a second baby. (PT 38)

* The second child's name is **Richard**. (TB 39)

* Now there are three children; the family has to evacuate from London to **Mrs. (Laura) Morland's** house. (CBI 40)

Mr. Knox's Annie: *See* **Annie, Mr. Knox's.**

Mr. Knox's Annie's Aunt: *See* **Mallow, Mrs.**

Kpozcz, Czemschk

* The well-paid producer of a film featuring **Glamora Tudor** and **Pietro Nasone**, whose pronounced Italian accent

in the role of Cyrano de Bergerac he explains by making Cyrano an Italian *condottiere*. (CQ 58)

Krcks

* The greatest playwright in Mixo-Lydia. He rewrote *Hamlet* so that Hamlet could kill Ophelia too. (CQ 58)

Kreelson, Phil

* The new actor co-starring with **Glamora Tudor** in *One Night in the Vatican*. (HRt 52)

Krogsbrog, Anders

* A rich Swedish economist and owner of iron-ore deposits. His daughter is **Petrea Krogsbrog**. (LAR 48)

Krogsbrog, Hvord

* Wrote a symphony for two orchestras, a military band, and the chimes of Big Ben. (ESR 55)

Krogsbrog, Petrea

* Swedish sociologist, daughter of **Anders Krogsbrog**. She is a friend of the actress **Selma Lundquist** and of **Richard Tebben,** whom she controls and to whom she eventually becomes engaged. (LAR 48)

* They are married, and **Mrs. (Winifred) Tebben** is devoted to her. (OBH 49)

Kropóv, Dr. (Ph.) Professor

* "That arch-imposter of a Mixo-Lydian refugee"; the **wife of the Master of (St.) Barabbas College** gets him a special chair of Romano-Lydian culture. (TH 44)

Lancelot, Professor

* Art restorer and discoverer of the murals by **Nicholas de Hogpen** in the Pomfret Madrigal church. (TB 39)

* He designs the embroidery for reupholstering the choir stalls in Barchester Cathedral. (CC 50)

* On a visit to **Mr. Gould's** church at High Rising, he discovers a bundle of old surplices in the cokeshed and a blotch on the wall that may be either the Seventh Day of Creation or the Day of Judgment. (LAAA 59)

Lane, Mr.

* Vicar of Pomfret Madrigal after **Mr. Moffatt** and before **Mr. (Justin) Miller**. (TB 39)

Larousse, Mlle.

* French mistress of the Preparatory School, Barchester High School. (WDIM 54)

Lazarus, the Master of

❖ Leftist head of an Oxford college; as the former headmaster of Southbridge School, he hired the young, communistic **Philip Winter**. (SH 37)

❖ According to **Mr. (Alister) Cameron**, he is incorrect on Plotinus. (BL 39)

❖ Here known as **Crawford of Lazarus**, he preceded **Mr. (Bill) Birkett** as headmaster of Southbridge. When he came to Lazarus, his leftist leanings drove **Simnet** to leave his position as scout and go to Southbridge. His students tend to do Modern Greats, and he maneuvers to get them moved out to St. Swithin's so that the Institute for Ideological Interference can be billeted at Lazarus. (CBI 40)

❖ **Mr. Sidney Carton** criticizes his edition of **Fluvius Minucius**. (TH 44)

❖ His little book, *The Economic Outlook of Israel under Zerubbabel*, is reviewed by **Dr. Dale** in the *Church Times* with the contempt it deserves. (MB 45)

❖ During the war he became a Socialist Member of Parliament, and has now taken a Labour peerage; he will be known as **Lord Skinner**, though his wife wants to be called **Mrs. Skinner**; so apparently he's not Crawford any more. (PE 47)

❖ He invites people like the First Lord of the Treasury and a woman named **Mothersill** who is in the Cabinet to preach lay sermons in the college chapel. (DD 51)

❖ **Julian Rivers** is appointed Professor of Culture at Lazarus. (HRt 52)

Lazarus, the New Master of
❖ Calls himself a Liberal. (ADA 57)

Lazarus, the Wife of the Master of: *See* **Skinner, Mrs.**

Leadbitter
❖ Veterinarian; all right on horses, no good on dogs. (DD 51)

Lee
❖ One of the Lees up in the Woods beyond Grumper's End. Half-gypsy, his mother is a Margett, and his uncle is **Jasper Margett**. He drives a lorry and works for **Harcourt**, the **Duke of Towers**, on the estate. (LAAA 59)

Lee, Old Pharaoh
❖ Presumably another of the Lees up in the Woods beyond Grumper's End. Was sent to Barchester Jail again for stealing a broody hen and her eggs; it was his tenth conviction. (LAAA 59)

Lefter, V.
❖ Writes hate mail to **Mrs. (Laura) Morland**. (LAR 48)

Lefevre, Miss Babs
❖ Proprietor of Babs's Buttery, the best lunching place in Silverbridge. In her fifties, she lives with her dotty old father. (DD 51)

Lefroy, Mr. and Mrs.
❖ Of the Technical School; members of the London circle of **Mr.** and **Mrs. Bissell**. (CBI 40)

Legpul, Gudold
❖ The great mid-European woman writer. Her last book, *I Bare My Breasts*, was not, as rumored, smuggled into En-

gland via Barcelona, but was written at her home in Willesden. (MB 45)

Leslie

❖ The stationmaster's nephew at Hallbury; he delivers the newspapers. (MB 45)

Leslie, Agnes: *See* Graham, Lady Agnes.

Leslie, Clive: *See* Leslie Minimus.

Leslie, David

❖ Youngest child of **Mr. (Henry)** and **Lady Emily Leslie**; his older siblings are **John** and **Agnes (Graham)**, and he is close to the son of his (dead) eldest brother, **Martin Leslie**. Having been left money by a doting aunt, he is independent and a dilettante at twenty-seven. He has written a novel named *Why Name*, and gets himself turned down for a job at the BBC. He flirts with both **Mary Preston** and **Joan Stevenson**, but they go off him. He leaves for Buenos Aires on his father's business. (WS 34)

❖ His governess had been **Miss (Maud) Bunting**. He is now in the R.A.F., with military missions to the U.S. and Argentina. He comes back from Cairo with a case of jaundice. (MH 42)

❖ He is a flight-lieutenant at thirty-seven, and slightly balding. He owns land in South America. He flirts with **Anne Fielding** and with **Sylvia Halliday**, but **Rose Bingham** finally marries him. (PBO 46)

❖ Now living in Paris, with two children, **Dorothy ("Dodo")** and **Henry**. (LAR 48)

❖ He and Rose are in America with the children when his mother dies; he flies back and drives Gerry Coverdale's race car, but is too late for the funeral. (OBH 49)

❖ Now in America, where they can leave Dodo (now seven) and Henry (six) with **Martin Leslie's** mother when they travel. He is making lots of money somehow. They invite **Edith Graham** to stay with them. (ESR 55)

L

❖ He and Rose and Edith fly in for **Miss Merriman's** wedding. The children, aged about ten, are at camp. They all live a very rootless life in America. (ADA 57)

Leslie, Dorothy ("Dodo")
❖ Eldest daughter of **Rose Bingham** Leslie and **David Leslie**. (LAR 48)

❖ At seven, she and her six-year-old brother **Henry** visit **Martin Leslie's** mother in America. (ESR 55)

❖ They are now both about ten, at camp. (ADA 57)

Leslie, Eleanor
❖ One-year-old daughter of **Martin** and **Sylvia Halliday Leslie; Robert Graham** is infatuated with her. (LAR 48)

❖ She has a new little brother **Georgy**. (DD 51)

❖ A third child is to be called Leonard Martin or Emily. (ESR 55)

❖ She is now about seven. (ADA 57)

❖ She is eleven or twelve, and is a friend of **Amabel Rose Adams** at Barchester High School. (TSAT 61)

Leslie, Lady Emily

* Sister of **Giles, Seventh Earl of Pomfret**, and of **Lady Agnes**, who died young; wife of **Henry Leslie**, of Rushwater; mother of an eldest son who died (and whose son, **Martin Leslie**, was raised at Rushwater), and then of **John, Agnes (Graham)**, and **David**. Splendid in her divagations, she tries to arrange everything and everyone, though she herself lives in a welter of scarves, shawls, embroidery, canes, and footstools. She dabbles in all the arts, sometimes literally, and is the exasperation and delight of her entire family. Her lady's maid is **Conque**. (WS 34)

* She and her husband are living at Holdings with their daughter. She is writing her autobiography, and is rather tired and frail, but her flame is not quenched. (MH 42)

* She is arthritic but well. (TH 44)

* Her husband has died, and she is not very well. (PBO 46)

* She has neuritis and is a bit fuzzy in her mind, but celebrates her eightieth birthday with a family reunion at Rushwater. (LAR 48)

* Very frail and living mostly in the past, she dies. (OBH 49)

* Her eldest son's name is finally given as **Giles**. (ESR 55)

Leslie, Georgy

* Second child of **Martin** and **Sylvia Halliday Leslie**; brother of **Eleanor**. (DD 51)

* A third child is to be called Leonard Martin or Emily. (ESR 55)

* He is at Southbridge School, where his friend is **Nicholson Minor**. (TSAT 61)

Leslie, Giles

* Unnamed eldest son of **Lady Emily** and **Mr. (Henry) Leslie**, and father of **Martin Leslie**. (WS 34)

* Still unnamed; he died at Arras. (MH 42)

* He died in 1918. (OBH 49)

* His name is finally given. (ESR 55)

Leslie, Mr. Henry

* Husband of **Lady Emily Leslie**; farmer and breeder of champion bulls, of Rushwater House. Father of an eldest son who died, and then of **John, Agnes (Graham),** and **David**. His heir to Rushwater is his eldest son's son, **Martin Leslie**. He leaves on a tour of Northern Capitals until his wife finishes her enameling phase. (WS 34)

* His bull, Rushwater Rubicon, causes **Jessica Dean's** accident. (AF 36)

* He and his wife are living at Holdings with their daughter Agnes. (MH 42)

* His heart is causing anxiety. (TH 44)

* He is now dead since early in the war. (PBO 46)

* He used to take a house in Cadogan Square every summer for the Season. (HRt 52)

* His eldest son's name is finally given as **Giles**. (ESR 55)

* Rushwater was his mother's place. (ADA 57)

Leslie, Henry

* ✤ Younger son of **Rose Bingham** Leslie and **David Leslie**. (LAR 48)

* ✤ At six, he and his seven-year-old sister **Dorothy ("Dodo")** visit **Martin Leslie's** mother in America. (ESR 55)

* ✤ They are now both about ten, at camp. (ADA 57)

Leslie, Henry: *See* Leslie Major.

Leslie, James: *See* Leslie Major and Graham, James.

Leslie, Mr. John

* ✤ Second child of **Mr. (Henry)** and **Lady Emily Leslie**; elder brother of **Lady Agnes Graham** and **David Leslie**; his late elder brother's son is **Martin Leslie**. He was in the Navy in World War I, then went into business. Now at thirty-four or thirty-five, he was married to his wife Gay for only a year when she died, seven years ago. He becomes engaged to **Mary Preston**. (WS 34)

* ✤ He and Mary are a very nice, rather dull couple who have two young children and represent the Leslies at the Agricultural Dinner at **Lord Bond's**. (BL 39)

* ✤ He is regional commissioner. (MH 42)

* ✤ Their three sons, **Leslie Major, Minor**, and **Minimus**, are at Southbridge School. (PBO 46)

* ✤ He corners **the Bishop** at the Palace garden party about not merging their parish with the neighboring one. (CC 50)

* He is a senior churchwarden, living in the Old Rectory over Greshamsbury way. (JC 53)

* He is a justice of the peace. (NTL 56)

* He is now retired from business. (CQ 58)

Leslie, John: *See* Leslie Minor.

Leslie Major (Henry)

† Eldest son of **John** and **Mary Preston Leslie**; his younger brothers are **Leslie Minor** and **Minimus**. All are at Southbridge School. He is a seemingly dull boy in the Upper Fourth who collects Empire stamps and takes a Greek testament to church, but he puts down **Miss Banks** for mispronouncing Uranus. (PBO 46)

* He baits **Chaplain "Holy Joe" Smith** by pretending to have a conscience. (PE 47)

* His name is given as **James**, and he is in the army, but this is probably a mistake for **James Graham**. (DD 51)

* His name is now given, after his father's father. He is at Oxford with an exhibition scholarship. (JC 53)

* He is scheduled to play for the Old Boys in the Southbridge School cricket match, but it is rained out. (ESR 55)

* He now plays in the cricket match and catches **Mr. Feeder** out. (NTL 56)

* He is doing well at Oxford. (ADA 57)

* He is now down from Oxford after three years, with a good First. (CQ 58)

Leslie, Martin

❖ Son of the eldest son of **Mr. (Henry)** and **Lady Emily Leslie**, and raised by them at Rushwater, to which he is the heir. His mother has remarried, to an American, and lives there. He is closest to his uncle, **David Leslie**. He celebrates his seventeenth birthday with a big party (and, as encouraged by **Jean-Claude Boulle**, an abortive royalist demonstration) at Rushwater. (WS 34)

❖ He is down from Oxford and working in his grandfather's estate office. His mother has American children as well. (BL 39)

❖ His father died at Arras. He has been awarded the George Medal "for doing something very meritorious with a bomb." (MH 42)

❖ He is now at the War Office, though it was touch and go while he was in Africa. (MB 45)

❖ He is at least twenty-seven years old, and inherited Rushwater on Mr. Leslie's death. He was machine-gunned in the foot at Anzio, and he and **Robin Dale** commiserate on their injuries. He gets engaged to **Sylvia Halliday**. (PBO 46)

❖ He and Sylvia are married, and their daughter **Eleanor** is one year old. They live at and manage Rushwater, where they hold Lady Emily's eightieth birthday reunion. He stands for County Council. (LAR 48)

❖ He is now thirty-odd, and his father died in 1918. He is on the Rural District Council, but **Mr. Macpherson** advises him to stand for the County Council. (OBH 49)

* He and Sylvia have a new baby boy, **Georgy**. His mother's American son is in the army during the Korean war. The Rushwater kitchen gardens and fruit trees are leased to **Mr. (Donald) MacFadyen's** Amalgamated Vedge Ltd. He visited the Argentine before the war, and during it served as an officer and regimental adjutant. (DD 51)

* His father's name is finally given as **Giles**. His and Sylvia's third child is to be called either Leonard Martin or Emily. (ESR 55)

* He sits on the Bench. His leg is better since they got a splinter out of it, though he still limps. (NTL 56)

* Now it's his foot that's entirely gone, so he has an artificial one; no doubt he is confused with Robin Dale. (LAAA 59)

* Their Rushwater Cowslip wins first prize for milk yield at the High Rising Agricultural. (TSAT 61)

Leslie, (Mrs.) Mary: *See* Preston, Mary.

Leslie Minimus (Clive)

* Youngest son of **John** and **Mary Preston Leslie**; his elder brothers are **Leslie Major** and **Minor**. All are at Southbridge School. He is always in trouble. (PBO 46)

* As the only brother who has no head for heights, he has to be rescued when he tries to climb the Temple at Rushwater. (LAR 48)

* He feeds the fish at the Palace garden party. (CC 50)

* He is finally named, after a Preston uncle killed in World War I.

* Despite his acrophobia, he is considering the R.A.F. (JC 53)

* He is in his last term at Southbridge. (CQ 58)

Leslie Minor (John)

* Middle son of **John** and **Mary Preston Leslie**; his brothers are **Leslie Major** and **Minimus**. All are at Southbridge School. He is a seemingly dull boy who collects European stamps (especially Mixo-Lydia), but is a terrific climber, and goes up the Rushwater tower. (PBO 46)

* At the Southbridge School Speech Day, he manages to fall down the platform steps with a pile of books. (PE 47)

* He climbs the Temple, Rushwater. (LAR 48)

* He climbs the tulip tree at the Palace garden party. (CC 50)

* He once climbed the chapel spire at Southbridge School. He is now in the army, but see later entries; may be confused with **John Graham**. (DD 51)

* He is finally named, after his father, and is considering Oxford. (JC 53)

* He and **George Halliday** climb the cathedral roof. (ESR 55)

* He is to graduate from Southbridge School next year. (NTL 56)

* He is due to go up to Oxford with a scholarship in the autumn. (ADA 57)

* He is at Oxford, and is known as "Johnny" to distinguish him from his father. His friend from Southbridge School days is **Wilson**. (CQ 58)

Leslie, (Mrs.) Rose: *See* **Bingham, Rose.**

Leslie, (Mrs.) Sylvia: *See* **Halliday, Sylvia.**

Librarian of the Barchester General Hospital
* At the Red Cross Library Show of Bookbinding, he unwittingly insults **Mrs. (Hermione) Rivers** by telling her that his brother in the Army of the Rhine said her book was hilarious. (PE 47)

Lily
* Works for **Captain** and **Mrs. Jane Gresham** at Greshamsbury House. Also obliges (and eats) at **Father Fewling's**, but that may not be why she's getting so fat. (ADA 57)

Lily
* Has been help to the **Pallisers** at Gatherum Castle since she was a girl. Once lady's maid to **Lady Mary Palliser**, she now has sciatica but still understands the Begum cooker. (CC 50)

Lily-Annie
* Kitchenmaid to the **Birketts** at Worsted; she can't read, and has an illegitimate little girl. Perhaps identical to **Lily-Annie Pollett**. (LAR 48)

Lob, Herr
* A band conductor; when **Rose Birkett** was sent to school in Munich, she got engaged to him and to an officer, **Lieutenant von Storck**, at the same time. (SH 37)

Longford, Mr.
* A teacher at Coppin's School when **Mr. (Gregory) Villars** was headmaster. He was so devoted to **Mrs. (Verena)**

Villars that he kept her handkerchief, but later found it was Matron's. He married Porton Major's elder sister and went into Mr. Porton's business. Also see **Mr. Lumford**. (NR 41)

Longtooth, Thorstein
* Viking whose (putative) bones have been found in Bloody Meadow; **Lord Stoke** shows them to **Mr. (Gilbert) Tebben**. (BL 39)

Lorimer, Mr.
* Senior Classical Master of Southbridge School, author of a Latin Grammar and unseens. He takes boys to his home in Scotland for the holidays. Later, he dies there, and **Philip Winter** takes over his Classical Sixth class. (SH 37)

* He died of a heart condition. (DD 51)

Louis, Prince, of Cobalt
* Father of **Princess Louisa Christina**. (BL 39)

Louisa
* Maid to **Anne Todd** and her mother. (HR 34)

Louisa Christina, Princess
* Daughter of **Prince Louis of Cobalt**; one of her ladies in waiting was **the Honourable (Miss) Juliana Starter**. (BL 39)

* She is Princess of Cobalt-Herz-Reinigen. (JC 53)

* Her mother named as a Hatz-Reinigen. She goes with Miss Starter on an (uninvited) weekend with the **Harcourts, Duke and Duchess of Towers**. (LAAA 59)

* She visited **Lady Bond**, who took her to see **Lord Stokes'** Rising Castle. (TSAT 61)

Lover, Mrs. Audrey

* Mother of **Aubrey Clover**, whose real name is **Caleb Lover** (when signed "C. Lover" it looked like "Clover"). No name is yet given for her. She is the widow of a bank manager in **Miss Hampton's** father's parish, is religious, and doesn't approve of the theatre. (PE 47)

* She has arthritis. (LAR 48)

* She died last winter. (OBH 49)

* She seems to be alive again, and is known to **Isabel Dale** as **Mrs. Audrey Lover**. When baby **Sarah Siddons Clover** and her Nannie want a breath of country air, they go to her house. (CC 50)

Lover, Caleb: *See* **Clover, Aubrey**.

Lufton, the Honourable Justinia

* Second (as yet unnamed) child of **Lord** and **Lady Lufton**, who was taken by **Nannie Allen** from the month; her sister **Lucy Maria** is two years older. (GU 43)

* Her father dies, and her younger brother **Ludovic** inherits the title. Her grandmother's money is settled on her and her sister. She is named for her great-grandfather's sister, who married Sir George Meredith (*cf.* Trollope). She did a year's secretarial training, and turned down a job at Red Tape and Sealing Wax to come to the Close as **Dean (Josiah) Crawley's** secretary. (DD 51)

﹡ She is a good dancer, and looks like her great-grandmother Lucy Robarts (*cf.* Trollope). She has had proposals from a budding missionary who stayed two nights at the Deanery, and from **Lord Dumbello,** who wants to marry her as soon as he's ten. As well as her work for the Dean, she works at the St. John and Red Cross Hospital Libraries. When her brother marries, she plans to live with her mother at Framley Parsonage. (HRt 52)

﹡ She is engaged to **Eric Swan.** (JC 53)

﹡ They are married and living at Harefield House School, where they are rapidly catching up with **Charles** and **Clarissa Graham Belton's** two children. (CQ 58)

Lufton, Lord

﹡ He married **Lady Lufton** in 1921. Their first child was **Lucy,** then another girl two years later that **Nannie Allen** took from the month. (GU 43)

﹡ A baron, he died recently; his son **Ludovic** inherits the title but little else, as he sold Lufton Park during the war, and his father had already given up the hounds and the place in Perthshire, Scotland. His mother was an heiress, however, and her money was settled on her granddaughters. His father's mother was Lucy Robarts, the parson's sister (*cf.* Trollope). (DD 51)

Lufton, the Honourable Lucy Maria

﹡ First child of **Lord** and **Lady Lufton**; her sister is two years younger. (GU 43)

﹡ Her father dies, and her younger brother **Ludovic** inherits the title. Her grandmother's money is settled on her and her sister **Justinia**. Though known as Maria, she was named for her great-grandmother Lucy Robarts, the parson's sister (*cf.* Trollope). She runs the Young Conservatives and breeds cocker spaniels. She saves **Oliver Marling** from having to let the Cedars to **Frances Harvey** by claiming first refusal herself. She and Oliver then become engaged. (DD 51)

❧ They are married, and she has a baby girl three weeks late; at **Mr. (William) Marling's** suggestion, the baby's second name is Mora. (HRt 52)

❧ They have two children. (ESR 55)

❧ She judges the spaniels at the Nutfield Gymkhana. (TSAT 61)

Lufton, Ludovic, Lord
❧ Third child and only son of **Lord** and **Lady (Mary) Lufton**; his elder sisters are **Lucy Maria** and **Justinia**. Inherits the title but little else when his father dies, as his father had sold Lufton Park during the war, and his grandfather had already given up the hounds and the place in Perthshire, Scotland. He got out of the army in 1946, went to agricultural college, and studied under **Roddy Wicklow**. Now twenty-six, he intends to farm and go on the Bench like his father. They have had to lease half of Framley to **Mr. (Donald) MacFadyen**, the Manager of Amalgamated Vedge; when he sits in the Lords, he has to board with his mother's old cousin in Buckingham Gate. He is friends with Princess Margaret, and is very interested in **Grace Grantly**. (DD 51)

✢ Now it's his father's cousin in Buckingham Gate, who turns out to be **Miss (Juliana) Starter**. She is starving him on the small rent he pays, and he can't afford to lodge with **Colin** and **Eleanor Keith**, but **Oliver Marling** lets him stay at his London flat for free. He gets engaged to Grace Grantly, and asks **Eric Swan** to be his best man. (HRt 52)

✢ They are married and living at Framley Court; she is pregnant. (JC 53)

✢ They have two daughters. (CQ 58)

✢ Their brood is still increasing. (TSAT 61)

Lufton, Maria: *See* **Lufton, the Honourable Lucy Maria**.

Lufton, Lady Mary

✢ She married **Lord Lufton** in 1921. Their first child was **Lucy**, then another girl two years later, that **Nannie Allen** took from the month. (GU 43)

✢ She insisted on being godmother to **Ludovic Foster, Lord Mellings**. (TH 44)

✢ Her husband has died recently, and her third child, **Ludovic**, has inherited the title. She was married at nineteen; her daughters' names are **Lucy Maria** and **Justinia**. (DD 51)

✢ She is only practical at running Women's Institutes; she plays *Lieder* accompaniment, once for a famous singer who was a friend of her mother's. She plans to move from Framley to the Old Parsonage (now a dower house) when Ludovic is married. (HRt 52)

* For the first time, her first name is given. She is a justice of the peace, and sits on the Bench regularly. She had a younger sister Susan who died long ago. (JC 53)

* She's getting on for seventy. (CQ 58)

Lufton, Young Lady: *See* **Grantly, Grace.**

Lumford, Mr.
* Science master at Coppin's School when **Mr. (Gregory) Villars** was headmaster. Like his near-homonym **Mr. Longford**, "devoted" to **Mrs. (Verena) Villars.** (NR 41)

Lundquist, Selma
* Actress in the plays of **Hjalmar Gunnarssen**, and friend of **Petrea Krogsbrog.** (LAR 48)

M., Miss: *See* **Mowbray, Miss.**

Macalister, Pixie

＊ A schoolmate of **Miss (Cecily) Holly** and **Mrs. (Molly) Watson** at Fairlawns School. Now games mistress at a mental home and member of the Ludo Club. (MB 45)

MacFadyen, Mr. Donald

＊ Manager of Amalgamated Vedge, Ltd., which leases the fruit trees and kitchen gardens of Rushwater from **Martin Leslie**. A Scot, from Perthshire. He rents half of Framley Hall from **Ludovic, Lord Lufton**. (DD 51)

＊ His line goes back to a burgher of Perth in the early seventeenth century, with each generation having a farmer and a minister. His father was killed in the Boer War and his mother was turned out of their house with only her pension. He gave her a home, and worked under the head gardener **Methven** in the policies of Auchsteer to support her. She died when he was twenty, and he went South to work under a Scots market gardener. Now known to his family as "Jock o'London," he deals kindly but firmly with his father's stepsister's nephew's son **Robert McGuffog**. He takes a lease on the stabling at Framley Parsonage and installs central heating there and at Framley Hall, mainly for the benefit of **Lady Lufton**. (HRt 52)

* His brothers and sisters had all died in infancy. He gets engaged to **Margot Phelps**. (JC 53)

* He is going into business with **Sam Adams** and **Old Pilward**; they want to rent most of Pomfret Towers for offices and an experimental station for Amalgamated Vedge. (WDIM 54)

* He was able to get away from Amalgamated Vedge for his honeymoon. (ESR 55)

* He is considerably older than Margot. He becomes ill and dies. He is buried at Framley. (CQ 58)

MacFadyen, (Mrs.) Margot: *See* Phelps, Margot.

MacGregor, Mr.
* General manager, **Johns** and Fairfield Publishing. (PT 38)

Macheath, Sister
* Nurse, Barchester General Hospital. (GU 43)

MacHenry
* Real name of **Stoker's** father, who got his sobriquet from shoveling coke at the gasworks. (HR 33)

* He was a drinker; his wife and daughter had to identify him at a mortuary on the Tuesday after Easter. (NTL 56)

Macpherson, Mr.

* Agent of Rushwater, devoted to the **Leslies**, especially **Lady Emily**. Afflicted with sciatica. Originally of Dunbar, he hasn't visited Scotland for forty years. (PBO 46)

* He learned his job under a good factor in Scotland, came to Rushwater at age thirty, and has worked there fifty years. He intends his house to go to **Emmy Graham** when he dies. (OBH 49)

* Delicate though still working, he attends his eighty-third birthday dinner at Rushwater. He dies peacefully. (DD 51)

Macpherson, Nurse

* Night nurse for **Tommy Needham** at the convalescent hospital. (LAR 48)

Mallow, Mr. Jos.

* Cowman to **Lord Stoke**, best in the county. He wins first class in all entries in the Skeynes Agricultural Show. Married; cousin to **Mr. Mallow** the stationmaster. (BL 39)

* He dies, leaving cow honors open to all comers. (PE 47)

Mallow, Mr.

* Stationmaster at High Rising; nephew by marriage to **Mrs. Mallow**. (HR 33)

* Friend of **Tony Morland**. (DH 34)

* His cousin is **Lord Stoke's** cowman, **Mr. Jos. Mallow**. (BL 39)

* His station's name is Stoke Dry. (TSAT 61)

Mallow, Mrs.

* Mr. Knox's **Annie's** aunt; a widow, and housekeeper to **Dr. Ford**. Her cousin is a builder. Also aunt to Annie's sister **Flo** and (by marriage) to the stationmaster **Mr. Mallow**. (HR 33)

* She has a halfwit nephew down in the village, and she sometimes has to take him outside when he talks in church. (LAAA 59)

Man with the Brick-Red Face, the: *See* Brick-Red Face, the Man with the.

Manhole, Mr.

* Housemaster at Eton. **Robert** and **James Graham** are in his house. (PBO 46)

* Robert and **John Graham** are in his house. (LAR 48)

Manners

* Son of a greengrocer, one of the Hosiers' Boys' Foundation School's most brilliant students. Elected to an open scholarship at Cambridge. (CBI 40)

* His father is a greengrocer and furniture remover in the Isle of Dogs. He is given a free place at the Southbridge School; his parents at first object to his being a "charity-boy," though not to his state scholarship. He wins an open scholarship in History at Lazarus College, Oxford (but *see* above). (PE 47)

* His parents left London for Wales for the duration. **Snow** let him learn carpentry in his shop at Southbridge School, and they kept in touch. According to Snow, he had a

scholarship to "Oxford or Cambridge or one of them colleges" and is now teaching "Replied Physic" and history at Upping College, Redbrick University (where **Hacker** is as well). (NTL 56)

Manton, Octavius
* ❖ "*The* Manton," according to **Mr. (Caleb) Oriel**. Fourth son of a large family, he got a fellowship at Oxford, then married, took orders, and got a College living. Maternal grandfather of **Dorothea, Dowager Duchess of Towers**; he taught her some Latin. The **Duke of Towers** read with him, but he died before the Duke and Duchess were married; *see* **Harcourt**. (LAAA 59)

March, Dr.
* ❖ General practitioner working with **Lucy Marling** at the Cottage Hospital. (MH 42)

Marco Aurelio
* ❖ Chemist and part-time bandit in Calabria. He and his wife rent lodgings to **Mrs. (Felicia) Grant**. (CBI 40)
* ❖ Now known simply as **Aurelio**, he has killed five men. (CC 50)

Margarison, Old
* ❖ Former owner (before the **Tebbens**) of Lamb's Piece, Worsted. "Married his housekeeper—high time too," according to **Lord Stoke**. (BL 39)

Margett, Alf
* ❖ Younger son of **Mr. Margett** the builder; his older brother is **Bert**. On leave from the Tank Corps, he snared six rabbits and sold them at Beliers Priory, for which deed he

was beaten up and then taken to shoot rooks by **Jasper Margett**. (GU 43)

Margett, Bert

❖ Son of **Mr. Margett** the builder; head porter, Worsted station. He is a second cousin of **Mrs. Phipps**, and is walking out with her daughter **Doris Phipps**. He is in the chorus of *Hippolytus*. (AF 36)

❖ He has been going with Doris for six years. He has a younger brother, **Alf**. (GU 43)

❖ He and Doris are married and have children. He became the Worsted station master once **Mr. Patten** retired. (LAR 48)

❖ Yet a Bert Margett is porter at Stoke Dry station, High Rising. (TSAT 61)

Margett, Eliza

❖ Sister of **Mr. Margett** the builder, and a notable cook over Winter Overcotes way. Her daughter is cook to the **Grahams**, Holdings. **Jasper Margett** the gamekeeper is her first cousin. (DD 51)

Margett, Jasper

❖ Gamekeeper to the **Warings**, Beliers Priory, where he lives in a picturesque but unhygienic cottage. His grandmother was a half-gypsy witch from Golden Valley, whose only child married a poacher who broke his neck falling down the Woolpack steps. His aunt is **Mrs. Margett** the underhousemaid to the **Palmers**. Though his granny died sixty years ago, she still appears as a black hare, and his chief ambition is to shoot it. He does so, and proposes to **Selina Allen**, but is rejected. (GU 43)

❖ His nephew is the horse-coper **Jasper Margett**. (OBH 49)

❖ **Mr. Margett** the builder and **Eliza Margett** are his first cousins. (DD 51)

Margett, Jasper (Old Jasper)

❖ Gypsy horse-coper, nephew of the gamekeeper **Jasper Margett**. His mother was **Nannie Peters'** aunt by marriage. He gets a pony for **Giles Foster**. (OBH 49)

❖ According to **Mr. (Harold) Welk**, he's a great hand with wood. (CQ 58)

❖ He lives out in the woods near Beliers, where Giles visits him. His own nephew fell down a hillside shaft into the canal, after which his father beat him. (LAAA 59)

Margett, Mr.

❖ Builder, father of **Bert**. He installed a leaky basin in the **Palmers'** barn, and divided the **Tebbens'** dining room. He plays a huntsman in *Hippolytus*. (AF 36)

❖ His younger son is **Alf**. (GU 43)

❖ He built Mr. Palmer's new barn around '35, and a poor job too. His sister was **Eliza Margett**, and his first cousin is the gamekeeper **Jasper Margett**. (DD 51)

❖ His uncle is **Old Margett**. (WDIM 54)

Margett, Mrs.

❖ Under-housemaid to the **Palmers**; aunt of the gamekeeper **Jasper Margett**. She loses her ration cards and clothing coupons. (GU 43)

Margett, Mrs.

❖ Postmistress at Marling. (OBH 49)

Margett, Old

* A deaf old codger who competes with **Old Patten** for honors in the folk-song field, though none seems to pre-date Queen Victoria. His father farmed Pooker's Piece in 1902, and his mother said her grandmother told her that a highwayman was buried there. He once ate three live frogs for a wager. (BL 39)

* His nephew is **Mr. Margett** the builder. **Aubrey Clover** pumps him for bawdy songs. (WDIM 54)

Margett, Tommy

* A naughty little boy whose father works with the bodgers up at Grumper's End. His mother is elsewhere and his aunt is supposed to look after him, but she has nine of her own. He crawls into the ring at the Nutfield Gymkhana and a horse steps on his hand. He goes to Barchester General for X-rays, but there's no serious damage. (TSAT 61)

Marks, Miss

* A former teacher at the Hosiers' Girls' Foundation School. She left for the Board of Trade. (TH 44)

Marleen

* Kitchenmaid to the **Grahams**, Holdings. Fifteen years old. (LAR 48)

* Her name is now spelled "Marlene" and she's been pro-moted to general utility. (DD 51)

Marling, (the Honourable) Mrs. Amabel

* Wife of **Mr. (William) Marling** and mother of **Bill, Let-tice Watson, Oliver**, and **Lucy**. Of Marling Hall. A daughter of **Lord Nutfield**, she is vaguely connected to the

Leslies. She had a nephew in the Consular Service who died of fever, leaving an Austrian widow but no children. (MH 42)

❖ She brings in **Isabel Dale** to help with Lucy's wedding. (CC 50)

Marling, Bill

❖ Eldest child of **Mr. (William)** and **Mrs. (Amabel) Marling**; his younger siblings are **Lettice Watson, Oliver**, and **Lucy**. A soldier, he married a bishop's daughter, known universally as **Mrs. Bill**. They have four children, and live in Camberley. (MH 42)

❖ Their children are boys. (LAR 48)

❖ Their children are now girls. He is now a colonel. (CC 50)

❖ They now have three children. (DD 51)

Marling, Mrs. Bill (actually Deirdre)

❖ Daughter of a bishop, she married **Bill Marling**. They have four children under the care of **Nana** and **Everleen**, and live in Camberley. (MH 42)

❖ Their children are boys. (LAR 48)

❖ Their children are now girls. Her real name is now revealed. Her parents had arranged her wedding up North in Camberley at **Mrs. (Amabel) Marling's** most inconvenient time. (CC 50)

❖ They now have three children. (DD 51)

Marling, Deirdre: *See* Marling, Mrs. Bill.

Marling, Fitzherbert

* Uncle of **Mr. (William) Marling** and rector of Courcy Abbas for sixty years. He hunted until he was eighty. (LAR 48)

* An archdeacon, he had the same parish for fifty years and was buried there (but *see* above). He left Mr. Marling his port. He once wagered **Mr. (Fred) Belton's** father that he could ride five miles, drink a quart of claret, and marry a couple within an hour. (CC 50)

* He used to be carried to bed by two footmen. (DD 51)

Marling, Lucy Emily

* Youngest child of **Mr. (William)** and **Mrs. (Amabel) Marling**; her older siblings are **Bill, Lettice Watson,** and **Oliver**. About twenty-five, she works around the estate and at the Cottage Hospital. She has a dog, Turk, and will tell you what. She likes **Tom Barclay**, but gives him up to her sister Lettice. (MH 42)

* She is a goddaughter of **Mrs. (Lucy) Belton** and a friend of **Octavia Needham**. (TH 44)

* She is going abroad with the Red Cross. (MB 45)

* She manages the Marling Red Cross Fete, and agrees to work for **Sam Adams** as manager of market gardens. (LAR 48)

* Now about thirty, she is growing vegetables for Adams and for **Pilward** and Sons, with the overflow going to Amalgamated Vedge Ltd.; she also plans for livestock. She agrees to marry Sam Adams. (OBH 49)

* She gets a makeover from **Jessica Dean** and is married at Easter. (CC 50)

* She has a baby girl, **Amabel Rose**. (DD 51)

* Their second child is a boy. (NTL 56)

* Their children are Amabel Rose, then **William** (after her father), and a girl, **Leslie** (after the Rushwater family). She wins first prize for veg. at the High Rising Agricultural. (TSAT 61)

Marling, Mrs. Maria: *See* **Lufton, the Honourable Lucy Maria**.

Marling, Old Mrs.
* Mother of **Mr. (William) Marling**; she turned the Marling Hall lamproom into a lay chapel. **Miss (Maud) Bunting** sees a resemblance to her in her granddaughter, **Lettice Watson**. (MH 42)

* She was engaged at nineteen and had six children before she was thirty. All are now dead except for William. (CC 50)

* She has been dead for thirty years. (DD 51)

Marling, Oliver
* Third child of **Mr. (William)** and **Mrs. (Amabel) Marling**; his elder siblings are **Bill** and **Lettice Watson**, his younger sister is **Lucy**. He was in business in London, but

now works for the Regional Commissioner's Office in Barchester. He was turned down for the army because of age and bad eyesight. He is an expert, in a dilettantish way, on **the Rev. Thomas Bohun's** life and works. He is pursued by **Frances Harvey**, but eludes her. (MH 42)

✦ Now in his thirties, and back at the London firm of which he's a partner. He is infatuated with **Jessica Dean**, but she refuses him. (LAR 48)

❖ He proposes to Jessica again, to find she married **Aubrey Clover** a week before. (OBH 49)

❖ Now thirty-six, he has **Isabel Dale** type his book on Bohun; she says it's too short for **Adrian Coates** to publish. He almost proposes to her, but for his sins gets stuck with Frances Harvey at the Conservative Do at Gatherum. (CC 50)

❖ He has had his opuscule on Bohun printed at his own expense. His father gives him The Cedars, and **Maria Lufton** saves him from having to lease it to Frances Harvey. He and Maria get engaged. (DD 51)

❖ They are married, and she has a baby girl three weeks late; at **Mr. (William) Marling's** suggestion, the baby's second name is Mora. He only goes to London two days a week, and lets **Ludovic, Lord Lufton**, have the flat for the rest of the time. (HRt 52)

❖ They have two children. (ESR 55)

Marling, Mr. William
❖ Husband of **Mrs. (Amabel) Marling** and father of **Bill, Lettice Watson, Oliver**, and **Lucy**. Of Marling Hall. (MH 42)

* He presides at the Red Cross Fete at Marling, and his Marling Magnum is first at the Pig Show and Conservative Rally. He had an Uncle William who made his butler sit up and see him to bed. Another uncle was **Fitzherbert Marling**. (LAR 48)

* He is increasingly deaf. (OBH 49)

* He had five siblings, all now dead. His Aunt Lucy married the Duke of Omnium's youngest son, **D. D'Algy Palliser**; they had no children, and both went down with the *Titanic*. (CC 50)

* He is over seventy, having volunteered for the Barsetshire Yeomanry for the Boer War. He makes over The Cedars, which was to have been his Aunt Lucy's, to Oliver. (DD 51)

* His Marling Magister, a White Porkminster, wins best in show at the High Rising Agricultural. (TSAT 61)

Marston, Professor
* Renaissance scholar and author of monumental books, all footnotes. Friend of **Mrs. (Susan) Barton**. (PT 38)

* Assisted **Professor Milward** with the **Pomfret** history. (LAAA 59)

Mary Joseph, Sister
* Head of the St. Quantock (Catholic) School. She takes her pupils to the Southbridge Christmas Treat. (CBI 40)

Mason
* Sergeant of the Lower School, Southbridge. (HR 33)

* Now Sergeant of the entire School since he came up with the **Birketts**. He visits his mother in Manchester. (CBI 40)

Mason, Lady Peggy

* During World War I she lost two husbands, and married the third before the armistice. She had a very common grandfather on her mother's side. (MH 42)

M.F.H., the: *See* **Brick-Red Face, the Man with the.**

Master of Lazarus: *See* **Lazarus, the Master of; Crawford of Lazarus;** and **Skinner, Lord.**

Master, the Junior: *See* **Junior Master of Beliers Priory School, the.**

Master, the Senior: *See* **Senior Master of Beliers Priory School, the.**

Master, Dr.

* Of London. Consulted about **Mrs. (Rachel) Dean's** heart and **Jessica Dean's** concussion. (AF 36)

Masters, Old

* Tenant farmer of **Admiral Palliser.** He has a cow, Daisy, that just calved, and is visited by **Lord Stoke** in the middle of the Barsetshire Archaeological meeting. He donates a goat harness to the Cottage Hospital Raffle. (MB 45)

Matcham, Mrs. Colonel

* In India, habitually flirted on the veranda with **Captain Fred Arbuthnot.** (PE 47)

Matron of the Barchester Infirmary/General Hospital

* The bane of trainees **Octavia Crawley** and **Geraldine Birkett.** (CBI 40)

* She is now in charge of the convalescent home for soldiers at Beliers Priory. She has ribbons from the First World

War. **Private Jenks** shoots her cat, and she adopts a new one, Winston, from **Mrs. Phipps**. (GU 43)

❖ The Infirmary was amalgamated with Barchester General earlier in the war. (TH 44)

❖ While **Cecil Waring** is in surgery, she reminisces with **Lady Glencora Palliser** about the laughs in the plastic surgery ward when **Corporal Hoggett** put plasticine scars on his face and scared **V.A.D. Coxon**. (DD 51)

Matron of the Beliers Priory School
❖ About thirty and nice looking. She was at Knight's, and spends her holidays working at a small nursing home that a friend of hers from there owns. She has an elder niece with children, and writes to her Mums about **Mrs. (Mary) Grantly's** hat. (HRt 52)

Matron of the Cottage Hospital
❖ Supervised **Octavia Crawley** and **Lucy Marling**. (LAR 48)

Matron at Knight's
❖ A strict taskmaster, she trained both **Nurse Chiffinch** and **Miss (Poppy) Dudley**. She is now retired, living with a friend in Folkestone, and serving on the Town Council. (DD 51)

Matron of the Southbridge Lower School
❖ According to **Tony Morland**, she "goes off pop." She has a married sister at Weston-super-Mare. (HR 33)

❖ She has a "historic leg," and is in a state of war with **Mr. Ferris**. (DH 34)

Matron of the Southbridge Senior School: *See* **Dudley, Miss Poppy.**

McBean
* Head gardener, Southbridge School. (CBI 40)

McClan, Professor Macphairson Clonglocketty Angus
* Scottish Home Rule Member of Parliament for Aberdeathly; son of an elderly laboring man. (CC 50)

McGuffog, Robert
* **Mr. (Donald) MacFadyen's** father's stepsister's nephew's son, who's gone to the bad in Glasgow. (HRt 52)

Measel, Miss
* A teacher at the Hosiers' Girls' Foundation School who leaves to nurse her old mother. (TH 44)

Mellings, Lord: title of the heir to the **Earl of Pomfret;** *see also* **Foster, Ludovic.**

Mellings, Harry, Lord
* Only child of **Giles, Seventh Earl of Pomfret,** and of **Edith, Lady Pomfret.** Once a friend of **Mrs. (Susan) Barton.** Killed in a frontier skirmish in India. (PT 38)

* Like the late **Colonel Stonor** and **Mr. (Alister) Cameron's** father, he was in the 23rd regiment. (BL 39)

* Killed on the northwest frontier in India, in the same battle as the Detrimental who was engaged to his aunt **Lady Agnes (Pomfret).** (DD 51)

Mells, Miss
* Informally known as "Smells" or "Old Smelly." Trained with **Miss Heath,** and specialized in surgical cases. Was matron to V.A.D. **Lydia Keith** Merton. (NTL 56)

Menski, Sasha

❖ Author of *Worm that Eateth the Flesh*, for which **Bolikoff** designed the book jacket. (PT 38)

Merivale, Annie

❖ Eldest daughter of **Mrs. Merivale**; her younger sisters are **Peggie, Evie,** and **Elsie.** She is abroad in A.T.S. and gets engaged to a young man in Signals. (MB 45)

Merivale, Elsie

❖ Youngest daughter of **Mrs. Merivale**; her elder sisters are **Annie, Peggie,** and **Evie.** She is overseas in the WAAFs and gets engaged to a flight lieutenant named **Peter.** (MB 45)

Merivale, Evie

❖ Third daughter of **Mrs. Merivale**; her elder sisters are **Annie** and **Peggie,** the younger one is **Elsie.** She is in the Foreign Office in Washington D.C., and marries an American named **Constant Cutsam.** (MB 45)

Merivale, Mrs.

❖ A widow, about fifty, of Valimere, Riverside Close, Hallbury. Her late husband was a clerk in **Sir Robert Fielding's** office. She has four daughters: **Annie, Peggie, Evie,** and **Elsie,** all serving abroad and all getting engaged or married. She takes in paying guests, including **Canon Banister's** mother, some of **Dean (Josiah) Crawley's** daughters and their children, and, most recently, **Heather Adams** and **Miss (Cicely) Holly.** (MB 45)

Merivale, Peggie

❖ Second daughter of **Mrs. Merivale**; her elder sister is **Annie,** the younger ones are **Evie** and **Elsie.** She is a Wren in Gibraltar, and gets engaged to a thirty-two-year-old paymaster general there, **Don**. (MB 45)

Merriman, Miss ("Merry")

❖ Secretary to **Edith, Lady Pomfret**, and general factotum of Pomfret Towers. Her first name is known to no one. She has an invalid sister, and a soft spot for **Gillie Foster**. (PT 38)

❖ After Lady Pomfret died, she went to Lady Harberton, the former **Phoebe Rivers**. She is now companion to **Lady Emily Leslie** at **Lady Agnes Graham's** house, Holdings. (MH 42)

❖ After the death of Lady Emily, she returns to Pomfret Towers to help Gillie and the former **Sally Wicklow**, now **Lord** and **Lady Pomfret**. (OBH 49)

❖ She goes with the Pomfrets to winter at Cap Ferrat. (CC 50)

❖ Her only relative is her married sister, who now has grandchildren. For **Mr. (Herbert) Choyce**, she agrees to give a talk on Pomfret Towers at the Mothers' Union Annual Meeting at Hatch End. Tired out, she goes to Holdings for a rest, and becomes engaged to Mr. Choyce. Her first name, Dorothea, is revealed. (NTL 56)

❖ In a wedding arranged by Lady Agnes, Dorothea Frances Merriman marries Mr. Choyce. (ADA 57)

Merriman, Mr.

❖ Provençal scholar, author of *Cultural Influence of the Court of King René*, which gets a bad review from **Mr. (Harold) Downing**. (NR 41)

Merton, Harry

* Second child of **Noel** and **Lydia Keith Merton**; his older sister is **Lavinia**. When his mother gets the measles, his aunt **Kate Keith** Carter takes both children to Devonshire with their cousins. (PE 47)

* He is three; there is a third child, called **Kate**, in the perambulator. (OBH 49)

* He is seven, and his little sister is now **Jessica**. (WDIM 54)

* The Mertons and Carters joke about marrying their children to their cousins. He is better at sports than at lessons. (LAAA 59)

* He is going to Cambridge for his science degree next year. His sister's name is reconciled as **Kate Jessica**. (TSAT 61)

Merton, Kate Jessica

* Third child of **Noel** and **Lydia Keith Merton**; younger sister of **Lavinia** and **Harry**. She is simply called **Kate**, in the perambulator, and can't talk yet. (OBH 49)

* She is five, and is now called **Jessica**, after **Jessica Dean**. (WDIM 54)

* The Mertons and Carters joke about marrying their children to their cousins. (LAAA 59)

* Her name is finally reconciled as **Kate Jessica**; she chose to go by her second name early in her schooldays. She is now sixteen, and tiresomely modern. She will be a bridesmaid for her sister Lavinia's wedding. (TSAT 61)

Merton, Jessica: *See* **Merton, Kate Jessica**.

Merton, Lavinia

❖ First child of **Noel** and **Lydia Keith Merton**; six months old. She is named for **Mrs. (Lavinia) Brandon**. (TH 44)

❖ She gets a baby brother, **Harry**. She also gets the measles, and gives them to her mother; her aunt **Kate Keith Carter** takes her and Harry to Devonshire with their cousins. (PE 47)

❖ She is five; there is a third child, called **Kate**, in the perambulator. (OBH 49)

❖ Her little sister is now **Jessica**. She is ten, and attends the Preparatory School of the Barchester High School. (WDIM 54)

❖ The Mertons and Carters joke about marrying their children to their cousins. She is about fifteen or sixteen, close in age to **Ludovic Foster, Lord Mellings**. She studies French with **Mlle. Chiendent** and German with **Fräulein Katzenjammer** at the Barchester High School. (LAAA 59)

❖ She is about twenty, back from six months in Paris with the **Pierre Boulle** family. She gets engaged to Ludovic. Her sister (whose name is reconciled as **Kate Jessica**) is to be a bridesmaid. (TSAT 61)

Merton, (Mrs.) Lydia: *See* **Keith, Lydia**.

Merton, Noel

❖ Barrister, a guest at **Mr. (Henry)** and **Mrs. (Helen) Keith's**. He flirts lightly with their daughter **Kate** and becomes friends with **Lydia**, who is fifteen years younger than he. (SH 37)

* His father is a solicitor, and he is legal adviser to **Miss (Amelia) Brandon**. He flirts with **Mrs. (Lavinia) Brandon**. (TB 39)

* He attends **Rose Birkett's** wedding. He is made second lieutenant, then captain, in Intelligence. He marries Lydia, then is saved from Dunkirk. (CBI 40)

* He and Lydia are in Scotland. (NR 41)

* He is now a major, and he and Lydia are billeted on the **Warings** at Beliers Priory. They buy Northbridge Manor from **Robert Keith**, and Lydia becomes pregnant. (GU 43)

* They are now settled at Northbridge Manor, and their daughter **Lavinia** is six months old. (TH 44)

* Lydia is pregnant, due in January. (PBO 46)

* Their new baby is **Harry**. They have been married for seven years, and he has a flirtation with **Peggy Arbuthnot**. He is told off by **Jessica Dean**, and gives Lydia a bolt of purple silk in tacit apology. He "takes silk" and becomes K.C. (PE 47)

* He formally apologizes to Lydia. They have a third child, called **Kate**, in the perambulator. (OBH 49)

* His father hardly ever goes to the office now, but the other partner in Merton and Merton is very nice. (CC 50)

* He runs for Parliament for Morristown, London. (HRt 52)

* Their third child is now **Jessica**, after Jessica Dean. He gets a Coronation knighthood. (WDIM 54)

* Their third child's name is reconciled as **Kate Jessica**. (TSAT 61)

Methven

* Head gardener in the policies of Auchsteer, under Ben Gaunt, just by Loch Gloom. He trained the young **Donald MacFadyen**. (HRt 52)

Michel, Mlle.

* French miotress, Hoslers' Girls' Foundation School. (TH 44)

Mickleham, Lord

* Victorian statesman, littérateur and bearded impostor. Author of *Cimabue: a Poetical Drama in Prologue, Five Acts and Epilogue*, performed once (and never again) by Irving. He proposed once to **Lord Stoke's** mother, but he was poor and ineligible. Nonetheless, he married three times; **Miss (Juliana) Starter** is the youngest of his eighteen children. (BL 39)

* His wife was a Victorian beauty, **Miss Foster**. (HRt 52)

* Miss Starter is now the daughter of *old* Lord Mickleham, whose *son* married the heiress **Dolly Foster**. (LAAA 59)

Mickleham, the present Lord

* **Miss (Juliana) Starter's** income is a first charge on his (diminished) estate. (JC 53)

Micky

* A guest at **Pomfret** Towers. **The Screaming Girl (Miss Faraday-Home)** squirts him and **Peter** in the bath with the puff-billiards puffers, and has a bet with him (or Peter) about the chances for Monday. They all use the letters from a game for a paper chase. (PT 38)

Middleton, Mrs. Catherine

* Wife of **Mr. Jack Middleton**, of Laverings. An orphan, over thirty when she married. She has an affection toward her sister-in-law **Lilian Stonor's** stepson **Denis Stonor**. (BL 39)

* She is friends with **Anne Todd** Knox. (MB 45)

* She meets Denis again. (LAR 48)

Middleton, Mr. Jack

* Husband of **Catherine Middleton**, of Laverings. Garrulous architect, senior partner to **Mr. (Alister) Cameron**. He married after his mother died, when he was under fifty. His married sister is **Lilian Stonor**, who brings her stepson and -daughter **Denis** and **Daphne Stonor** to stay nearby. He has pretensions towards being a gentleman farmer, with his dog Flora and his heifer Lily Langtry. (BL 39)

* His lecture to convalescent soldiers on the antiquities of Skeynes is not very successful. (GU 43)

* He meets **George Knox** in a talking contest on the field of the Barsetshire Archaeological. (MB 45)

Milburds, the

* Owners of Harefield Park before **Belton the Nabob** bought it, 150 years before. They were ruined in the South Sea Bubble, but the father hung on for some years before committing suicide. His son shut the house and lived in the lodge. (TH 44)

Miller, Mr. Justin

* Vicar of Pomfret Madrigal. He has a stepmother in Harrogate, and a soft spot for **Mrs. (Lavinia) Brandon**, to

whom he tries to read his book on John Donne. He was once a student of the **Rev. Justin Morris**, but they fell out over his high church views. He was also estranged from Mr. Morris' daughter **Ella**, but they remeet and agree to marry. (TB 39)

❖ At college with **Tommy Needham's** father, he was known as "Goggers." Now married, he and his wife house evacuees. (CBI 40)

❖ He takes **Miss Horniman's** funeral at Lambton. (GU 43)

❖ When young, he lived in the slums of a large seaport, so as a chaplain in World War I he could outswear any of his regiment. (PE 47)

❖ He is on holiday when Mrs. Brandon's grandchild is christened. (LAR 48)

❖ **Lord Pomfret** appoints him Vicar of St. Ewold's near Barchester; he is succeeded at Pomfret Madrigal by **Mr. (Theodore) Parkinson**. (CC 50)

❖ His first name is given for the first time; it happens to be the same as his late unlamented father-in-law. At St. Ewold's, they live in the vicarage Archdeacon Grantly prepared for Mr. Arabin (*cf.* Trollope). They give a dinner party to celebrate their twelfth anniversary. (HRt 52)

Milner, Miss
  ❖ Dancing teacher at Rushwater. (MH 42)

Milvin, Sir Barclay
  ❖ Attending physician in London to **Miss (Juliana) Starter**. (BL 39)

Milward, Professor

❖ An agreeable young historian who visits Pomfret Towers to look at the **Pomfret** family papers. (PT 38)

❖ Assisted by **Professor Marston** and the **Duke of Monte Cristo**, he has collected, constructed, and collated the Pomfret family history. (LAAA 59)

Miranda, Miss

❖ Operator of a beauty parlor in Barchester. *See also* **Miss Amanda**. (LAR 48)

Mitton, Ted

❖ Railway engineer of the *Gatherum Castle* before it was sent abroad for the war. (GU 43)

Mitzi

❖ Austrian maid of the **Gissings**. Heavily overworked. (CBI 40)

Mixo-Lydian Ambassador: *See* **Bonescu, Gradka**.

Mixo-Lydian Fleet, Admiral of the: *See* **Prsvb, Admiral**.

Mngangaland, the Bishop of: *See* **Joram, Bishop**.

Mngangaland, the Eightieth Son of the Head Chief of: *See* **Head Chief of Mngangaland, the Eightieth Son of the**.

Mngangaland, the Head Chief of: *See* **Head Chief of Mngangaland, the**.

Mngangaland, the Head Witch Doctor of: *See* **Head Witch Doctor of Mngangaland, the**.

Mngangaland, the Prime Minister of: *See* **Prime Minister of Mngangaland, the.**

Moffatt, Mr.
* ❖ Vicar of Pomfret Madrigal before **Mr. Lane** and **Mr. (Justin) Miller.** (TB 39)

Monte Cristo, the Duke of
* ❖ Cosmopolitan doyen of the diplomatic world. Friend of **Mrs. (Susan) Barton.** (PT 38)

* ❖ He helped **Professor Milward** with the Italian side of the **Pomfret** family history. (LAAA 59)

Moore, Miss
* ❖ Teacher at Barchester High School, cheeked by **Amber Dandridge** in the bookroom. (SH 37)

Morgan, Dr.
* ❖ Female doctor, called in to see **Heather Adams** when **Dr. Perry** can't be found. An amateur psychoanalyst. She wears the same Robin Hood hat as **Miss Pettinger** to Bobbin Day at the Hosiers' Girls' Foundation School. (TH 44)

* ❖ She takes out the tonsils and adenoids of **Ellie**, daughter of **George, Lord Norton**. She then gets a job in the Ministry of Nutritional Hygiene under **Dr. Mothersill.** (DD 51)

Morland, Dick
* ❖ Third son of the late **Henry** and **Mrs. (Laura) Morland.** His elder brothers are **Gerald** and **John**, the youngest is **Tony.** He is in the Navy, on the China station. (HR 33)

* ❖ He just rejoined his ship at Malta. (TB 39)

* ❖ He is a lieutenant on the *Flatiron* on the China station. He met the **Phelpses** in Malta. (CBI 40)

* He is at sea somewhere. (GU 43)

* In Australia with his ship, he sends home for his childhood pictures, probably to show to a fiancée. (MB 45)

* His three brothers are married but he is not. (OBH 49)

* Now all four are married, and among them, have produced ten children. (NTL 56)

* All except Tony are usually away on foreign jobs. (TSAT 61)

Morland, Gerald
   * Oldest son of the late **Henry** and **Mrs. (Laura) Morland**. His younger brothers are **John, Dick,** and **Tony**. Educated at the Southbridge School and Oxford, he is now in Mexico with an American. (HR 33)

* Now in Tibet. (DH 34)

* He is secretary to an American explorer. (TB 39)

* He is well over military age, currently exploring in central South America. (CBI 40)

* He and John both married shortly before the war, variously in Canada and South Africa, and have three children between them. He must now be in the service, as Mrs. Morland says that all her sons are fighting somewhere. (MB 45)

* He is about forty-four years old. (ESR 55)

* Among them, the four boys have produced ten children. (NTL 56)

* He is nearer fifty than forty; all the brothers except Tony are usually away on foreign jobs. (TSAT 61)

Morland, Mr. Henry

* Late husband of **Laura Morland**. Characterized variously as good-looking, expensive, "a suet pudding," and "ineffectual and unlamented." Father of **Gerald, John, Dick,** and **Tony**, he died when the latter was a baby, leaving Mrs. Morland not much of anything. (HR 33)

* Characterized by **Old Mrs. Knox** as "*excessivement nul.*" (MB 45)

* He was an only child. (NTL 56)

Morland, John

* Second son of the late **Henry** and **Mrs. (Laura) Morland**. His elder brother is **Gerald**, and younger brothers are **Dick** and **Tony**. He is in the army in Burma. (HR 33)

* He is doing very well there. (TB 39)

* He and his regiment are still in Burma. (CBI 40)

* He and Gerald both married shortly before the war, variously in Canada and South Africa, and have three children between them. (MB 45)

* He now has a good job in oil. He put on weight while in Germany. Among them, the four boys have produced ten children. (NTL 56)

* All the brothers except Tony are usually away on foreign jobs. (TSAT 61)

Morland, Mrs. Laura

* Widow of **Henry Morland**, and mother of **Gerald, John, Dick,** and **Tony**. Left without resources after her hus-

band's death, she began to write the Madame Koska series of mysteries, which are published, generally yearly, by **Adrian Coates**. She raised her children on the income, and now only Tony is left (at least during school holidays) at High Rising with her and her faithful **Stoker**. Adrian proposes to her, but she refuses. (HR 33)

* She copes with Tony. Her maiden name also began with an M. (DH 34)

* She is in America. (SH 37)

* She attends **Mrs. (Lavinia) Brandon's** picnic and the Vicarage Fete at Pomfret Madrigal. She suggests that **Hilary Grant** write up his study of **le Capet** as a historical novel. (TB 39)

* When war breaks out, she goes to help the **Birketts** at Southbridge School while Adrian Coates and his family take her house. (CBI 40)

* She lectures to the convalescent soldiers at Beliers Priory, and is a big hit. (GU 43)

* She has three grandchildren she's never seen, and all her sons are fighting somewhere. (MB 45)

* She joins the Women's Section of the High Rising Branch of the Barsetshire Conservative Association. (PBO 46)

* She gets hate mail from **V. Lefter** and **E.G. Towel**. (LAR 48)

* Three of her sons are married. She never saw her own mother-in-law. (OBH 49)

* She has an Aunt Edith. She was almost brought to court for libel, but she apologized, perhaps to **the Dowager Lady Norton**. (CC 50)

* She corrected the Prime Minister in a misquotation at a public speech. (DD 51)

* She lectures for the Pomfret Madrigal Women's Institute. (HRt 52)

* Her boys are from about thirty-four to forty-four years old. (ESR 55)

* She was an only child, as was her husband. She has ten grandchildren whose ages she can't remember. Before the war, she wrote a biography under the pen name **Esme Porlock**, and a memoir about getting mixed up with an Anglo-Mixo-Lydian Association. **Lord Crosse** proposes to her, but she refuses. (NTL 56)

* She lends her house to **Mr.** and **Mrs. Choyce** for their honeymoon. (ADA 57)

From *Three Houses*

* She wants to start a pony club at High Rising, but drops the idea. (LAAA 59)

* The pony club actually gets off the ground. She spent her childhood in Kensington, and had an old uncle in Sussex

who was President of the Society for Correcting Translations. She was once almost proposed to by **Lord Stoke**, although perhaps Lord Crosse is meant here. Her three sons other than Tony are usually away on foreign jobs. She has Tony's son **Robin Morland** to visit over the holidays, and celebrates her seventieth birthday with a party at the **Adams'** Old Bank House, where she is given a retrospective Barsetshire album. (TSAT 61)

Morland, Robin

❖ Unnamed and unsexed first child of **Tony Morland**; at one year, taken by Tony to Mixo-Lydia on a job for the Tape and Sealing Wax Office. (LAR 48)

❖ They are now in London. (OBH 49)

❖ There are two children. (DD 51)

❖ There are "thousands of children." (HRt 52)

❖ There are three or four children, and the family is still in London. (WDIM 54)

❖ His mother and the four children are at the seaside. (NTL 56)

❖ The three younger children get measles. While they and their mother go to Littlehampton to recover, Tony sends the eldest, now finally named, to stay with his grandmother **Mrs. (Laura) Morland** during his school holidays. He is ten or eleven, and helps organize Mrs. Morland's seventieth birthday party. (TSAT 61)

Morland, Tony

❖ Fourth and youngest son of the late **Henry** and **Mrs. (Laura) Morland**. His elder brothers are **Gerald, John,** and **Dick**. His father died when he was a baby. He goes to the Southbridge School, where his best friend is **Robert Wesendonck**. He spends his holidays with his mother and **Stoker** at High Rising. (HR 33)

❖ Now thirteen years old, and generally causing trouble. (DH 34)

❖ He is in **Robin Dean's** form at Southbridge. (AF 36)

❖ He is a senior in **Everard Carter's** House, and a friend of **Eric Swan**, with whom he visits the **Keiths**. (SH 37)

❖ Seventeen and in his last year at Southbridge, he attends **Mrs. (Lavinia) Brandon's** picnic and the Pomfret Madrigal Vicarage Fete, where he wins a coconut. (TB 39)

❖ He leaves Southbridge for a Formership to Paul's College, Oxford, but he attends **Rose Birkett's** wedding reception in rather disreputable clothes. (CBI 40)

❖ Still at Oxford, but may be called up soon. (NR 41)

❖ After a muddle, he is now in the Field Artillery O.C.T.U. and about to go to Powderham in Middleshire. (MH 42)

❖ Now a second lieutenant in the Gunners, on leave. (GU 43)

❖ First in Holland, then sent to India and Burma. He was prefect and captain of boating at Southbridge. (MB 45)

❖ He is in Burma. He met **Ted Hopkinson** while on his cadet course in Middleshire, Wales. (PBO 46)

❖ Now demobilized, engaged, and working in the Red Tape and Sealing Wax Office (thanks to an interview with a former secretary of **George Knox**). (PE 47)

* Now married with a one-year-old baby, whom he takes to Mixo-Lydia on a job for the Red Tape and Sealing Wax Office. (LAR 48)

* He is now in London with his wife and the baby. (OBH 49)

* There are two children. (DD 51)

* There are "thousands of children." (HRt 52)

* There are three or four children, and the family is still in London. (WDIM 54)

* He is now about thirty-four years old. (ESR 55)

* He now works at the Ministry of General Interference, London. **George Halliday** knew him during the war, at Vache-en-Étable. His wife and four children are at the seaside; among them, he and his brothers have produced ten children. (NTL 56)

* The three younger children get measles. While they and their mother go to Littlehampton to recover, Tony sends the eldest, **Robin**, now ten or eleven, to stay with Mrs. Morland during his school holidays. He drives down to attend his mother's seventieth birthday party. (TSAT 61)

Morple, Bill

* Ticket clerk at Melicent Halt. His mother was a Margett, niece of **Mr. Patten**, the Worsted station master; his father was **Edward Morple**. He admires the Russians. (MH 42)

* He is now filling in at Winter Overcotes, where **Mr. Beedle** suspects him of pilfering. He plays the pools and is in with a bad crowd from London, who may have damaged

the station and stolen its prize cup. He is caught stealing by **Sergeant Hopkins**, but Mr. Beedle lets him go. Before he leaves for the Army, he returns the cup. (GU 43)

✤ He got in with a bad lot, and got seven years for robbing a post office with violence. (LAR 18)

✤ He had half-killed the postmaster during the crime. (OBH 49)

Morple, Edward

✤ "A foreigner" who married a Margett, niece of **Mr. Patten**, the Worsted station master; they produced **Bill Morple**. (MH 42)

Morris, Miss Ella

✤ Daughter of the **Rev. Justin Morris**. She loved his student **Mr. (Justin) Miller**, but took her father's side when they quarreled. Left nearly penniless after her father's death, she serves as companion to many old ladies, the last of whom is **Miss (Amelia) Brandon**. She has a breakdown after Miss Brandon's death, but is left ten thousand pounds, and comes into her own managing the Pomfret Madrigal Vicarage Fete. She reconciles with Mr. Miller, and they agree to marry. (TB 39)

✤ Now married, she is the Billeting Officer for Pomfret Madrigal. (CBI 40)

✤ She knows the country within bicycling radius inside-out. (PE 47)

✤ She is given a gold watch when she and her husband leave for his new post at St. Ewold's. (CC 50)

* They give a dinner party to celebrate their twelfth anniversary. (HRt 52)

Morris, the Rev. Justin
* A selfish and fanatically low-church clergyman, father of **Ella Morris**. His student is **Mr. (Justin) Miller**, until they quarrel over church doctrine and break off relations. His death left his daughter almost penniless. (TB 39)

Morton, Miss
* Youngest sister of **Old Mrs. Brandon**. She married Robert Grant of the Barsetshire Regiment, and their son was **Edward Grant**. (TB 39)

Moss, Private
* He and **Corporal Jackson** work for **Philip Winter** at the Hush-Hush camp. (GU 43)

Mothersill, Dr.
* A woman in the Cabinet, invited to preach a lay sermon in the college chapel by the **Master of Lazarus**. She gets **Dr. Morgan** a job in her Ministry of Nutritional Hygiene. (DD 51)

Mould, Mr. and Mrs. (and their foreman)
* Undertakers, carriers, and general removers, Edgewood. (OBH 49)

Mowbray, Miss ("Miss M.")
* Daughter of a doctor in the East Riding; first-class cook and general factotum to **Jessica Dean**, whom she worships. (CC 50)

Moxon, Mr.
* A curate whose chief aim is to promote good fellowship. He ran a boys' club in the East End, and now the Worsted

* He has a prophetic poem on the Coronation—but What Did It Mean? (WDIM 54)

Nannie: *See also* **Nana** and **Nanny** and **Nurse.**

Nannie
* Nurse to **Francis** and **Peggy Arbuthnot Brandon's** three children at Stories. Feuds with the Brandons' old nurse **Miss Vance**; gives notice, then takes it back, then gives it again to go and work for Young Lady Bond, the former **Daphne Stonor**. Miss Vance is left in triumph at Stories. (CC 50)

Nannie
* Nurse to **Robert** and **Agnes Graham's** children. Superior of the nursery maid **Ivy**. She quarrels with **Mrs. Siddon** about the children's breakfasts. (WS 34)

* Now also called **Nurse**. She is Chapel, and only comes to Church for discipline and disapproval. (PBO 46)

Nanny: *See also* **Nana** and **Nannie** and **Nurse.**

Nanny
* Nurse to the children of **Mr. (Frank)** and **Mrs. (Rachel) Dean**. She supervises **Jessica's** donkey rides, but can only scream when Jessica is thrown in front of the bull and saved by **Richard Tebben**. (AF 36)

* Now nurse to the children of **Noel** and **Lydia Keith Merton**. Middle-aged and uncompromising. She takes **Harry** when **Lavinia** gets measles, then when Lydia also gets them, lets **Nanny Twicker** have Harry. Finally she takes both children to the seaside with **Kate Keith** Carter and her family. (PE 47)

Nasone, Pietro

* Costar of **Glamora Tudor** in a **Czemschk Kpozcz** production about Cyrano de Bergerac; his pronounced Italian accent is explained by making Cyrano an Italian *condottiere*. (CQ 58)

Needham, Thomas ("Tommy")

* A young clergyman, secretary to **Dean Crawley**. He has two sisters, and his father, then known as "Mangle," went to college with **Mr. (Justin) Miller**. His uncle is **Thomas Oldmeadow**. He gets engaged to **Octavia Crawley**, and enlists as an army chaplain. (CBI 40)

* He is stationed in Reykjavik. (MH 42)

* He was sent to Africa to the Free French and was wounded. They amputated his left arm in Tunisia. His parents have been dead for ten years, and his only home is with his married sister. He boards with **Nannie Allen** until **Sir Harry Waring** gives him the living at Lambton. (GU 43)

* He and Octavia are recently married. (TH 44)

* They have a baby boy. He has a new artificial arm which he hates and gives up. (MB 45)

* As Vicar of Lambton, he opens the Red Cross Fete at Marling. Their two elder children are of nursery-school age. His arm was wounded by a shell splinter in the Libyan desert. (LAR 48)

* There are now four children. He takes the Rushwater Harvest Service for **Mr. Bostock**. (DD 51)

* Octavia is pregnant again. (HRt 52)

* Now it's his right arm that's gone! (ADA 57)

* She is expecting their seventh baby any minute, but it turns out to be twins (a boy and a girl), thus achieving her desired eight finally and in the nick of time. (TSAT 61)

Nice Not-Quite-So-Young Girl, the
* A colleague of **Susan Dean** at the Red Cross library. She plays tennis. (PE 47)

Nicholson Minor
* Friend of **Georgy Leslie** at Southbridge School. (TSAT 61)

Norris, the Honourable Mr.
* A student at Lazarus College scouted by **Simnet**, and a friend of **Colin Keith**. He is engaged to **the Honourable Eleanor Purvis**. (SH 37)

* They are now married. When he was in college, he nearly got entangled with a married lady at the Devorguilla Arms. (TH 44)

Norton, Eleanor, Lady
* Wife of **George, Lord Norton**, of Norton Park. The household is very miserly. (MH 42)

* She is jealous of Lady Pomfret, the former **Sally Wicklow**. (PE 47)

* Their dreadful daughter lives in sin and Chelsea with a Slavo-Lydian intellectual. (LAR 48)

* She will take over from Lady Pomfret as head of the Red Cross Hospital Libraries. (CC 50)

* They now have two dull girls, **Vicky** and **Ellie**, both in boarding school. (DD 51)

* They have a flat across the lightwell from **Miss (Juliana) Starter's** in London. According to **Lord Stoke**, they have no children (but *see* above) and the title dies with him. (NTL 56)

* She calls her mother-in-law "Moggs." (CQ 58)

Norton, Ellie
* One of the two dull daughters of **George, Lord Norton**, and **Eleanor, Lady Norton**; her sister is **Vicky**. Both are in boarding school. She had her tonsils and adenoids taken out by **Dr. Morgan**. (DD 51)

Norton, George, Lord
* Son of **Lord Norton** and **Victoria, the Dowager Lady Norton**, and husband of **Eleanor, Lady Norton**. He inherited the title, Norton Park, and perhaps the garden, on his father's death, but the household is very miserly. He is a cousin of **Geoffrey Harvey**, and also of **Oliver Marling**, with whom he was at school. (MH 42)

* He ploughed his field adjoining **Mr. (Fred) Belton's** for wheat, but got only weeds and stones. (TH 44)

* Their dreadful daughter lives in sin and Chelsea with a Slavo-Lydian intellectual. (LAR 48)

* He is chairman of several committees where with a good secretary he can't do any harm. They now have two dull girls, **Vicky** and **Ellie**, both in boarding school. (DD 51)

* Though his father is long dead, he is still known as Young Lord Norton. (WDIM 53)

* They have a flat across the lightwell from **Miss (Juliana) Starter's** in London. According to **Lord Stoke**, they have

no children (but *see* above) and the title dies with him. (NTL 56)

Norton, Lady: *See* usually, **Norton, Victoria, Lady.**

Norton, Lord

❖ An ex-governor, deceased husband of **Victoria, Lady Norton.** (WS 34)

❖ He has been dead for two years (but *see* above), and the title passed to a nephew. (TB 39)

❖ Now the title passed to his son, **George.** (MH 42)

❖ His was a Lloyd George peerage. (DD 51)

❖ Yet **Mr. (Fred) Belton** remembers that when he was a boy, Old Lord Norton bought broken glass from Mr. Belton's father for a six-mile wall around Norton Park. (CQ 58)

Norton, Vicky

❖ One of the two dull daughters of **George, Lord Norton,** and **Eleanor, Lady Norton;** her sister is **Ellie.** Both are in boarding school. She has a gold band on her front teeth. (DD 51)

Norton, Victoria, Lady

❖ "The Dreadful Dowager." Widow of an ex-governor, and gardening enthusiast. (WS 34)

❖ She was widowed two years ago (!), and a nephew inherited the title (but *see* below). She is a friend and hostess to **Mrs. (Felicia) Grant.** (TB 39)

❖ She now has a son, **George,** who inherited the title and is married to **Eleanor, Lady Norton.** She is a cousin of **Mr.**

(William) Marling. Her book, *Herbs of Grace*, is filled with "godwots" and misprints. (MH 42)

❖ Her latest book is *Along My Borders*. (PBO 46)

❖ She models her dress, hair, and hats on the Queen Mother. (PE 47)

❖ She has an Alpine rock garden. (LAR 48)

❖ Aged seventy and a former lady-in-waiting to Queen Alexandra. She covets **Miss (Hilda) Sowerby's** *Palafox borealis*. (OBH 49)

❖ Her daughter-in-law calls her "Moggs." She paid one hundred pounds to have *Herbs of Grace* published, and now wants to sue **Mrs. (Hermione) Rivers** for putting a character named "Lady Norton" in a book. (CC 50)

❖ She was snubbed by the exclusive dressmaker Padella (on Via Perduta and Via Abbandonata, Florence). She makes an offer on a house in the Close, Barchester, but is outdone by **Tubby Fewling**. (CQ 58)

❖ She visits from Cheltenham; the widowed **Lucasta, Lady Bond** stayed with her in her private hotel suite there. (TSAT 61)

Nurse: *See also* **Nana** and **Nanny** and **Nannie**.

Nurse
 ❖ To **Mr. (William)** and **Mrs. (Amabel) Marling**. She cares for their granddaughters **Diana** and **Clare Watson** when **Lettice** Marling **Watson** comes to visit. She has a proper sense of decorum with **Miss (Maud) Bunting**. Her brother Sid was made a sergeant. She was temporary nurse to **Lady Agnes Graham** one summer. (MH 42)

✤ She is great-niece of **Nannie Allen**. Sid is now a sergeant-major. (GU 43)

✤ Now nurse to Lettice's children with **Tom Barclay**, she revisits Marling Hall with the family. (CC 50)

Nurse
✤ To the children of **Lord** and **Lady Pomfret**, the former **Gillie Foster** and **Sally Wicklow**. She came to Pomfret Towers when **Ludovic, Lord Mellings**, was three weeks old. Her cousin's niece is **Jessie**, properly **Jessica**. (LAAA 59)

Nurse to Mrs. (Lavinia) Brandon's family: *See* **Vance, Miss**.

Nurse to the Honourable Mrs. Richard Carter's children: *See* **Hubback, Miss**.

Nutfield, Lord
✤ Father of **the Honourable Amabel Marling**. His niece is **Mrs. (Hermione) Rivers**. (MH 42)

✤ Some connection with **Mrs. (Lucy) Belton**. (DD 51)

✤ The Nutfield title is now extinct. (TSAT 61)

Nutfield, Mr., the Honourable
✤ Employed **Florrie Simnet** as cook-housekeeper before she married. (CC 50)

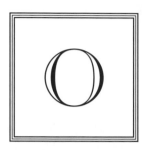

O'Brien, Mr.
 * Student at Coppin's when **Mr. (Gregory) Villars** was headmaster. He came to the school entertainments in a saffron kilt because his ancestors had been kings of Ireland. (NR 41)

Oldmeadow, Mr. Thomas
 * Brother of **Thomas Needham's** mother, now in the reserve of officers in Switzerland. When he was at Southbridge School under the **Birketts,** he had measles twice in one term, was the best footballer the school ever produced, and was captain of games in his last year. (CBI 40)

 * He played rugger for England. (GU 43)

 * He was a connection by marriage of the late **Captain Fred Arbuthnot**. (PE 47)

Omnium, Duke and Duchess of: *See* **Palliser**.

Organist of Saint Hall Friars, the

❖ A stationer with a half-wit brother. He spent three days at a Three Choir Festival and when he came back played too slowly and changed the music. He was blasted back into place by **Dr. Dale**, who also helped when his brother tried to throw himself out of a window and had to be taken to the County Asylum. (MB 45)

Oriel, Mr. Caleb

❖ Vicar of Harefield, seventy years old. His great-uncle was Bishop Oriel, who married Beatrice Gresham (*cf.* Trollope) and had fifteen children, whom he called "his fifteen little Christians." He is also related through the Greshams to the late **Edith, Lady Pomfret**. When a young clergyman, he lived with his mother and sister, then with his sister after their mother died; but the sister died too, just before the war. He has nieces. He directs the Fifth and Sixth Forms of the Hosiers' Girls' Foundation School in a performance of *As You Like It.* (TH 44)

❖ He had been incumbent of the Old Rectory, Greshamsbury, and fixed up the house with money his grandfather, an Anglo-Indian general, left to him. (JC 53)

❖ He went to Balliol, his father's old college. He says that his years are approaching the alloted span, though he actually attained it in 1944 (*see* above). He christens the baby of **Lord William Harcourt**, and is discreetly adored by his sister **Lady Gwendolen Harcourt**; when given a cutting of *Fibrositis vomitaria* by **Margot Phelps** Fewling, he gets engaged to Lady Gwendolen over their common hatred of it. (LAAA 59)

O'Seianmhe, Dhoidreagh

* Pen name of **Bert Hobson**, *q.v.* (WDIM 54)

Oswald, Uncle

* Uncle of **Mrs. (Helen) Keith**. Her grandfather married
  three times, and he was the eldest son of the first family. He
  was headmaster of a large mission school in Calcutta, and
  eventually became a bishop. He knew **Lady Sibyl Carter's**
  family in India, and gave her a yellow shawl. He died when
  Colin Keith was little. (SH 37)

Other Girl, the: *See* **Pollett, Norma.**

Other Niece, the

* Niece of **Mrs. (Poppy) Turner**. She and her sister **Betty**
  were taken in by Mrs. Turner when their parents died of
  influenza. She becomes engaged to **Lieutenant Greaves**.
  (NR 41)

* Now married, they live in an expensive flat with small
  rooms and a restaurant downstairs so she needn't cook. No
  children yet. (WDIM 54)

Otis, Mr. Amery P.

* Of Brookline, Massachusetts, U.S.A. He owns an imper-
  fect manuscript with descriptions of murals in Northum-
  berland by an unknown monk that seem similar to those in
  the church at Pomfret Madrigal, but won't let anyone see
  it. (TB 39)

Outhwaite

* Owner of the works at Newcastle where **Sam Adams** had
  special castings done. He had been chief engineer of the
  Ironsides, supply ship of the *Flatiron* and all the other Iron
  Class ships, under **Admiral Palliser**. (MB 45)

Packer, Ed: *See* **Pollett, Ed.**

Packer, Joe
- ✦ Stationmaster, Southbridge Station. (OBH 49)

Packer, Mr.
- ✦ Operator of a roundabout (carousel), Packer's Universal Royal Derby, which plays the tunes "Farewell My Bluebell" and "The Honeysuckle and the Bee." Sets up at the Vicarage Fete, Pomfret Madrigal. (TB 39)

- ✦ He sets up at the Marling Red Cross Fete, where the carpenter **Fred** does some repairs on the horses. The carousel now plays "Handhold in the Twilight." (LAR 48)

- ✦ Mr. Packer's father had owned and operated the carousel before him. Its tunes are always ten years behind the times: in **Mr. (William) Marling's** youth it played "Tommy Make Room for your Uncle" and "Ta-ra-ra-boom-de-ay," for **Bill Marling** the songs were "Tommy Atkins" and

"Sweet Marie," and for **Oliver** and **Lucy Marling** it
was "The Honeysuckle and the Bee." It now plays "Over
There." (CC 50)

❖ He is booked up for Coronation Day, at Northbridge for
the afternoon and at Southbridge for the evening. (WDIM
54)

❖ Though delinquents at Hogglestock damaged it, the carousel was repaired for the High Rising Agricultural, and
now plays "Love's Roundabout." (TSAT 61)

Packer, Mr.
❖ Runs the taxi service at Hallbury. His son is an apprentice
in **Sam Adams'** nuts-and-bolts shop. (MB 45)

Palfrey, Miss
❖ Maid to **Lilian Stonor** and friend to **Sarah Pucken**. She
comes from Foxling-in-Henfold, and her father is captain
of an oil tanker. (BL 39)

Palliser, Admiral
❖ A widower, Royal Navy (retired), of Hallbury House, Hallbury (which has been in the family since Commodore
Augustus Palliser did well in prize money under Lord
Howe). His younger daughter is **Jane Gresham**; his elder
daughter is married to a naval man in Sussex, with a young
family; and both his sons are in the Navy (their wives are an
Admiral's daughter and the granddaughter of the captain
of his father's first ship). He is now an engineer, treasurer
for Barsetshire, and serves on a board of directors in
Barchester. His mother ran Hallbury affairs during the
First World War. (MB 45)

Palliser, Lord Algernon
+ Youngest brother of **Plantagenet Palliser, Duke of Omnium**. An aged bachelor and flirt. (ESR 55)

Palliser, Lady Arabella
+ Daughter of **the Duke and Duchess of Omnium**, and sister of **Lady Glencora, Lady Griselda**, and **Lord Henry**, plus two nameless brothers. She married well, has a flourishing nursery, and does war work. (MB 45)

+ This version of the family comes to an end. (CC 50)

Palliser, Lady Cora: *See* Palliser, Lady Glencora.

Palliser, D. D'Algy
+ Youngest son of one of the **Dukes of Omnium**, he married **Mr. (William) Belton's** Aunt Lucy; they had no children, and both went down with the *Titanic*. (CC 50)

Palliser, the Honourable George
+ Uncle of **Lady Glencora Palliser**; a notable drunk. He was once governor of Mngangaland and knew **Bishop Joram**. (CC 50)

Palliser, Lord Gerald
+ Third child of the **Duke and Duchess of Omnium**; his siblings are **Jeffrey, Lord Silverbridge** and **Lady Glencora**. He died in the war, on D-Day. (CC 50)

+ He had been at Eton. (DD 51)

Palliser, Gerald
+ Eldest-child-to-be of the **Earl and Countess of Silverbridge**, **Jeff** and **Isabel Dale Palliser**, expected in November. To be named after his father's late brother. (DD 51)

* **Gerald**, future Duke of Omnium, is born. (HRt 52)

* He gets a brother. (JC 53)

* His mother is pregnant again. (ESR 55)

* A Palliser son, presumably Gerald, is six or seven years old. (LAAA 59)

Palliser, Lady Glencora

* Daughter of the **Duke and Duchess of Omnium**; her siblings are given as **Lady Griselda** and **Lord Henry**. She was taken for walks by **Miss (Maud) Bunting**. (MH 42)

* Now there are three brothers, all in the army, and an additional sister, **Lady Arabella**; like her, she married well, has a flourishing nursery, and does war work. (MB 45)

* The family changes completely. Glencora's elder brother is now **Jeffrey, Lord Silverbridge**, and her younger the late **Lord Gerald**. She is known as **Lady Cora**. Her uncle is **the Honourable George Palliser**. She drove generals during the war, and received the *Croix de Guerre*, but both her brother Gerald and her boyfriend **Froggy** were killed. She is now thirty, running Hiram's Trust, and doing amateur theatricals with several Palliser cousins and with **Francis** and **Peggy Arbuthnot Brandon**. (CC 50)

* She gets **Sir Cecil Waring** to rent the Lodge to her brother Jeffrey and his wife, the former **Isabel Dale**. She gives advice to **Tom Grantly**, and rebuffs him gently. She drives Cecil to the hospital, and they get engaged. (DD 51)

* They are married, and she has a baby (**"the future Bart"**) a little early. (HRt 52)

* The future Bart is now named Plantagenet Cecil, or "P.C." (WDIM 54)

* She is pregnant again. (ESR 55)

* They have more than two children. (CQ 58)

Palliser, Lady Griselda
* Daughter of the **Duke and Duchess of Omnium**; her siblings are **Lady Glencora** and **Lord Henry**. Their governess is **Miss (Maud) Bunting**. She ran after **Lord Humberton or Harberton**, who married **Phoebe Rivers**, but now her own marriage is impending. (MH 42)

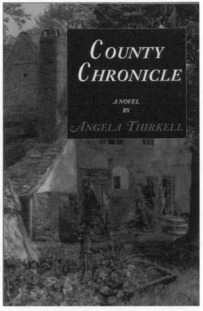

* Now there are three brothers, all in the army, and an additional sister, **Lady Arabella**. (MB 45)

* This version of the family comes to an end. (CC 50)

Palliser, Lord Henry
* Son of the **Duke and Duchess of Omnium**; his siblings are **Lady Griselda** and **Lady Glencora**. He gave **Miss (Maud) Bunting** a pipkin with a snail on it for her butter ration. (MH 42)

* Now there are two additional brothers and an additional sister, **Lady Arabella**; like his brothers, he is in the army. (MB 45)

* This version of the family comes to an end. (CC 50)

Palliser, Jeffrey

* Presumably a brother of **Plantagenet Palliser, Duke of Omnium**. He has the reversion of the dukedom after his nephew, **Jeffrey, Lord Silverbridge**. (CC 50)

Palliser, Jeffrey, Lord (the Earl of) Silverbridge

* Eldest child of **Plantagenet Palliser, the Duke of Omnium** and his **Duchess, Louise**; his siblings are **Lady Glencora** and the late **Lord Gerald**. He either is or wants to be the Conservative Member of Parliament for Barchester. He works for **Johns** the publisher. He was in the Barsetshire Yeomanry during the war, in the same regiment as **Isabel Dale's** fiancé **John**. He is writing a regimental history on which Isabel collaborates, and they become engaged. (CC 50)

* Now married. They rent the Lodge at Silverbridge from **Cecil Waring**. She expects a baby in November, to be named **Gerald Palliser** after his brother. He was at Eton, and served in Italy during the war. He is selected as the Conservative candidate for Barchester. (DD 51)

* He narrowly loses the election, thanks to **the Reverend (by courtesy) Enoch Arden. Gerald**, future Duke of Omnium, is born. (HRt 52)

* They have another boy. (JC 53)

* She is pregnant again. (ESR 55)

Palliser, Louise, Duchess of Omnium and Gatherum

* No first name given. Her home is Gatherum Castle, and her husband the nameless **Duke of Omnium**; their children in this version include **Lady Glencora, Lady**

Griselda, and **Lord Henry**, all under the care of **Miss (Maud) Bunting**, with whom she agreed about **Lord Humberton or Harberton**. (MH 42)

❖ Now there are two additional sons (all three in the Army) and an additional daughter, **Lady Arabella**. There are several grandsons. They can still afford to live at Gatherum. (MB 45)

❖ The family changes completely. Her three children are now **Jeffrey, Lord Silverbridge**, Lady Glencora, and the late **Lord Gerald**. The family lives in the former servants' quarters of Gatherum, while the Ministry for General Interference has its offices in the rest. She has a Grade A dairy herd, rents her gardens to a veg. service, and belongs to the Cathedral embroidery guild. (CC 50)

❖ They have a place in Fife. Their yacht *Planty Pal* was sunk while on war work. She employed a nurserymaid, Hattie, who got pregnant and had to be sent away. (DD 51)

❖ Her name is finally given; she was godchild of a royal Princess Louise. (HRt 52)

Palliser, Lady Mary

❖ Possibly the present **Duke of Omnium's** Aunt Mary, who did watercolors and had sciatica. **Lily** was her lady's maid. (CC 50)

Palliser, Plantagenet, Duke of Omnium and Gatherum

❖ No first name given. His home is Gatherum Castle, his wife the nameless **Duchess of Omnium**, and in this version their children include **Lady Glencora, Lady Griselda**, and **Lord Henry**, all under the care of **Miss (Maud)**

Bunting. He presents Matchings to the National Trust. (MH 42)

❖ Now there are two additional sons (all three in the army) and an additional daughter, **Lady Arabella**. There are several grandsons. They can still afford to live at Gatherum. Miss Bunting had to keep Lord Henry and the Ladies Griselda and Glencora out of the Duke's way after the Derby when his horse Planty Pal was unplaced. (MB 45)

❖ The family changes completely. He is named, and said to be a grandson (less consistently, a great-grandson) of his Trollopean namesake. His three children are **Jeffrey, Lord Silverbridge**, Lady Glencora, and the late **Lord Gerald**. He has (presumably) a brother, **Jeffrey Palliser**, who has the reversion of the dukedom after his son Jeff. Matching Priory was sold to a school, he leases his Scotch property for the shooting, and the Horns was requisitioned and now is a County Mental Hospital. The National Trust wouldn't take Gatherum because he couldn't make over enough money for its upkeep, but the Ministry of General Interference took it for offices, while the family lives in the servants' quarters. He gives his 1668 edition of **Thomas Bohun** to **Oliver Marling**. (CC 50)

❖ He served in France from 1915 to 1917. They have a place in Fife, and are related to the Lord of the Isles via the former Lady Glencora Macluskie (*cf.* Trollope). Their yacht *Planty Pal* was sunk while on war work. (DD 51)

❖ His youngest brother is **Lord Algernon Palliser**. (ESR 55)

Palmer
* Parlormaid to the **Keiths,** Northbridge Manor. (SH 37)
* She resents sewing parties in her drawing room. (CBI 40)
* When **Noel** and **Lydia Keith Merton** buy the manor from **Robert Keith**, she presumably stays with it. (TH 44)
* She packs for guests, whether they like it or not. (PE 47)
* She is still contemptuous of visitors. (WDIM 54)

Palmer, Mr. Fred
* Justice of the peace and dairy farmer, of the Manor House, Worsted. Husband of **Mrs. (Louise) Palmer**, and older brother of **Mrs. (Rachel) Dean**. He and his wife are childless, and their heir is **Laurence Dean**. (AF 36)
* They dine at eight, war or no war. (GU 43)
* His ancestor was **Horatio Palmer, Gent.** (MB 45)
* They use their tithe barn for the Worsted Coronation pageant. (WDIM 54)

Palmer, Horatio, Gent.
* Ancestor of **Mr. (Fred) Palmer**. He founded the Barsetshire Archaeological Society in 1759, and believed that whatever he found was Roman. (MB 45)

Palmer, Mrs. Louise
* Of the Manor House, Worsted. Wife of **Mr. (Fred) Palmer**. They are childless, and their heir is **Laurence Dean**. She produces amateur theatricals in their barn. The current production is *Hippolytus*, in which she leads the chorus and berates **Margaret Tebben** until she gives up her role, but is later forgiven. (AF 36)

* She is putting on *Twelfth Night*. (BL 39)

* They dine at eight, war or no war. (GU 43)

* They use their tithe barn for the Worsted Coronation pageant. (WDIM 54)

Panter, Cissie
* Daughter of **Mr. Panter** the carter and **Mrs. Panter** (née Hubback), so presumably a sister of **Odeena, Fred**, and (perhaps) **Jimmy**. She is a niece of **Mr. Geo. Panter** of the Mellings Arms. Her mother's sister **Miss Hubback** is nurse for **the Honourable Mrs. Richard Carter**, who is also keeping an eye on her as a possible servant. (NTL 56)

Panter, Fred
* Son of **Mr. Panter** (the one-armed carter) and **Mrs. Panter** (née Hubback); his (younger?) brother is **Jimmy**. He sends his proxy to vote Labour, but his mother votes him Conservative. (PBO 46)

Panter, Mr. Fred: *See* Panter, Mr.

Panter, Mr. Geo.
* Landlord of the Mellings Arms, Hatch End. Cousin of **Mr. Panter** the carter and also of **Mrs. Hubback** of The Shop. (PBO 46)

* His premises are a sort of clearing house for poachers, by special arrangement with the local constable, whose wife is his wife's cousin. (ESR 55)

* His mother is **Old Mrs. Panter**, and his niece is **Cissie Panter**. (NTL 56)

Panter, George: *See* Panter, Mr.

Panter, Jimmy

❖ Son of **Mr. Panter** (the one-armed carter) and **Mrs. Panter** (née Hubback); his (elder?) brother is **Fred**. He is very bad and ruined his bicycle. (PBO 46)

❖ Now he is the grandson of the one-armed carter, and his mother (not his grandmother the carter's wife) was a Hubback. His father was killed in World War II and he's now up for a scholarship. (ESR 55)

Panter, Mr.

❖ Carter to **Mr. (Leonard) Halliday** of Hatch House; husband of **Mrs. Panter**. They live in No. 6, Clarence Cottages, Hatch End. No first name yet. Their sons are **Fred** and **Jimmy**, and his cousin is **Mr. Geo. Panter**. He lost an arm at Ypres but still handles horses well. (PBO 46)

❖ He is called **George** but more consistently **Fred**, and Jimmy is now his grandson. He and his wife courted at the Barchester Odeon, so they named their daughter **Odeena**. (ESR 55)

❖ They have another daughter, **Cissie**. (NTL 56)

❖ They have (vaguely) other boys and girls beyond Odeena. (ADA 57)

❖ He is now carter for **George Halliday**. (TSAT 61)

Panter, Mrs.

❖ Daughter of **Mrs. Hubback** of The Shop, and wife of **Mr. Panter**. They live in No. 6, Clarence Cottages, Hatch End. Their sons are **Fred** and **Jimmy**. Fred sends his proxy to vote Labour, but she votes him Conservative. (PBO 46)

P

* Her husband is called **George** but more consistently **Fred**, and Jimmy is now her grandson; though like her, his mother (her daughter-in-law) was a Hubback. She takes in laundry. She and her husband courted at the Barchester Odeon, so they named their daughter **Odeena**. (ESR 55)

* They have another daughter, **Cissie**. She is a cousin of **Albert** at Rising Castle, and thus also of his sisters, Mr. Knox's **Annie** and **Flo**. She has a much younger sister (presumably a **Miss Hubback**) who is Nurse to **the Honourable Mrs. Richard Carter**. (NTL 56)

* They have (vaguely) other boys and girls beyond Odeena. (ADA 57)

Panter, Odeena
* Daughter of **Mr. Panter** the carter (**George**, or later **Fred**) and his wife **Mrs. Panter**; they courted at the Barchester Odeon, which is where they got her first name. Presumably her brothers are **Fred** and **Jimmy**. She works as kitchen-maid to the **Grahams**, Holdings, and is walking out with **Harry Hubback**. (ESR 55)

* She is the niece of Mr. Knox's cook (presumably **Annie**), and is as bad a parlormaid as her aunt is a cook. She has another sister, **Cissie**. (NTL 56)

Panter, Old Mrs.
* Mother of **Mr. Geo. Panter** of the Mellings Arms. She has a hook nose and a grey beard. (NTL 56)

* Still alive, and a gormed old nuisance she is. (ADA 57)

Parfitt
* Butler at Holdings, home of the **Grahams**. (MH 42)

Pardon, Mr. and Mrs.

❖ Servants to **Mr. (William) and Mrs. (Amabel) Marling**; he is a gardener, and she is a coachman's daughter. (CC 50)

Parkinson, Connie

❖ One of the two skinny children of **Teddy** and **Mavis Welk Parkinson**. The other is **Harold**. She is named for her father's hard-working mother. (CC 50)

❖ They get a new young brother, **Josiah**. (HRt 52)

Parkinson, Harold Winston

❖ One of the two skinny children of **Teddy** and **Mavis Welk Parkinson**. The other is **Connie**. He is named for his mother's father, **Mr. (Harold) Welk**. (CC 50)

❖ His parents met at the Young Conservatives, thus his middle name. They get a new young brother, **Josiah**. (HRt 52)

Parkinson, Josiah Welk

❖ Third child of **Teddy** and **Mavis Welk Parkinson**. His siblings are **Harold** and **Connie**. Born rather suddenly, he is named for his godfather, **Dean Crawley**. (HRt 52)

❖ He is known as Joey or Joe. (CQ 58)

❖ He is mistakenly called their first child. He is now at a local grammar school, on the Dean's presentation. (LAAA 59)

Parkinson, Miss

❖ As yet a nameless colonel's daughter from Leamington. In January she married **Mr. Tompion**, Vicar of Little Misfit. (TB 39)

❖ She is named. (CBI 40)

Parkinson, (Mrs.) Mavis: *See* **Welk, Mavis**.

Parkinson, Theodore ("Teddy")

❖ Theological student with a hard-working mother and state scholarships. He is coached by **Colonel Crofts**, but still mispronounces "Onesiphorus." He is engaged to **Mavis Welk**. (PE 47)

❖ Now married, with two skinny children, **Harold**, after her father, and **Connie**, after his mother. He is very low church, but is appointed vicar of Pomfret Madrigal to replace **Mr. (Justin) Miller**. (CC 50)

❖ His father had been a bookseller in a small way, but they had to sell up when he died. He and his wife met at a Young Conservatives meeting (their son's full name is Harold Winston). He had pneumonia shortly after he took up his new office. He and his wife, though poor, are well-respected; he keeps Evensong high to accommodate **Mrs. (Lavinia) Brandon**, and reads dictionaries to better his pronunciation. They have their third child quite suddenly, and name him **Josiah Welk**, as **Dean Crawley** will be his godfather. (HRt 52)

❖ He is getting the church three-quarters full on Sundays. (ADA 57)

❖ He is now vicar of Greshamsbury New Town, and doing well, though they are still poor. **Mary Preston** Leslie gives her a winning lottery ticket for a new washing machine. (CQ 58)

❖ Back when he was a bachelor, it was due to Dean and **Mrs. Crawley's** influence that he didn't take a position in the ultra-high church in Hallbury New Town. (LAAA 59)

❖ They are now in a comfortable new house. (TSAT 61)

Parradine, Miss Pinkie
  ❖ Dance teacher at Barchester High School. She has an extensive and peculiar wardrobe. (HRt 52)

Parry, Mr.
  ❖ City Librarian of the Barchester Central Public Library. (HRt 52)

Parson, Pippa
  ❖ A new film star whose Veronica Lake hairstyle is copied by **Marigold Smith**. (DD 51)

Parting, Cyril ("Baby")
  ❖ One of the three children in **Miss Feilding's** nursery school left with **Mrs. (Lavinia) Brandon** at Stories. Three years old. He leaves with the others for Suffolk. (PE 47)

Passmore, Colonel H.W.
  ❖ Of the Barsetshire Regiment. He served with them from 1914 to 1918, then became a solicitor, and, when World War II was declared, he re-enlisted through territorial enthusiasm. His office staff is billeted on **Mr. (Gregory)** and **Mrs. (Verena) Villars**. He has grandchildren, and pesters his junior partner by advising him on cases he had been handling. He gets the flu. (NR 41)

Patten, Mr.
  ❖ Stationmaster at Worsted; his nephew is **Ed Pollett**. His old mother dies and is the first to be buried (by **Mr. Phipps**) in the new cemetery. (AF 36)

  ❖ His grandfather is **Old Patten**. (BL 39)

* His niece was a Margett, and her son is **Bill Morple**, the Russia-loving ticket clerk at Melicent Halt. (MH 42)

* He is mistakenly called **Mr. Pollett**. He fills in at Lambton when **Ernie Pollett** goes on leave. (GU 43)

* He retires, and is replaced by **Bert Margett**. (LAR 48)

Patten, Old
* Grandfather of **Mr. Patten**. He has a folk song, in competition with **Old Margett**. (BL 39)

Patten, Percy
* Second gardener to **Mr. (Fred)** and **Mrs. (Louise) Palmer**. He boards with **Mrs. Phipps**. He plays the henchman in Mrs. Palmer's production of *Hippolytus*. (AF 36)

Pattern and Son
* Builders and estate agents, Hallbury. They have Ideas. Old Mr. Pattern is dead, and Young Mr. Pattern married above him into a bank manager's family. (MB 45)

Patterne, Rear-Admiral Sir Crossjay
* What he said about the naval program. (DD 51)

Pavois, Zizi
* Acted in the film *Descente de lit*. (TP 39)

Paxon, Mr.
* Husband of **Mrs. ("Minnie") Paxon**; a bank manager in Barchester. He and she get the flu. (NR 41)

* He is a Mason, and soon to retire. (WDIM 54)

Paxon, Mrs. "Minnie"
* Wife of **Mr. Paxon**. With regard to the war effort, she is the feminine of *largo al factotum* for Northbridge; wears a

uniform and rides a bicycle. She puts up two aunts and various evacuees. She and her husband get flu and she stays with the **Talbots** to be nursed. She got her nickname by playing Minnehaha in the South Wembley Amateur Choral Society's production of *Hiawatha*. (NR 41)

❖ She is on Civil Defense, Friends of Barchester General Hospital, and the Joint Coronation Committee, Northbridge. In the Coronation pageant, she brings down the house with her portrayal of a hysteria case (to "the Ride of the Valkyries"). (WDIM 54)

❖ She will help the **Parkinsons** with their Christmas pageant at Greshamsbury. (CQ 58)

Paxton, Ivy
❖ A schoolmate of **Miss (Cicely) Holly** and **Mrs. (Molly) Watson** at Fairlawns School. She died, and it was such a shock to her mother. (MB 45)

Pecker, Mr., and His Daughter
❖ Members of the London circle of **Mr. and Mrs. Bissell**. He works in the Free Library; his daughter taught music and folk dancing at LCC evening classes. (CBI 40)

Pedro
❖ A hairdresser in Las Palombas. He missed **Rose Birkett** Fairweather's appointment because he was watching a naval battle. (CBI 40)

Peel, Florence
❖ Principal girl of the South Wembley Amateur Dramatic Society, in which **Mrs. ("Minnie") Paxon** also featured. Played Rosalind in *As You Like It*, and Helena in *All's Well*

that Ends Well. She married, and her only son was **Mr. (Henry Peel) Highmore**. (WDIM 54)

Pemberton, Miss Ianthe

❖ Of Punshions, Northbridge. Secretary of the *Journal of the English Word-Lovers' Association* and author of a biography of Elizabeth Rivers, Edward IV's queen, she is currently writing on the painter **Giacopone Giacopini**, and gives a talk on him to the Barchester Choristers' Parents' Club. She also writes a wartime cookbook for **Adrian Coates'** firm. She is landlady and Egeria to **Mr. (Harold) Downing**, and collaborates with him on a *Biographical Dictionary of Provence*; she allows him into the orbit of **Mrs. (Poppy) Turner**, but eventually he returns to her and to his work. (NR 41)

❖ She and Mr. Downing are invited to Lille by **M. Bontemps**, to celebrate their completion and publication of the *Féau-Filhz* volume of the *Biographical Dictionary*. They also attend the Conservative Do at Gatherum. (CC 50)

❖ She is on the Northbridge Coronation Committee, in charge of historical episodes for the pageant. The *Dictionary* is now up to the *Mas-Moult* volume. She is ill, and gives Mr. Downing over to Mrs. Turner while **Nurse Heath** comes to look after her. (WDIM 54)

❖ After being ill and practically bed-ridden for some time (though still sensible), she died. Nurse Heath and **Nurse Ward** take over Punshions. (NTL 56)

❖ She left her cookbook royalties (almost twelve pounds per year) to Mr. Downing. (ADA 57)

Pendry

❖ Odd-job man for the **Duke of Omnium** at Gatherum Castle. He used to run along the kitchen passage and suddenly fall flat on his back to amuse the children. (LAAA 59)

Peppercorn

❖ A boy at **Everard Carter's** House, Southbridge School. He has a rash, not measles. (GU 43)

Perfect, Miss

❖ Secretary at **Mr. (Frank) Dean's** office who takes care of the Health Insurance. (OBH 49)

Perry

❖ Butcher at Northbridge. (NR 41)

Perry, Dr.

❖ Physician, of Plassey House. Husband of **Mrs. (Maud) Perry** and father of **Robert, Jim**, and **Gus**. His father was a doctor, and so are all of his sons. (TH 44)

❖ His son Gus is now general practitioner in his practice, and he is thinking of retiring. (LAAA 59)

Perry, Gus (Augustus)

❖ Son of **Dr.** and **Mrs. (Maud) Perry**; his elder brother is **Robert**, and his twin is **Jim**. All three brothers are in medical careers, and all wanted to enlist when war broke out, but they submitted to authority. He is currently doing a course on leprosy. (TH 44)

❖ Now a dermatologist, and married to a doctor's daughter. (LAR 48)

* His proper name is given, but he is listed as the third son, and unmarried. He is a general practitioner in his father's practice, which he will go on with when his father retires. (LAAA 59)

Perry, Jim

* Son of **Dr.** and **Mrs. (Maud) Perry**; his elder brother is **Robert**, and his twin is **Gus**. All three brothers are in medical careers, and all wanted to enlist when war broke out, but they submitted to authority. He wins a medal in anatomy. (TH 44)

* Now a surgeon, and married to a doctor's daughter. (LAR 48)

* Now called the second son, he is head surgeon at Knight's. (LAAA 59)

Perry, Joyce: *See* **Smith, Mrs. Joyce Perry**.

Perry, Mrs. Maud

* Of Plassey House. Wife of **Dr. Perry** and mother of **Robert, Jim**, and **Gus**. She is given to causes, most prominently the Mixo-Lydians. Her sister-in-law is staying with them. (TH 44)

* She recommends **Gradka (Bonescu)** to the Fieldings. (MB 45)

Perry, Robert ("Bob")

* Eldest son of **Dr.** and **Mrs. (Maud) Perry**; his juniors (by fifteen months) are the twins, **Jim** and **Gus**. All three brothers are in medical careers, and all wanted to enlist when war broke out, but they submitted to authority. He is house physician at Knight's. (TH 44)

* He is engaged to a doctor's daughter; his father-in-law will be the well-known medical consultant **Sir Featherly Hargreaves**. (LAR 48)

* Now a consultant in Harley Street; his fiancée is **the Honourable Clara**. (DD 51)

* She is now Mrs. Bob, her last name turns out to be **Bronson-Hewbury** rather than Hargreaves, and she is alienating him from his family. He is still nice, however, and was a consultant in **Eric Swan's** case during the war. (HRt 52)

* He is one of the highest-paid consultants in Harley Street. (LAAA 59)

Peter
* A guest at **Pomfret** Towers. **The Screaming Girl (Miss Faraday-Home)** squirts him and **Micky** in the bath with the puff-billiards puffers, and has a bet with him (or Micky) about the chances for Monday; they all use the letters from a game for a paper chase. (PT 38)

Peter
* A flight lieutenant whose mother was on the stage. He gets engaged to **Elsie Merivale**. (MB 45)

Peters
* Butler at Pomfret Towers. (PT 38)

* His sister is **Nannie Peters**. (OBH 49)

* Now fifty-seven, he is butler to **Lord Crosse**. (ESR 55)

* He was in the Home Guard during the war, worked in **George, Lord Norton's** London flat for two months, then came to Lord Crosse and married a local woman, who also

works at Crosse Hall. He is breaking in a new pantry boy, known as **the Boy**. (NTL 56)

* He got a new lease on life when Mrs. **John-Arthur Crosse**, the former **Grace Crawley**, came to Crosse Hall. (TSAT 61)

Peters, Nannie

* Sister of **Peters** the former butler at Pomfret Towers, where she is now nannie to **Ludovic, Emily**, and **Giles Foster**, the children of **Lord** and **Lady Pomfret**. Her aunt by marriage, now dead, was the mother of **Jasper Margett** the gypsy horse-coper. (OBH 49)

* She is now nannie to **Roddy** and **Alice Barton Wicklow's** family. (WDIM 54)

* She is back at Pomfret Towers, riding herd on Giles and Emily. (LAAA 59)

* Still at the Towers; Ludovic and **Lavinia Merton** secure her as housekeeper (and future nannie) for themselves after their marriage. (TSAT 61)

Pettinger, Miss Bertha ("Beast Pettinger")

* Headmistress of the Barchester High School. **Lydia Keith** and **Delia Brandon** are fellow sufferers/alumnae. (TB 39)

* A.k.a. the Old Kit Bag. She refused swimming colors to **Amber Dandridge** because she cheeked **Miss Moore** in the bookroom. She goes to tea at **Mr. (Henry)** and **Mrs. (Helen) Keith's**. (SH 37)

* She (overbearingly) houses the Hosiers' Girls' Foundation School, and goes to **Rose Birkett's** wedding. (CBI 40)

* She is bosom friends with **the Bishop's wife**. (GU 43)

* **Miss (Madeleine) Sparling**, Headmistress of the Hosiers' Girls' School, was her unwilling guest for two years, so she tries to push herself into the Bobbin Day festivities, to which she wears the same Robin Hood hat as **Dr. Morgan**. She is a past President of the Headmistresses' Association. (TH 44)

* She got an O.B.E. (MB 45)

* At the urging of her Governors, she tries to arrange a student exchange with the Hosiers' Girls' School, but Dr. Sparling refuses, as it would set her whole school back a year. (PE 47)

* She went to school with **Miss Hopgood's Aunt (Helen)**; good at math, she went to college on a scholarship. (WDIM 54)

Phelps, Admiral ("Irons")

* Rear-admiral, Royal Navy; retired two years ago. Husband of **Mrs. Phelps** and father of **Margot**. He was captain of the *Andiron*, and was with the *Gridiron* on her trials. Wounded at Jutland, and now they are badly off. They renamed The Hollies Jutland Cottage when they moved in. He is small and industrious, on every committee and service. (CBI 40)

* He was commander of the *Scrapiron* when **Tubby Fewling** was assigned to her. (NR 41)

* He commanded the Home Guard during the war, and is a churchwarden at Southbridge. (PE 47)

* He has always served with destroyers in the Iron class since he was lieutenant in the *Flatiron*, so is known in the family

as "Irons". He has bronchitis, and they only have his
pension to live on. They had a boy who died before Margot
was born, and are now about to have their golden wedding
anniversary. (JC 53)

❖ When Margot marries **Mr. (Donald) MacFadyen**, they
will have a petty officer's widow come in as cook and
housekeeper. (WDIM 54)

❖ They are doing well on their own with a char to help out,
but Mrs. Phelps dies suddenly. He goes to visit Tubby
Fewling until Margot can get a house, but goes gently
loony and then dies. (CQ 58)

Phelps, Margot
❖ Daughter of **Admiral** and **Mrs. Phelps**. They renamed
The Hollies Jutland Cottage when they moved in. Like her
mother, she is bouncing, masterful, and wears trousers,
though she is not yet so fat. She is nearly thirty and keeps
goats. (CBI 40)

❖ She is just forty and overworked, what with her ailing
parents, the house, the garden, and keeping goats and hens.
The Friends of the Phelpses (mainly **Rose Birkett** Fairweather, **Tubby Fewling**, and **Mr. Wickham**) organize to
help and to distract her. She writes a book on her gardening
and animal husbandry, which will be published by **Johns**
and Fairfield. Tubby Fewling falls in love with her, Wickham proposes, and she accepts **Mr. (Donald) MacFadyen**.
(JC 53)

❖ They are not yet married. (WDIM 54)

❖ Married; he was able to get away for their honeymoon.
(ESR 55)

❖ She and her husband traveled extensively. Now he falls ill and dies. She is getting on for fifty. Her mother dies suddenly, then her father. She gets engaged to Tubby Fewling. (CQ 58)

❖ They are married. (LAAA 59)

Phelps, Mrs.
❖ Wife of **Admiral Phelps** and mother of **Margot**. They renamed The Hollies Jutland Cottage when they moved in. They are badly off. She is big, bouncing, wears trousers, and heads the A.R.P. and the village Red Cross. (CBI 40)

❖ She has a heart condition, and they only have his pension to live on. They had a boy who died before Margot was born, and are now about to have their golden wedding anniversary. Her elder sister Poppy died in India when Margot was three. (JC 53)

❖ When Margot marries **Mr. (Donald) MacFadyen**, they will have a petty-officer's widow come in as cook and housekeeper. (WDIM 54)

❖ They are doing well on their own with a char to help out, but she dies suddenly, and her husband soon thereafter. (CQ 58)

Philpott, Eve
❖ A woman in the WAAFs with **Sylvia Halliday**; Sylvia and **Rose Bingham** despise her. (PBO 46)

Phipps, Doris
❖ Daughter of **Mr. and Mrs. Phipps**, sister of **Ernie**. She works as kitchenmaid for the **Deans**, and plays Aphrodite

in **Mrs. (Louise) Palmer's** production of *Hippolytus*. She is walking out with **Bert Margett**. (AF 36)

* She and **Lily-Annie Pollett** work as porters at the Winter Overcotes station. Her uncle is **Ernie Pollett**. She has been walking out with Bert for six years. (GU 43)

* She is now married, has children, and works at an airplane factory. (LAR 48)

Phipps, Ernie
* Son of **Mr. and Mrs. Phipps**, brother of **Doris**. (AF 36)

Phipps, Marlene
* Along with **Sabrina Pollett**, successor to **Doris Phipps** and **Lily-Annie Pollett** as porters at Winter Overcotes station. (TSAT 61)

Phipps, Miss
* Postmistress who runs the shop at Skeynes. She takes a broad view of post office regulations, and so can remove posted letters for **Daphne Stonor** and for **Mrs. (Catherine) Middleton**. (BL 39)

Phipps, Mr.
* Husband of **Mrs. Phipps**, father of **Doris** and **Ernie**. Gardener and sexton. (AF 36)

Phipps, Mrs.
* Wife of **Mr. Phipps**, mother of **Doris** and **Ernie**. She is daily help for the **Tebbens**, though she is often snatched away from them by **Mrs. (Louise) Palmer**, for whom she does the costumes for *Hippolytus*. She is second cousin to **Bert Margett**. (AF 36)

❖ She chars for the **Warings** and brings the kitten Winston to **Matron (of the Barchester Infirmary)** at the convalescent home, Beliers Priory. (GU 43)

❖ She made the flan for **Lady Glencora (Palliser)** Waring's dinner party. (HRt 52)

Phipps, Palmyra

❖ Omniscient operator of the Worsted telephone exchange. Niece of **Mrs. Phipps**, she was named after **Mrs. (Louise) Palmer**. (AF 36)

❖ Her sister was second housemaid at **Everard Carter's** house, Southbridge School, and now has triplets. (GU 43)

❖ She is just back from a holiday. (HRt 52)

❖ She has been promoted to be a kind of Queen Telephonist, but she still does favors for old friends. (CQ 58)

❖ The **Other Girl** who relieves her is **Norma Pollett**. (TSAT 61)

Pickaback, Buck

❖ Scion of an old Pennsylvania Dutch family, co-starring in *Pearl of Paris* with **Glamora Tudor**. (ADA 57)

Pickering

❖ Friend of **Addison** and **Young Dean** at Beliers Priory School. He keeps skinning his knees. (LAR 48)

❖ In his last term, and to go on to Southbridge School. (DD 51)

Pickthorn, Miss

❖ Secretary to **Sam Adams** at Hogglestock Rolling Mills. Previously worked on the teleprinter at the Regional Commissioner's Office, Barchester. (LAR 48)

❖ She helps with the garden party at the Old Bank House. Her mother is ill. (OBH 49)

❖ Her sister worked with **Isabel Dale** in the Red Cross during the war. (CC 50)

❖ She goes to the Adams' house after their baby **Amabel Rose** is born. (DD 51)

❖ She is secretary-in-chief, with **Sylvia Gould** as her counterpart at the **Pomfret** Towers offices. (TSAT 61)

Picton, Dr.
❖ Of Tunbridge Wells; recommends Ita-Lot starch-free bread to **Miss (Juliana) Starter**. (BL 39)

Pictor Ignotus
❖ Primitive painter (1409–1451?) of a celebrated picture bought by **Woolcott Jefferson van Dryven** from the **Duke of Towers'** collection. (LAAA 59)

Pie, Mr. Omicron
❖ Brilliant young orthopedic surgeon who worked on **Robin Dale**. His grandfather is **Sir Omicron Pie**. (MB 45)

Pie, Sir Omicron
❖ Well-known consultant physician, often called in by Barchester doctors. His grandson is **Mr. Omicron Pie**. (MB 45)

❖ He was brought in on **Tommy Needham's** case. (LAR 48)

Pilbeam (or Pilman), Mr.
❖ Oculist to **Oliver Marling**, currently in the army and unavailable. Later, as Pilman, gets out of the Army. (MH 42)

❖ Just released from the R.A.M.C. **Mrs. (Laura) Morland** consults him, as Pilman. (MB 45)

❖ He is Pilman again. (LAR 48)

Pildown, Miss
❖ The always cheery cafeteria lady at the Red Cross Library. (OBH 49)

Pilldozer, Hick
❖ New co-star of **Glamora Tudor** in *The Cardinal's Mate, A Factual Comment on Life Under the Borgias*. (LAAA 59)

Pilman, Mr.: *See* **Pilbeam, Mr.**

Pilsener, Hank
❖ Plays Voltaire opposite "that ageless vedette" **Glamora Tudor** in *A Mistress of Voltaire*. (TSAT 61)

Pilson, Gertie
❖ Operator at the Harefield telephone exchange. (TH 44)

Pilward, Edward Belton
❖ Son of **Heather Adams** Pilward and **Young Ted Pilward**. (DD 51)

Pilward, (Mrs.) Heather: *See* **Adams, Heather**.

Pilward, Mr. Ted (Old Pilward)
❖ Of Messrs. Pilward and Sons Entire. Their dray, drawn by two grey carthorses, delivers in the Barchester area. (TB 39)

❖ His son is **Young Ted Pilward**. (MB 45)

❖ A good customer of **Sam Adams'** Hogglestock Rolling Mills. (PBO 46)

* Adams calls him "Bert." He is a Liberal. He is interested in **Mr. (William) Marling's** land for a brewery, but Adams outdoes him. (LAR 48)

* He is now Councillor Pilward. (HRt 52)

* He goes into business with Adams and **Mr. (Donald) MacFadyen** of Amalgamated Vedge. (WDIM 54)

* He is in a poor way. (ADA 57)

* But he's still around. (CQ 58)

* He joins the Syndicate formed by **Sam Adams** to buy **Wiple** terrace away from **Lord Aberfordbury** and give it to Southbridge School. (TSAT 61)

Pilward, (Young) Ted

* Son of **Old Pilward**, of Messrs. Pilward and Sons Entire. He is on leave from the army with an impacted wisdom tooth. He partners **Heather Adams** in the New Town tennis tournament. (MB 45)

* He and Heather are engaged, and he is getting out of the army next year. (PBO 46)

* He spent two years at Cambridge, five in the army, and one more year of college before going into his father's business. He is now going to America to study breweries, but intends to be married in a year. (LAR 48)

* His degree was in physics and chemistry, and he was in Iceland with **Tom Grantly**. He is due to be married in September; the wedding is to be in Hogglestock, where they will live after the honeymoon. (OBH 49)

❖ He has a crabby old aunt (by marriage). He and Heather get married. (CC 50)

❖ Their first child, **Edward Belton Pilward**, is born. (DD 51)

❖ He and Heather go to the Riviera with her father and stepmother. (HRt 52)

❖ They now have two children. (TSAT 61)

Pitcher-Jukes, Miss Effie ("Pidge")

❖ Classicist at the Oxford college that **Betty Dean** attends. She was a fellow student of **Ivy Punch**, who idolized her, and of **Winifred (Ross) Tebben**, who beat her out for the Octavia Crammer Fellowship. (AF 36)

Plane, Hilda

❖ Former under-nurse, now maid, to **Frances** and **Geoffrey Harvey**. She was devoted to her older nephew Albert, who was killed at Ypres. (MH 42)

Platfield, General

❖ **Sir Robert Graham's** superior at the War Office. He is the Second Earl, and his son **Lord Humberton (or Harberton)** married **Phoebe Rivers**. (ESR 55)

Podgens

❖ Superannuated stableman who cares for **Maria Lufton's** dogs at Framley. Podgenses have always been Framley grocers and sextons, while the Mrs. Podgenses clean the church and are pew openers. (DD 51)

❖ She took him to Marling when she married, to be studgroom to her spaniels. **The Dowager Lady Lufton's** old

P

housemaid was a Podgens. His son (presumably) is **Young Podgens**. (HRt 52)

Podgens, Mrs.

✦ Wife (presumably) of **Young Podgens**. Housekeeper to the **Luftons** at Framley Hall, where her husband, family and hangers-on all work. (HRt 52)

✦ Her daughter is **Phoebe**. (JC 53)

Podgens, Old

✦ Gardener to **the Dowager Lady Lufton** at Framley Parsonage. (TSAT 61)

Podgens, Phoebe

✦ Daughter of **Mrs. Podgens**, and working as general utility for **the Dowager Lady Lufton** at Framley Parsonage. (JC 53)

Podgens, Young

✦ Son (presumably) of **Podgens**, and husband of **Mrs. Podgens**. He is occasional chauffeur to the **Luftons** at Framley Hall, where his wife, family, and hangers-on all work. (HRt 52)

✦ Their daughter is **Phoebe**. (JC 53)

Points

✦ Third out-of-wedlock child of **Ellen Humble's** Aunt Sarah; *see also* **Mrs. Humble**. (LAR 48)

Poirot, Old Madame

✦ Of Vache-en-Foin. During the war, both **John-Arthur Cross(e)** and **George Halliday** took baths in her kitchen. (ESR 55)

Poles, the Reverend
* ✦ **The Bishop's** evangelical chaplain, who handles his letters. (CC 50)

Pollett
* ✦ Old parlormaid to the **Fieldings**, Number Seventeen, the Close. A "distant but very despising" cousin of **Ed Pollett**. (PBO 46)

* ✦ She announces the guests at **Anne Fielding** and **Robin Dale's** wedding reception. (LAR 48)

Pollett
* ✦ Commissionaire to the consortium of **Sam Adams, Mr. (Donald) MacFadyen**, and **Old Pilward** at Pomfret Towers. A cousin of his father's was a verger named Sexton. (ADA 57)

Pollett, Belle
* ✦ One of the children of **Ed** and **Millie Poulter Pollett**, named after **Mrs. (Amabel) Marling**. Her elders are the twins **Donald** and **Mickey, Luce, Ol**, and **Will**; the youngest is **Cassie**, and there is soon to be **Winnie**. (LAR 48)

* ✦ There's another on the way. (OBH 49)

Pollett, Cassie
* ✦ Currently the youngest child of **Ed** and **Millie Poulter Pollett**, named after **Lucasta, Lady Bond**. Her elders are the twins **Donald** and **Mickey, Luce, Ol, Will**, and **Belle**; there is soon to be **Winnie**. (LAR 48)

* ✦ There's yet another on the way. (OBH 49)

Pollett, Ed

❖ Son of **Mr. Pollett** and (presumably) **Mrs. Pollett**. He is the village idiot, though good with machines, and works as under-porter at Worsted station (his uncle is **Mr. Patten** the stationmaster). He is in the chorus of **Mrs. (Louise) Palmer's** production of *Hippolytus*. (AF 36)

❖ He serves as fill-in chauffeur to **Lord Bond**; his brother is chauffeur to the **Middletons**, Laverings. His mother takes all his wages. Ed was the result of her liaison with one of **Lord Pomfret's** under-keepers who had to be discharged for selling pheasants. He is sort of a second cousin to **Jim Pollett**. He sings **Old Margett's** folk song to **Denis Stonor** in exchange for a harmonica. (BL 39)

❖ Lord Bond took him on as second chauffeur. At the onset of war, he transferred to the **Marlings**. He was rescued from the army by **Sir Edmund Pridham**. (MH 42)

❖ A year or two ago, he married **Millie Poulter**, who is as wanting as he, and they already have a couple of nice children (also wanting) and expect another in March. He has natural water sense, and finds a forgotten cesspool in the **Thatchers'** back yard, as well as working on **Dr. Dale's** Rectory well for the Barsetshire Archaeological. (MB 45)

❖ His "distant but very despising" cousin is **Pollett**. (PBO 46)

❖ Now has seven children: the twins **Donald** and **Mickey, Luce, Ol, Will, Belle**, and **Cassie**, plus one on the way (probably to be **Winnie**). He is handyman to the Marlings. (LAR 48)

* He is mistakenly called **Ed Packer** as well as his proper name. Millie had one child before they married, (yet the eldest are twins). She is pregnant again and they will name it Adams if a boy, Beedle if a girl. (OBH 49)

* On the night before **Lucy Marling's** wedding, he calls her and **Emmy Graham** out to help deliver a goat while Millie is out and two of the children have whooping cough. (CC 50)

* He now has eight or nine beautiful, happy, dirty children, and drives **Mr. (William) Marling** everywhere. (DD 51)

Pollett, Donald
* One of the elder children of **Ed** and **Millie Poulter Pollett**. His twin brother is **Mickey**, and the younger ones are **Luce, Ol, Will, Belle, Cassie**, and soon to be **Winnie**. (LAR 48)

* His parents had one child before they married, presumably him, but he's a twin. There's another on the way. (OBH 49)

Pollett, Ernie
* Uncle of **Doris Phipps**. He works at Lambton station. If he is on leave, the station master at Worsted (here misidentified as **Mr. Pollett**, actually **Mr. Patten**) fills in. (GU 43)

Pollett, George F.
* Husband of **Mrs. Pollett**, and landlord of the Sheep's Head pub. (GU 43)

Pollett, Jim
* Drives the bus between Worsted and the Ram and Twins pub. (AF 36)

❖ Is sort of a second cousin to **Ed Pollett**, and drives the Winter Overcotes bus. (BL 39)

Pollett, Lily-Annie
❖ Porter at Winter Overcotes station, along with **Doris Phipps**. (GU 43)

❖ The kitchenmaid to the **Birketts** at Worsted is named Lily-Annie, no last name specified. She can't read, and has an illegitimate little girl. (LAR 48)

Pollett, Luce
❖ One of the children of **Ed** and **Millie Poulter Pollett**, named after **Lucy Marling**. Her elder twin brothers are **Donald** and **Mickey**, and the younger ones are **Ol, Will, Belle, Cassie**, and soon to be **Winnie**. (LAR 48)

❖ There's another on the way. (OBH 49)

Pollett, Mickey
❖ One of the elder children of **Ed** and **Millie Poulter Pollett**. His twin brother is **Donald**, and the younger ones are **Luce, Ol, Will, Belle, Cassie**, and soon to be **Winnie**. (LAR 48)

❖ His parents had one child before they married, presumably him, but he's a twin. There's another on the way. (OBH 49)

Pollett, Millie: *See* **Poulter, Millie**.

Pollett, Mr.
❖ Husband (presumably) of **Mrs. Pollett** and father of **Ed Pollett**. He keeps the shop at Worsted, and plays Theseus in **Mrs. (Louise) Palmer's** production of *Hippolytus*. (AF 36)

* Another son is chauffeur to the **Middletons**, Laverings. Ed turns out to be product of an illicit liaison. (BL 39)

* Mistake for **Mr. Patten**, the Worsted Stationmaster. (GU 43)

Pollett, Mr.: *See* **Patten, Mr.**

Pollett, Mrs.
* Wife (presumably) of **Mr. Pollett** and mother of **Ed Pollett**; Another son is chauffeur to the **Middletons**, Laverings. She takes all Ed's wages. She isn't at all particular, Ed being the result of one of **Lord Pomfret's** under-keepers who had to be discharged for selling pheasants. (BL 39)

Pollett, Mrs.
* Wife of **George F. Pollett**, and landlady of the Sheep's Head pub. She is a notable cook, and runs an informal officers' mess for the Hush-Hush camp. (GU 43)

* She finds a good young cook for **Lady Glencora Palliser** Waring. (HRt 52)

Pollett, Norma
* She is on the telephone exchange with **Palmyra Phipps**. Her people live down the Worsted line. (DD 51)

* She is the **Other Girl** who relieves Palmyra at the telephone exchange. (TSAT 61)

Pollett, Ol
* One of the children of **Ed** and **Millie Poulter Pollett**, named after **Oliver Marling**. His elders are the twins **Donald** and **Mickey**, and **Luce**; the younger ones are **Will**, **Belle, Cassie**, and soon to be **Winnie**. (LAR 48)

* There's another on the way. (OBH 49)

Pollett, Sabrina
* With **Marlene Phipps**, successor to **Lily-Annie Pollett** and **Doris Phipps** as porters at Winter Overcotes station. (TSAT 61)

Pollett, Sid
* Engine driver, cousin of **Mr. Patten** the stationmaster. (AF 36)

* He is on the local run. (GU 43)

Pollett, Will
* One of the children of **Ed** and **Millie Poulter Pollett**, named after **Mr. (William) Marling**. His elders are the twins **Donald** and **Mickey, Luce**, and **Ol**; the younger ones are **Belle, Cassie**, and soon to be **Winnie**. (LAR 48)

* There's another on the way. (OBH 49)

Pomfret, Lady Agnes
* Second child of **the Sixth Earl** and **Lady Pomfret**; younger sister of **Giles (later the Seventh Earl of Pomfret)** and elder sister of **Lady Emily (Leslie)**. She died young. (PT 38)

* **Guido Strelsa** gave her a little dog, Carlo, who died of overeating (perhaps the pug she holds in an old photo). (OBH 49)

* She was engaged to a Detrimental who was killed on the northwest frontier in India, in the same battle as **Harry, Lord Mellings**. She died unmarried, and left her money to her niece **Agnes Graham's** daughters when they marry or turn twenty-five. (DD 51)

* Now she was engaged to a Palliser, but her brother Giles made a fuss because the Omniums were parvenus, and she took to curates and church embroidery instead. (ESR 55)

* Now she got engaged to a clergyman at age seventeen, but did bad watercolors and died an old maid. (NTL 56)

Pomfret, Alured de
* Ancestor of the Earls of Pomfret. (WDIM 54)

Pomfret, Edith, Lady (née Thorne)
* Wife of **Giles, Seventh Earl of Pomfret**, and mother of one son, the late **(Harry) Lord Mellings**. She is an invalid, who mainly lives in Florence and only visits her English home, Pomfret Towers, occasionally. Her companion and secretary is **Miss Merriman**. (PT 38)

* She has died. Lord Pomfret gives Pooker's Piece to the National Trust in her memory. (BL 39)

* She was one of the Thornes of Ullathorne. (TH 44)

* As Edith Thorne, she had good blood but no money, though her settlement from Lord Pomfret was very good. **Lord Stoke** had given her a pearl necklace, which she returned, presumably on her engagement to Lord Pomfret. **Guido** Pomfret (actually **Strelsa**) had lent her his villa, the Casa Strelsa, every year. (NTL 56)

Pomfret, Eustace, Count Strelsa
* Of the cadet branch of the family. A Catholic, he fled with James II in 1688, and settled in Italy in 1689. His descendants are the **Strelsas**. (PT 38)

* He married into the Strelsa family. (NR 41)

P

❖ **Ludovic Foster,** Lord Mellings, is named for him (among others). (NTL 56)

❖ His elder brother was the Pomfret who in 1689 was created earl for services rendered to the Prince of Orange. He himself took the name Strelsa, the title of count, and the land, from the wealth of his wife. (LAAA 59)

Pomfret, Fulke de

❖ He impounded some of the Abbey pigs for incursions into his Lady's herb garden, so he may be the upside-down figure in **Nicholas de Hogpen's** mural in Pomfret Madrigal church. (TB 39)

Pomfret, Giles de

❖ Founder of the family (but also see **Neville de Pomfret**). He built a Norman fortress in the twelfth century to guard lands given by Henry II. (LAAA 59)

Pomfret, Giles, Lord (the Seventh Earl of Pomfret)

❖ Of Pomfret Towers. Husband of **Edith, Lady Pomfret** and father of the late **(Harry) Lord Mellings**. Son of the **Sixth Earl** and **Lady Pomfret**, his younger sisters are the late **Lady Agnes (Pomfret)** and **Lady Emily Leslie**. Lord lieutenant of the county, Knight of the Garter, aged almost eighty. His heirs are a cousin, **Major Foster**, and his son **Gillie Foster. Mr. Johns** publishes his memoir, *A Landowner in Five Reigns*, to unexpected success, and he gives all the royalties to Nutfield Cottage Hospital. (PT 38)

❖ Now widowed, he goes on a cruise with Gillie and **Sally Wicklow** Foster. He bullies **Sir Ogilvy Hibberd** into selling him Pooker's Piece and gives it to the National Trust in Lady Pomfret's memory. (BL 39)

* He is a governor of South-bridge School, and though abroad, sends **Rose Birkett** a wedding present. He has not been well since Lady Pomfret died. He dies in May, and is buried in the parish church, with memorials at St. Margaret's Westminster and in Barchester Cathedral. (CBI 40)

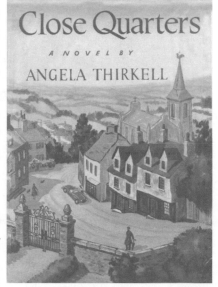

* When Queen Victoria had asked him what he thought of Stanley's *History of the Jews*, he said "The Bible is good enough for me, Ma'am, or bad enough," thus losing a possible marquisate. (OBH 49)

* He died in the spring of Dunkirk. (LAAA 59)

Pomfret, Guido: *See* **Strelsa, Guido**.

Pomfret, Harry: *See* **Mellings, Harry, Lord**.

Pomfret, Lady (the Countess of Pomfret): *See* **Pomfret, Edith, Lady,** (after CBI 40, **Old Lady Pomfret**), or **Wicklow, Sally,** thereafter.

Pomfret, Lady
* Wife of **the Sixth Earl of Pomfret** and mother of **Giles** (later **the Seventh Earl of Pomfret**), **Lady Agnes,** and **Lady Emily Leslie**. She did watercolors, and her three-

volume novel, *A Step Too Far*, shocked Mr. Gladstone. (PT 38)

❖ She took lessons from a Royal Academician, did frescoes in her bedroom, and outlived her husband. (WDIM 54)

Pomfret, Lord (the Third Earl of Pomfret)

❖ In 1760, he won an obelisk from the contemporary **Duke of Omnium**. He put it up with the inscription that the goddess of Fortune had reft this Egyptian stone from Dux Omnium to bestow it upon Comes Pontefractus whose victories not by the sword of Mars but by the peaceful dice were here commemorated; *alea jacta est*. (LAAA 59)

Pomfret, Lord (the Fifth Earl of Pomfret)

❖ Died of drink at his coming of age. His posthumous son was **the Sixth Earl of Pomfret**. (PT 38)

Pomfret, Lord (the Sixth Earl of Pomfret)

❖ Posthumous son of **the Fifth Earl of Pomfret**. He and his wife **Lady Pomfret** had the children **Giles (later the Seventh Earl of Pomfret), Lady Agnes**, and **Lady Emily Leslie**. "An affectionate husband and father, an excellent landlord, and one of the most insufferable prigs that Queen Victoria's reign produced." A philanthropist. On the site of Pomfret Castle, he built Pomfret Towers (on the model of St. Pancras station) and filled it with expensive uncomfortable pre-Raphaelite furnishings. (PT 38)

Pomfret, Lord (the Seventh Earl of Pomfret):
See **Giles, Lord Pomfret**.

Pomfret, Lord (the Eighth Earl of Pomfret):** *See* **Foster, Gillie**.

Pomfret, Neville de
* According to **Ludovic Foster**, Lord Mellings, "some kind of ancestor" who founded the Pomfret family (but also see **Giles de Pomfret**) and for whom (among others) he was named. (NTL 56)

Pond, Hastings
* **Glamora Tudor's** new male star in the movie *What Men Desire* (about the love life of Marcus Aurelius).

Pooker, the Reverend Horatio
* Vicar of Skeynes Agnes, 1820–1843. He bought Pooker's Piece out of spite, because both the **Bonds** and **Palmers** wanted it, then left it to the Charity Commissioners. (BL 39)

Pooter, Nellie
* Cousin of the wife of **Councilor Budge** of the Gas Works. She visits them, but is almost deaf, so she can't go to **Eric Swan's** lecture at the Barchester Central Library. (HRt 52)

Porlock, Esme
* Purportedly a one-book man; actually the pen name used by **Mrs. (Laura) Morland** before the war, for her biography of Molly Bangs, one of three ladies of the town (Mrs. Bangs, Mrs. Patten, and Mrs. Pancras) in early nineteenth century London. (NTL 56)

Porter, Horatio, Esq.
* A freethinker and gambler, notorious in Hallbury history. He died of a stroke while having a debauch in the kitchen with his cook, accompanied by a thunderstorm and the birth of a six-legged calf. (MB 45)

P

Porter, Sir Joseph, K.C.M.G.

❖ Grandson of the First lord of the Admiralty (*cf.* Gilbert and Sullivan). As permanent secretary of the Red Tape and Sealing Wax Department, he thwarts good relations between it and the Admiralty. (DD 51)

Porter, Mr. L.N.B., C.B.E.

❖ Retired member of the Civil Service who was up at Oxford with, and is two years younger than, **Mr. (Leonard) Halliday**; which is why the latter is cheered to hear of his death of a fractured leg, result of a street accident. (NTL 56)

Porter, Walden Concord

❖ American who employs seven thousand workers, owns most of Porterville, and endowed the American observatory where **Miss Hopgood's Aunt** and her husband were. He puts up the money for **Miss (Ianthe) Pemberton** and **Mr. (Harold) Downing** to finish the *Biographical Dictionary of Provence* in order to spite **Professor Gawky**. (NR 41)

❖ Porterville is in Texas. (CC 50)

❖ He is coming over for the Coronation. He sends Miss Pemberton a dozen of port per month after Prof. Gawky's disparaging remarks, and he invites Mr. Downing to give the **Lincoln Fish Doppelgänger** Lectures on Provençal poetry. His secretary was Miss Texas in the Stenographers' Olympic Beauty Contest. (WDIM 54)

❖ Though he is away, he leaves his (now) Portersville house, cars, and secretaries at the disposal of Mr. and Mrs. Downing (the former **Mrs. Turner**) when they visit. (ADA 57)

Potin, Angele ("Nini le Poumon"): *See* **le Capet, Jehan.**

Potter
- ⁜ The man over near Rushwater who used to shoot foxes. **Miss (Amelia) Brandon's** funeral is almost as poorly attended as his. (TB 39)

Potter
- ⁜ Chemist at Harefield, cousin to **George Potter.** (TH 44)

Potter, Alec ("Old Alec")
- ⁜ He has a cow in calf. **Lucy Marling** collects sugar for his housekeeper. (MH 42)

Potter, George
- ⁜ Runs a furniture moving and storage company. Cousin to **Potter** the chemist. (TH 44)

Potter, Job
- ⁜ Died young, drowned in Harefield lake when louts cracked the ice over the spring. He would have been ninety-two had he lived. (MH 42)

Potter, Mr.
- ⁜ **Lionel Harvest's** ally at the BBC, with whom he gets up a conspiracy against **Joan Stevenson.** (WS 34)

Potter, Miss ("Pots")
- ⁜ One of the two teachers in charge of six evacuees billeted on the **Keiths,** Northbridge Manor; her colleague is **Miss "Draky" Drake.** (CBI 40)

Potter, Tom
- ⁜ Stoker of the engine Rising Castle, and cousin to **Mrs. Beedle.** He was called up, and has been missing since Singapore. (GU 43)

P

Poulter
* Gardener at Rushwater for the **Leslies,** or at Holdings for the **Grahams.** (OBH 49)

Poulter, Millie
* Red-haired niece of **Mrs. Cox.** She works for **Frances** and **Geoffrey Harvey,** and reports on their activities to their landlady, **Joyce Perry Smith.** (MH 42)

* A year or two ago, she married **Ed Pollett,** who is as wanting as she. They already have a couple of nice wanting children, and expect another in March. (MB 45)

* She now has seven children: the twins **Donald** and **Mickey, Luce, Ol, Will, Belle,** and **Cassie,** plus one on the way (probably to be named **Winnie**). (LAR 48)

* She had one child before they married (yet the eldest are twins). She is pregnant again and will name it Adams if a boy, Beedle if a girl. (OBH 49)

* Two of the children have whooping cough. (CC 50)

* They now have eight or nine beautiful, happy, dirty children. (DD 51)

Poulter, Mrs.
* Mother of **Ted Poulter.** She currently does for **Mr. Bostock,** but when Ted and **Lily Brown** marry, they will replace her. (PBO 46)

* She is dying at home. (OBH 49)

Poulter, Nurse
* A recent addition to the convalescent hospital at Beliers Priory. (GU 43)

* Now Sister, she was head of the Hallbury Cottage Hospital previous to **Sister Chiffinch**. (MB 45)

* She was at Allington at **Mrs. (Priscilla) Dale's** death. (CC 50)

* Now at Barchester General Hospital. (DD 51)

Poulter, Ted

* Son of **Mrs. Poulter**, and gardener's boy for the **Leslies**, Rushwater; walking out with **Lily Brown**. By **Emmy Graham's** arrangement, when they marry, they'll replace his mother and live in with **Mr. Bostock**. (PBO 46)

* His mother is dying at home, Lily is helping out, and he's doing well. (OBH 49)

* According to **Edith Graham**, he beat Lily, but they got married, so it's all right. (ADA 57)

Pover, Alice Edith ("Edie")

* Kitchenmaid to the **Villars** at Northbridge Rectory and slave to **Mrs. Chapman**. Feeble-minded, she grew up in an orphanage. She gets flu, and becomes engaged to **Corporal Arthur Jackson**. (NR 41)

* She is happily married, with no children, and still working for the Villars. (CQ 58)

Powell-Jones, Captain

* Violently Welsh ex-don with rooms at Bangor; coach in Cymric. Now billeted on the **Villars** at Northbridge Rectory. (NR 41)

Powlett, Mr.

* Late husband of **Mrs. Powlett**. A verger, and a drinker. (TH 44)

P

✦ He died of cold on the stomach. (HRt 52)

Powlett, Mrs.
✦ Widow of **Mr. Powlett** and cook to **Mr. (Caleb) Oriel**, than whom she is five years older (so seventy-five). Her father was a sexton. Her mentally-defective nephew is a cleaner at **Sam Adams'** Hogglestock factory and is also a cousin of **Mr. (Fred) Belton's** gamekeeper, who allows him to do a little poaching. Her niece Olive works in the post office, and another niece, Sarah, is the cook for the Hosiers' Girls' Foundation School at Harefield Park and has an illegitimate son. (TH 44)

Poynter, Miss
✦ Very efficient secretary to **Sam Adams** at the Hogglestock Rolling Mills. (TH 44)

Prack
✦ Of Cincinnati. Mixo-Lydian refugee and psychoanalyst, expert on all memory fixations. (BL 39)

Pratt
✦ Fishmonger in Harefield High Street. (TH 44)

Precentor of Barchester Cathedral, the
✦ Disciplined by **the Bishop** for using extra petrol. (MB 45)

✦ He holds that **Dean (Josiah) Crawley** intromits in Close affairs. He has a mother. (HRt 52)

✦ He attends **the Oriels'** wedding reception at **the Jorams'**. (LAAA 59)

Prescott, Tommy
✦ Drinking buddy of **Mr. Wickham's**, the gears of whose car he stripped. (JC 53)

Preston, Colonel

 * Late husband of **Mrs. Preston** and father of **Mary**. Killed in World War I. (WS 34)

Preston, Mr. and Mrs. Jackie

 * Friends of **Major** and **Mrs. Major Spender** near Nutfield. Their children (including Joan, three years) are the same age as those of the Spenders, "but not so bright." (NR 41)

Preston, Mary

 * Daughter of **Colonel** and **Mrs. Preston**, niece of **Sir Robert Graham** on her mother's side. Released from attendance on her mother, she stays with the **Leslies** at Rushwater for the summer, flirts with **David Leslie**, and gets engaged to **John Leslie**. (WS 34)

 * She and John are a very nice, rather dull couple who have two young children and represent the Leslies at the Agricultural Dinner at **Lord Bond's** (BL 39)

 * Their three sons, **Leslie Major, Minor**, and **Minimus**, are at Southbridge School. (PBO 46)

 * They live in the Old Rectory over Greshamsbury way. (JC 53)

 * She gives **Mavis Welk** Parkinson a winning lottery ticket for a new washing machine. (CQ 58)

Preston, Mrs.

 * Eldest sister of **Sir Robert Graham**, widow of **Colonel Preston**, and mother of **Mary**. A peevish invalid. Her brother pays for her summer at a Swiss clinic. (WS 34)

Prettyman family

* Former owners of the Lodge, Silverbridge. The last of the family were two old maids who kept a school (*cf.* Trollope). They sold to **Sir Harry Waring**. (DD 51)

Pridham, Sir Edmund, Baronet

* Of Pomfret Madrigal. A widower, childless, but the busiest man in the county. He led the Barsetshire Yeomanry in World War I for two years before he was invalided out with a crippled leg. He is trustee to **Mrs. (Lavinia) Brandon**, whom he admires but understands. He proposes to her to keep her from accepting **Mr. (Justin) Miller**, and is relieved when she doesn't hear him. (TB 39)

* His ancestor was **Sir Walpole Pridham**. In a drought, he fights with the Barchester County Council and the water company. (CBI 40)

* He is busy keeping a sewage farm out of Starveacres Hatches. (PE 47)

* He was eighty-three on his last birthday and has driven the same car since the end of World War I. He proposes to Mrs. Brandon again to get her away from her unhappiness with her son and his wife at Stories, but is (happily) refused. (CC 50)

* He wrote his recollections of the Boer War, but no publisher would touch them. His uncle Alfred Pridham never cut his beard. Mrs. Brandon, now Mrs. Joram, gives a party (belatedly) for his 80th birthday. (HRt 52)

* Now eighty-six years old. (WDIM 54)

* Now eighty-five, according to his family Bible; but **Lord Stoke**, himself over eighty, says that Sir Edmund is a good ten years older than he. (NTL 56)

* Now over ninety. (ADA 57)

* He is quite deaf. He brings his man to consult with **Harcourt, Duke of Towers** over his trees, but actually fixes it all himself with **Lee** and the Duke's woodsman. (LAAA 59)

* He is in Scotland, salmon fishing. (TSAT 61)

Pridham, Sir Walpole
* Ancestor of **Sir Edmund Pridham**. Second president of the Barsetshire Archaeological Society. He believed that everything he found was British. (MB 45)

Prime Minister of Mngangaland, the
* He sent **Bishop Joram** a leopard skin on his birthday. (HRt 52)

Procrastinator
* Author of the *Analects*, an edition of which is published by **Mr. (Bill) Birkett**. (PE 47)

Propert, Captain
* Next-door neighbor of **Frances** and **Geoffrey Harvey**. (MH 42)

Propett, Aggie
* At Rushwater. She never knows whether she's pregnant or by whom. (ESR 55)

Propett, Old Mr.
* "Husband" of **Old Mrs. (Polly) Propett**; they never married, though they've been together over sixty years. Sexton

to **Colonel the Reverend Crofts**, Southbridge. His niece is **Young Mrs. Propett**. He first rang the churchbell at age thirty, and at ninety-two he's been ringing it for sixty years. Now ill, crotchety, and "the last of his name," he doesn't want **Bateman** to ring the church bell while he's alive, or the passing bell for him when he dies; he does, and Bateman doesn't, though he succeeds him as sexton. (PE 47)

 * His father at Northbridge made pony-mower shoes for the **Hallidays** at Hatch House. (NTL 56)

Propett, Old Mrs. (Polly)
 * "Wife" of **Old Mr. Propett** the sexton at Southbridge; they never married, though they've been together over sixty years. When he dies, she drinks a bottle of port and one of gin, and herself dies twenty-four hours later. (PE 47)

Propett, Young Mrs.
 * Niece of **Old Mr. Propett** the sexton at Southbridge. A robust grandmother, she is daily help to **Colonel Crofts** at the Vicarage. (PE 47)

Propria Persona, Sister
 * Author of *Selectivity in the Church Today*. (DD 51)

Prothero, Mr.
 * Master at Southbridge School. He was too old to go to World War I. (DH 34)

 * After spending a year at a Canadian school, he comes back to Southbridge. (SH 37)

Prsvb
 * "Intellectual of the first run which is dead at the age of twenty years," according to **Mme. Brownscu**. One of the greatest dramaturges of Mixo-Lydia. (TH 44)

by a matriarch who died at his marriage. His father had been smothered by an overturned haywagon. (BL 39)

Pumper, Derrick
* Evacuee child; he, **Derrick Farker**, and their cousin **Ron** are boarded by **Mrs. (Poppy) Turner** at the Hollies, Northbridge. (NR 41)

Punch, Ivy
* Fellow student of **Winifred Tebben**; she tried to drown herself out of love for **Effie Pitcher-Jukes**. But she recovered, got a good degree, became secretary to a literary man, and had an illegitimate daughter, Brynhild, who was at school with **Betty Dean**. (AF 36)

Purchase, Mr.
* American publisher of **Mrs. (Laura) Morland's** books. (NTL 56)

Purvis, the Honourable Eleanor
* Daughter of **Mrs. (Marian) Purvis**, and thus a half-great-niece or something to **Mrs. (Helen) Keith**. Engaged to **the Honourable Mr. Norris**. (SH 37)

* They are now married. (TH 44)

Purvis, Mrs. Marian
* Aunt of **Mrs. (Helen) Keith**, and third daughter of her father's second family; her daughter was **the Honourable Eleanor Purvis**, who married **the Honourable Mr. Norris**. (SH 37)

Raghams, the

✤ **Sir Robert Graham's** great-grandfather's illegitimate children were anagramatically named Ragham, and are now a plentiful, gypsy bunch in East Barsetshire. (ESR 55)

Ramsden, Madame

✤ French widow of a Sergeant-Major Ramsden. She runs the Pension Ramsden at Menton, patronized by **Miss Crowder** and **Miss Hopgood**. (NR 41)

✤ After the war, the business is flourishing under her and her daughter, who married an older Frenchman named Petitot during the occupation and has no children. (ADA 57)

Ramsay, Flora

✤ Maiden name of Mrs. **Swan**, mother of **Eric**. When her husband died during the war, she went to her family in Scotland. She is a friend of **Mrs. (Felicia) Grant**, who invites her to Rome for Christmas. (HRt 52)

Rear-Admiral's Wife, the

✤ Attends a working party at **Mrs. (Maud) Perry's**. She has been to India, China, Zanzibar, and Slavo-Lydia. Early in the war, her husband had **Freddy Belton** on a course on torpedoes. (TH 44)

Reid, Mr.

✤ Proprietor of the general store, High Rising. (DH 34)

✤ Now air raid warden. (CBI 40)

Rene

✤ A Lambton girl, new under-porter at Winter Overcotes, replacing **Bill Morple**. (GU 43)

Rivers, the Honourable George

✤ Cousin to **Giles, Lord Pomfret**, husband of **Mrs. (Hermione) Rivers**, and father of **Julian** and **Phoebe**. "A looker," but by preference he stays at home in Herefordshire. (PT 38)

✤ He gives a party at the Wigwam in London. (LAR 48)

✤ Now said to be of Shropshire. That is where his son-in-law **Lord Humberton (or Harberton)** lives. (DD 51)

✤ He does all he can for his tenants. (HRt 52)

✤ He has moved out of his old bedroom (which he presumably shared with Mrs. Rivers). His father died after his third stroke. His brother was living with a woman abroad while his first wife was still alive, and they had an illegitimate daughter whom they got into the peerage with the wrong date of birth after they finally married; but he died, leaving no money, and they now live in Majorca. (ESR 55)

R

* He is always in Herefordshire, while his wife is always in London. (ADA 57)

Rivers, Mrs. Hermione

* Wife of **the Honourable George Rivers**, and mother of **Julian** and **Phoebe**. Successful author of novels about young men who tempt chaste older women, set in North Africa, Danzig, Rome, Buenos Aires, on cruises to Norway and up the Amazon, and, most recently, at Angkor Wat. These have earned her the cognomen "the Baedeker Bitch" from her harassed publisher, **Mr. Johns**. She tries to make her daughter marry **Gillie Foster**, heir to **Lord Pomfret**, and to get her son away from **Alice Barton**, but she gets her comeuppance in every way. (PT 38)

* She is a niece of **Lord Nutfield**. (MH 42)

* She lives in a flat in London in Duck's Mews, now tarted up and renamed Duke's Close. She visits Liberal headquarters but then says she may not vote at all. (HRt 52)

* She did a lecture tour in America. Her husband has moved out of his old bedroom (which he presumably shared with her). (ESR 55)

* She is always in London, while her husband is always in Herefordshire. (ADA 57)

Rivers, Julian

* Son of **the Honourable George** and **Mrs. (Hermione) Rivers**; brother of **Phoebe**. A bad modern painter, his coterie is the Set of Five, and he exhibits in the Tottenham Court Road. He is worshipped by **Alice Barton**, but she finally berates him for not respecting his mother. (PT 38)

* He is an official war artist. (MH 42)

* He was unwillingly taken into the Army, then rescued as an Artist of National Importance by people who ought to have known better. He now calls himself Common Wealth. (PBO 46)

* He is now in the Society of Fifteen, which has exhibitions somewhere. He has a short, soft beard and wears a mustard-yellow kilt and a sports shirt open on his hairy chest. He offered to paint **Grace Grantly**, but was rejected. He is appointed Professor of Culture at Lazarus College. (HRt 52)

* He now has a gallery. (NTL 56)

* He is back with the Set of Five, exhibiting in an out-of-the-way gallery in the Tottenham Court Road. He tried to paint Harefield House but was warned off by **Mr. (Fred) Belton**. (CQ 58)

Rivers, Phoebe

* Daughter of **the Honourable George** and **Mrs. (Hermione) Rivers**; sister of **Julian**. An actress, in revolt from her mother, who wants her to marry **Gillie Foster**, heir to **Lord Pomfret**. She becomes friends with **Alice Barton**, and gets engaged, then unengaged, to **Guy Barton**. (PT 38)

* She married **Lord Humberton, Lord Platfield's** eldest son, who can't stand her mother either. They live in Shropshire. (CBI 40)

* Now he is both Lord Humberton and **Lord Harberton**. They have a child. (MH 42)

Robarts, Canon

❖ He has been gently mad for years, and thus doesn't hate **the Bishop**. (TH 44)

❖ He died, and his last words were "I've got him now!" with a blow to the bedclothes. The lower orders think he referred to the Devil in the form of a blow-fly, but the higher orders think that he was under the illusion that he'd had the Bishop removed by special act of Parliament. His nieces left to live in a private hotel in Bournemouth. (PBO 46)

❖ He previously occupied Number Seventeen the Close, now home of the **Fieldings**. He had six maids, all sleeping in one room, and a manservant who slept in the basement. (LAR 48)

Robarts, Dr.

❖ Dean of Barchester Cathedral a generation ago. A bachelor of limited means, but a connoisseur of wines. He translated the first book of the *Aeneid* into bad rhyming couplets. (HRt 52)

Robinson, Juan

❖ Of Buenos Aires. He and Mrs. Juan Robinson are friends of **the Archdeacon**. (PT 38)

❖ He takes **Rose Birkett** Fairweather out swimming in Las Palombas; his father is her doctor. (CBI 40)

Ron

❖ An evacuee child; he and his cousins, **Derrick Farker** and **Derrick Pumper** are boarded by **Mrs. (Poppy) Turner** at the Hollies, Northbridge. (NR 41)

Ronnquist, Doctor Professor

❖ Of Uppsala University. He is writing on Frederika Bremer's visits to England, and obliges with a copy of Uppsala's previously unseen manuscript of **Fluvius Minucius** for **Miss (Madeleine) Sparling** and **Mr. (Sidney) Carton**. (TH 44)

Root, Jefferson X.

❖ Author of *A Wastepaper Basket from Three Embassies*. He would have seen Lenin had he not been out of Moscow at the moment. (TB 39)

Roote, Mr.

❖ Of Amalgamated Vedge. Probably the successor to **Mr. (Donald) MacFadyen**. (TSAT 61)

Rose

❖ Tyrannical and devoted parlormaid to **Mrs. (Lavinia) Brandon** at Stories. In competition with **Nurse (Miss Vance)**. (TB 39)

❖ She is older than Mrs. Brandon, and had been **Mr. (Henry) Brandon's** parlormaid before his marriage. (PE 47)

❖ She follows Mrs. Brandon (now married to **Dr. Joram**) to the Vinery. **Mrs. (Florrie) Simnet** is her aunt's cousin. Her Aunt Poppy went into a decline. (CC 50)

❖ At odds with everyone, as usual. (HRt 52)

Rosina

❖ Cook-housekeeper in **Major Foster's** house in Italy, she was kind to young **Gillie Foster**. She married the innkeeper's son and had twelve children. Gillie was godfather to

one, Antonio, named after the local poacher (perhaps its
father—or perhaps the father was the Sindaco, who stood
in for Gillie at the christening). (ADA 57)

Ruth

* Maid to the **Perrys,** Plassey House. (TH 44)

* Devoted but sulky. (DD 51)

Saint Barabbas College, the Master (or President) and **His Wife:** *See* **Barabbas, Master of,** and **his Wife.**

la Salope, Mimi: *See* **le Capet, Jehan.**

Sampson and his Nephew
* Printer at Northbridge; his nephew is feeble-minded but a whiz at typesetting. (NR 41)

Samson, Mr.
* He owns the Garage, Greshamsbury. (CQ 58)

Sanders
* Chauffeur to the **Keiths**, Northbridge Manor. (SH 37)
* Now referred to as **Saunders**. (CBI 40)

Sarah
* Maid to **Mrs. Goble** the postmistress at Edgewood. (OBH 49)

Sartoria, Madame

* London dressmaker to **Lady Agnes Graham**; she makes bridesmaid dresses for **Lucy Marling's** wedding for **Emmy** and **Clarissa Graham**. (CC 50)

* She makes **Miss Merriman's** wedding dress. (ADA 57)

Saunders: *See* Sanders.

Scatcherd, Hettie

* Eldest niece, and a demon housekeeper, of **Mr. Scatcherd** the artist. She sings in the church choir. (PBO 46)

Scatcherd, Jean

* Young relative of an **Old Mr. Scatcherd**; she does V.A.D. in tube stations in London for two weeks. (NR 41)

Scatcherd, Mr.

* An artist, of Rokeby, Hatch End. His brother, **Mr. Scatcherd** of Scatcherd's Stores, bought Rokeby and lets him live there cheaply with his eldest niece **Hettie Scatcherd** as his housekeeper. He sells his pen-and-ink landscapes to **Lady Agnes Graham,** who lets them be raffled off at the Bring-and-Buy. He once spent a week in nervous sin in Boulogne; he is agnostic and Labour, except in opposition to **Sir Ogilvy Hibberd, Lord Aberfordbury,** whose National Rotochrome Polychrome Universal Picture Postcard Company is in competition with Mr. Scatcherd's own postcards. (PBO 46)

* Now the cousin of the current Mr. Scatcherd of Scatcherd's Stores. He does a portrait of **Miss Crowder** as Queen Elizabeth I, and five-minute likenesses at the Northbridge variety show for the Coronation. (WDIM 54)

❖ The current Mr. Scatcherd of Scatcherd's Stores is his brother again. (ESR 55)

❖ He speaks out against Lord Aberfordbury's putting a post-card factory in **Wiple** Terrace; then does an "Abstrack Conception" of the four Wiple Girls in front of the houses named for them, which **Mr. Wickham** buys as a memorial when the terrace is saved. (TSAT 61)

Scatcherd, Mr.
❖ The current proprietor of Scatcherd's Stores; his brother is the artist **Mr. Scatcherd**, and his eldest daughter is **Hettie Scatcherd**. He bought Rokeby and let his brother live there cheaply with Hettie as his housekeeper. (PBO 46)

❖ Now he is the artist's cousin. (WDIM 54)

❖ They are brothers again. (ESR 55)

Scatcherd, Old Mr.
❖ Of Scatcherd's Stores, established 1842. (NR 41)

Scatcherd, Old Mr.
❖ Of Scatcherd and Tozer, Caterers, where his partner is **Mr. Tozer**. He has been bedridden for years, but knows all the business. (CC 50)

❖ Still in charge, though he's been bedridden for seven years at least. (ADA 57)

Schreibfeder, Abner P.
❖ Of Seattle, Washington, U.S.A. He owns six cinemas, and is going to buy six more, as well as build a super-cinema with restaurant, pool, and planetarium on his own estate. (TSAT 61)

S

Screaming Girl, the: *See* **Faraday-Home, Miss**.

Scrimageour, "Sheep"
* He sends two bottles of brandy to his friend **Mr. Wickham** in time for **the Oriels'** wedding reception. (LAAA 59)

Scriptor Ignotus
* Of Aterra. A possible influence on the poetry of **Fluvius Minucius**, at least according to **Eric Swan**. (HRt 52)

Scumper, Croke
* Co-stars in *Legs Round Your Neck*, with **Glamora Tudor**. (HRt 52)

Senior Master of Beliers Priory School, the
* He got a second pip by the skin of his teeth before the peace, and so was outranked by the **Junior Master**. (LAR 48)

* He and a party, including the Junior Master, go to Switzerland on their holidays. (HRt 52)

Sergeant, the
* He takes the boxing at Southbridge School. (HR 33)

Shepherd, Dr.
* Medical man at Hallbury; an "old woman," according to **Dr. Ford**. (MB 45)

Shergold, Mr.
* Successor to **Everard Carter** as senior housemaster of Southbridge School. A bachelor and demobilized naval officer, he kept a jerboa aboard H.M.S. *Flatiron* (or *Gridiron*) and raced it with the jerboa kept by **George Empson**. His great-great-uncle Tom left all his money to the Ada

Clotworthy Mental Institution, so his father is one of its governors (see **Edna**). (PE 47)

* He is doing well at the Senior House. (CC 50)

* **Tubby Fewling** remembers him from the *Gridiron*. (JC 53)

Sid
* **Mrs. (Lavinia) Brandon's** garden boy at Stories. **Delia Brandon** has a morbid interest in the boil on his neck. (TB 39)

Sid
* A cousin of **Effie** and **Ruby Bunce**. He is **Mrs. Dunsford's** gardener and runs the Wolf Cubs. (WDIM 54)

Siddon, Mrs. ("Siddy")
* Housekeeper for the **Leslies**, Rushwater; formerly the stillroom maid. She quarrels with **Lady Agnes Graham's Nannie** over the children's breakfasts. (WS 34)

* She stayed on through the war, and is now looking after **Martin Leslie**. (PBO 46)

* She reminisces about **Lady Emily Leslie** in the old days. (OBH 49)

* She is misnamed as **Mrs. Simnet**. (CC 50)

Silverbridge, Lord (the Earl of): title of the heir of **the Duke of Omnium**; *see* **Palliser, Jeffrey**.

Simnet
* Butler to **Mr. (Bill) Birkett**, the headmaster of Southbridge School. Formerly a scout at Lazarus College, he left because the new master, **Crawford of Lazarus**, wrote for the leftist papers. (SH 37)

S

* He was stationed in France from 1915–1917, and on No. 7 staircase at Lazarus. He presides at **Rose Birkett's** wedding. (CBI 40)

* His mother lives in Barchester, and his brother **Mr. Simnet** is Apparitor of Worship to the Master of the Hosiers' Company. (TH 44)

* He presides at **Anne Fielding's** wedding reception. (LAR 48)

* He had been keeping company with **Eileen** of the Red Lion, but she gave him over to her sister **Florrie**, whom he married. They leave Southbridge and go to **Dr. Joram** in the Close; **Edward** takes his old position. (CC 50)

* He is president of the Close Upper Servants' Club, and presides at **Lady Gwendolyn Harcourt's** wedding reception at the Jorams'. (LAAA 59)

Simnet, Mrs. Dorothy

* Middle-aged, a Plymouth Sister, and subnormal. Before her marriage, she was maid to **Mr. (Caleb) Oriel**, vicar of Harefield, and under **Mrs. Powlett's** thumb. She then meets and marries **Mr. Simnet**, Apparitor of Worship to the Master of the Hosiers' Company. (TH 44)

* She serves (badly) at **Anne Fielding's** wedding reception. (LAR 48)

* They help at **Mrs. (Lavinia) Joram's** party for **Sir Edmund Pridham**. (HRt 52)

* They live in Barchester, where she gets on well with his mother. (CQ 58)

Simnet, Mrs. Florrie

❖ Sister of **Eileen** of the Red Lion, and former cook-housekeeper of the **Hon. Mr. Nutfield**. When she marries **Simnet**, they go into service for **Dr. Joram**. (CC 50)

Simnet, Mr.

❖ Apparitor of Worship to the Master of the Hosiers' Company, and brother of **Simnet**, the butler at Southbridge School. A widower, weedy and bespectacled; his mother lives at Barchester. He meets and marries **Dorothy**, maid to **Mr. Caleb Oriel**. (TH 44)

❖ They help serve at **Anne Fielding's** wedding reception. (LAR 48)

❖ They help at **Mrs. (Lavinia) Joram's** party for **Sir Edmund Pridham**. (HRt 52)

❖ They live in Barchester, and she gets on well with his mother. (CQ 58)

Simnet, Mrs.: *See* Siddon, Mrs.

Simon, Mr.

❖ Head of the Pocklington Road (Baptist) School. He takes his pupils to the Southbridge Christmas Treat. (CBI 40)

Simpson

❖ A boy at school with **Robin Morland**; very superstitious. (TSAT 61)

Simpson

❖ A youngish middle-aged man from the elder **Mr. Merton's** law office. He manages Brandon Abbey after **Miss (Amelia) Brandon's** death. (TB 39)

S

Skeynes, Lord Hugh

* **Miss (Maud) Bunting** used to read to him because he had bad eyes. (MH 42)

Skimpton, Old Mrs.

* Her old age pension and ten shillings a week from her son at the Hogglestock Iron Works will allow her to get blind drunk on Saturdays and DT's on Sundays. (LAAA 59)

Skinners, the

* People the **Bartons** used to know in Florence, too dull to explain. **Edith, Lady Pomfret** saw them in Florence and sends their regards. (PT 38)

Skinner, Lord: *See* Lazarus, the Master of

Skinner, Mrs.

* Wife of **the Master of Lazarus** College, Oxford. She rides a bicycle and wears a mackintosh (much like **the Wife of the President of Barabbas**). His Labour peerage makes him **Lord Skinner**, but she wants to be called **Mrs. Skinner**. (PE 47)

Skipper, Bobby

* A friend of Lieutenant **Robert Graham**, whom he owes ten pounds. (LAAA 59)

Slattery, Dr.

* "The man for tonsils. Has 'em out as soon as look at you."—**Lord Stoke**. (BL 39)

Smallbones, G.

* Monumental Mason, Orders Executed in All Styles, Winter Overcotes. (GU 43)

Smalley, Mr.

❖ Art master of Barchester High School, he was once engaged to the sixteen-year-old **Rose Birkett**. (SH 37)

Smith

❖ Maternal grandfather of **Mr. Brown** of the Red Lion pub,
Southbridge. He kept a tied house in Camden Town, and
his daughter sent his grandson back there on visits. (CBI
40)

Smith, Flo

❖ Daughter of the **Warings'** head carter; she has a sister
Marigold, and a younger brother **Percy**. She worked for
the **Hornimans** at the Vicarage, Lambton. (GU 43)

Smith, "Holy Joe"

❖ Chaplain of Southbridge School. (SH 37)

❖ He played football for Cambridge. He assists at **Rose
Birkett's** wedding. (CBI 40)

❖ Unmarried, he was in India for six months as secretary to a
perambulating bishop. He deals with **Leslie Major's** conscience. (PE 47)

❖ He assists at **Anne Fielding's** wedding to **Robin Dale**.
(LAR 48)

❖ He assists at the christening of the Dales' twins. (CC 50)

Smith, Mrs. Joyce Perry

❖ As Miss Perry, she taught infant school at Rushwater, then
married **Mr. Smith**. After his death, she rents their former
home, the Red House ("too off-white and Sloan Square")
to the **Harveys**, though she keeps nipping in from her

S

lodging with **Mrs. Cox** to take things. **Millie Poulter** is her informant at the Red House. (MH 42)

* She has her hooks out for **Dr. Joram**; the **Bissells** are now her tenants. (CC 50)

* She has sold the Red House and gone to Torquay. (DD 51)

* Has she returned to live in Greshamsbury? See the remarkably similar **Mrs. Smith** of Green Close. (CQ 58)

Smith, Marigold

* At fifteen, she is the village problem girl, film-struck and a giggler. Her father is the **Warings'** head carter, and she has a younger brother, **Percy**, and a sister, **Flo**. She works for **Nannie Allen** at Ladysmith Cottages, Lambton. (GU 43)

* She now works at the **Winters'** Beliers Priory School, where she is attracted to both **Charles Belton** and **Geoff Coxon**. (LAR 48)

* Now a parlormaid, she gets engaged to Geoff and is given a Mizpah brooch by his mother **Mrs. (Ruth) Coxon**. She is impressed by the **Duchess of Omnium**, who tells her that Lady Gwendoline Elphin's second girl was also **Marigold (Elphin)**, but everyone called her Boodle. (DD 51)

* Still engaged, still at Beliers, and slowly shaping up under **Lady Glencora Palliser** Waring's discipline. Yet she still chooses awful clothes, and once swapped sugar with salt while setting the table. (HRt 52)

Smith, Mr.

* A respectable corn merchant in Barchester, like his father before him. He marries **Joyce Perry Smith** and dies of DT's. (MH 42)

Smith, Mrs.

❖ Of Green Close, Greshamsbury. Like **Mrs. (Joyce Perry) Smith**, she is a widow whose husband used to drink. She babysits for the **Parkinsons'** children. (CQ 58)

Smith, Percy

❖ Son of the **Waring's** head carter, ten years old; his sisters are **Marigold** and **Flo**. (GU 43)

Smith, Pinky

❖ A man with a lump on his neck who sends **Mr. Wickham** rum from the West Indies. (CC 50)

Smith-Heatherington, Tubby

❖ A naval boy, no last name given, who was torpedoed a month before. He and his friend **Bill** stay with the **Phelpses**, Jutland Cottage. Not to be confused with **Tubby Fewling**. (CBI 40)

❖ He now gets a last name. His parents are dead. He is not to be confused with **Swift-Heatherington** either. (JC 53)

Snow, Jim

❖ Carpenter, Southbridge School. He can get extra wood because his wife's cousin is the local representative of the Ministry of Works. (PE 47)

❖ He and his mate **George** repair the **Phelpses'** rain barrel. **Mrs. Phelps** reminds him of his Aunt Emma, who just faded away. (JC 53)

Solway, General, and Lady Babs

❖ Former patients of **Nurse Heath**; she died, worn out, a week after he did. (NTL 56)

S

Sonia, that dreadful: *See* **Arbuthnot, Peggy.**

Sowerby, Miss Hilda

* Of the Old Bank House, Edgewood, which she sells to **Sam Adams.** Her family used to own Chaldicotes, and were Rangers of the Chase for a hundred years, before it was deforested. Her father Tom died in debt and his uncle ruined himself, all due to gambling. She gives her prized *Palafox borealis* plant to **Mrs. (Mary) Grantly** (and **Sid Thatcher**), and goes to live with her widowed sister in Worthing. (OBH 49)

* She is happy in Worthing, with her sister's pleasant house, a pew at St. Praxed's, and a Fortnum and Mason's case from Mr. Adams each Christmas; he also sends a car for her in spring and autumn, so she can come and see the Old Bank House garden. (TSAT 61)

Spadger

* Of Winter Overcotes; a foxy man with a red (now white) moustache, expert at building cowsheds, which he does for **Lucy Marling** and **Sam Adams.** His wife died five years before, and he has no family. (OBH 49)

Sparks

* Maid to **Miss (Amelia) Brandon,** whose will leaves her fifty pounds a year, the family photographs, and the two carved gorillas from Brandon Abbey. She goes to live with her married sister at Swanage. (TB 39)

Sparling, Miss Madeleine

* Headmistress of the Hosiers' Girls' Foundation School, which is evacuated to Barchester High School; she has to

board there with **Miss (Bertha) Pettinger** for two years. (CBI 40)

❖ Her school in London was bombed in 1940. She moves the school into Harefield Park, which is rented from the **Beltons**. She is about forty-five; her father, a wine merchant, and her mother, also Madeleine, both died when she was fifteen. She went into the care of her mother's father, **Canon Horbury**, who made her get scholarships and left her his books when he died. She finished his work on **Fluvius Minucius** in an article in the *Journal of Fourth Century Latin Studies*, which wins the admiration of **Mr. (Sidney) Carton**, to whom she becomes engaged. She is honored as the first woman freeman of the Worshipful Company of Hosiers at the School's Bobbin Day ceremonies. (TH 44)

❖ She received an honorary D. Litt. from Oxbridge last year; she spends her holidays with Mr. Carton's mother at Bognor. (MB 45)

❖ The Barsetshire branch of the Classical Association gave a dinner in honor of her retirement and marriage; she turned down a student exchange with the Barchester High School. (PE 47)

❖ Now she is Mrs. Carton, retired. (LAR 48)

Sparrow, Mr.
❖ Butler to the **Palmers**, the Manor House, Worsted; also the village's fastest cricket bowler. (AF 36)

Spatch, Professor
❖ Gives a radio talk on Chryzomes and Epizomes. (ESR 55)

Spencer

* Tyrannous butler at Staple Park, home of **Lord** and **Lady Bond**. His wife died in Wolverhampton two years before. (BL 39)

* The Bonds are now living in part of the servants' wing, so Lord Bond could fire him. (LAR 48)

Spender, Billy

* Eldest son of **Major** and **Mrs. Major Spender**; he has a younger brother **Billy**, then a younger sister **Clarissa**. But at the Villars' New Years' party, his mother calls him her second boy. (NR 41)

* He is now in prep school. (GU 43)

* He is with his brother at Harberton Grammar School, Dorset. (DD 51)

Spender, Clarissa

* Youngest child of **Major** and **Mrs. Major Spender**; her older brothers are **Billy** and **Jimmy**. Three years old. (NR 41)

* At Barchester High School, she passed her school certificate a year early. (DD 51)

Spender, Jimmy

* Middle child of **Major** and **Mrs. Major Spender**; older brother **Billy**, younger sister **Clarissa**. (NR 41)

* Now seven. (GU 43)

* With his brother at Harberton Grammar School, Dorset. (DD 51)

Spender, Major ("Bobbums" to his wife)

❖ Stationed at the Hush-Hush camp, and billeted on the **Villars**, Northbridge Rectory. Thin and sensitive; his wife, **Mrs. Major Spender**, is the opposite. They have three children: **Billy**, the eldest, then **Jimmy**, and three-year-old **Clarissa**. But at the Villars' New Year's party, Billy is their second boy. (NR 41)

❖ Jimmy is now seven, while Billy is in prep school. (GU 43)

❖ The boys are at Harberton Grammar School in Dorset, and Clarissa passed her school certificate a year early at Barchester High School. (DD 51)

❖ As an artillery major, he was stationed in France at Vache-en-Étable, where he met **Mr. (John-Arthur) Cross(e)** and **George Halliday**. (ESR 55)

Spender, Mrs. Major (née Williams)

❖ Loud and obnoxious wife of **Major Spender**, whom she calls **Bobbums**. They have three children: **Billy**, the eldest, then **Jimmy**, and three-year-old **Clarissa**. But when she visits for the **Villars'** New Year's party, Billy is their second boy. Her cousin George is consul to Mixo-Lydia, as was her father and her mother's uncle (since the Mixo-Lydian rising of 1848). (NR 41)

❖ Jimmy is now seven, while Billy is in prep school. (GU 43)

❖ She wants to send her youngest boy (but *see* above) to **Philip Winter's** Beliers Priory School. (LAR 48)

❖ She attends the Barsetshire Archaeological. The boys are at Harberton Grammar School in Dorset, and Clarissa passed her school certificate a year early at Barchester High School. (DD 51)

S

Spindler, Mr.

❖ Proprietor of the Cow and Sickle, Pomfret Madrigal. Husband of **Mrs. Spindler**, uncle of the Vicar's cook, and brother of the Assistant Scoutmaster at Little Misfit. They had some trouble with **Wheeler** at the garage over a cask. (TB 39)

Spindler, Mrs.

❖ Proprietor of the Cow and Sickle, Pomfret Madrigal. Wife of **Mr. Spindler**, she was kitchenmaid to **Lady Norton** for three years. They had some trouble with **Wheeler** at the garage over a cask. (TB 39)

Spragge, Miss

❖ Shop assistant in the Ladies' Underwear department of Bostock and Plummer; told the Bishop's wife that uplift brassieres were in Juveniles. Her mother has been ailing, at her daughter's expense, for twenty-five years, as well as being deaf and wanting in intellect. (JC 53)

Spurge-Mackworth

❖ Author of *A Concept of Neo-Phallic Thought*; lectured at **Mrs. (Elaine) Bissell's** training college. (CBI 40)

Stanhope, Mr. ("Squobs")

❖ Latin master at Southbridge School. He disciplines **Wilson**. (CQ 58)

Starter, (the Honourable) Miss Juliana

❖ Of 203 Ebury Street, Top Floor. Aged and impecunious daughter of **Lord Mickleham**, and former lady-in-waiting to **Princess Louisa Christina**, daughter of **Prince Louis of Cobalt**. Strict in diet as in behavior; her physicians are **Sir Barclay Milvin** in London and **Dr. Picton** in Tunbridge

Wells. Her grandfather was the author of *Essays in Anglican Agnosticism* and raised his entire family to be agnostic. She visits **Lady Bond** at Staple Park. (BL 39)

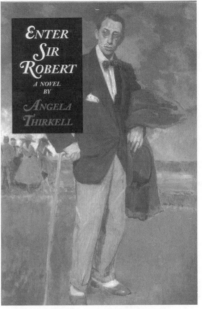

* Her mother was a **Miss Foster**, a Victorian beauty. She is a cousin of the **Luftons**, and puts up **Ludovic, Lord Lufton**, in her home in Buckingham Gate when he has to go to the House of Lords; for the small rent he pays, she takes his ration book, won't give him tea, and feeds him on cold cereal. (HRt 52)

* She is related to the **Pallisers** by marriage. Her income is a first charge on the diminished estate of **the present Lord Mickleham**, but she takes in paying guests, charges an outrageous rent, and complains of poverty nonetheless. (JC 53)

* She has a maid. (NTL 56)

* She is now the daughter of *old* Lord Mickleham, whose *son* married the heiress Dolly Foster. She goes with Princess Louisa Christina on an (uninvited) weekend with the **Harcourts, Duke and Duchess of Towers**. (LAAA 59)

Stevenson, Joan
* In charge of Uplift Poetry Readings at the B.B.C. She got a First in Economics at Oxford, and was secretary to Prof.

Gilbert. She comes to Rushwater, stays with the **Boulles**, flirts with **David Leslie**, but makes herself a companionate marriage with **Lionel Harvest**. (WS 34)

✢ As **Mrs. Harvest**, she has what she calls a salon in Bloomsbury. (DD 51)

Stoke, Dora
   ✢ Mother of **Captain Tom Barclay** and distant relation of **Lord Stoke**. (MH 42)

Stoke, Lady
   ✢ Of Rising Castle; wife of **Lord Stoke**. (HR 33)

   ✢ She has died. (BL 39)

   ✢ She never existed. (NTL 56)

Stoke, Old Lord
   ✢ With his first wife, the former **Miss Hooper**, father of **Thomas, Lord Stoke**; father of **Lucasta, Lady Bond** by a second marriage. (MH 42)

   ✢ His aunt went into a decline over a celibate curate; her father took away the curate's clothes while he was swimming in the river. (LAAA 59)

Stoke, Thomas, Lord
   ✢ An earl, of Rising Castle; there is also a **Lady Stoke**. He is quite deaf, but a good friend to **Mrs. (Laura) Morland**. (HR 33)

   ✢ He has Laura and **Tony Morland** and **Wesendonck** to see Rising Castle. (DH 34)

   ✢ He once played Disraeli to **Mrs. (Hermione) Rivers'** Hypatia at a Rising Castle houseparty. (PT 38)

❖ He puts off a trip to Aix for **Miss (Amelia) Brandon's** funeral. (TB 39)

❖ Now a widower. His half-sister is **Lucasta, Lady Bond**, and her son, **C.W. Bond**, is his heir. He has an Uncle Henry; also an Uncle Fred who left two illegitimate children: a boy who's now on the Stock Exchange, and a girl who married a man in India. An enthusiastic archaeologist, he shows the bones found in Bloody Meadow (perhaps those of **Thorstein Longtooth**) to **Mr. (Gilbert) Tebben**. (BL 39)

❖ He is enjoying an Agricultural Congress in Denmark, but sends **Rose Birkett** a wedding present. (CBI 40)

❖ His genealogy is given: his father, **Old Lord Stoke**, first married **Miss Hooper**, an heiress from Somerset, producing Lord Stoke. The Old Lord's second marriage produced Lucasta Bond. He is also a distant relative of **Dora Stoke, Tom Barclay's** mother. (MH 42)

❖ He lectures on the excavations at Bloody Meadow to convalescent soldiers at Beliers Priory. (GU 43)

❖ His title goes back to the Wars of the Roses; the family has been at High Rising since 1400. He, like all his family, went to Eton. Now over eighty, he rides or drives a barouche in order to save petrol. He is writing his autobiography, and is president for life of the Barsetshire Archaeological Society, whose meeting at Hallbury he presides over, showing **Frank Gresham** and **Tom Watson** the Old Rectory well (as he once showed Tony Morland and Wesendonck Rising Castle). (MB 45)

S

* He wins an ugly vase at the Holdings Bring & Buy Sale. (PBO 46)

* He (with his pig Pompey) presides at the Conservative Rally and Pig Breeders' Meeting at the **Bonds'** Staple Park. (LAR 48)

* (Still) over eighty and increasingly deaf; he never had any children and can't think why. (OBH 49)

* Now "well over eighty," though born in 1876, and never married. He was in love with **Edith Thorne**, later **Lady Pomfret**, and gave her a pearl necklace, which she returned, probably on her engagement; he gives the pearls to **Edith Graham**, her namesake. Now his is one of the oldest baronies in the West of England, and he is the thirteenth baron; his name is also changed to Algernon Courcy Stoke (**Old Lord de Courcy** was his godfather). His sister, the now-widowed Lady Bond, wanted to live in the village near him, but he hadn't a house empty, so she moved to Bath. The Friends of Rising Castle now pay half a crown to visit his house. He is rude to **Sir Ogilvy Hibberd** about the footpath under Bolder's Knob. (ESR 55)

* Lady Bond went to Bournemouth, where Lord Stoke would prefer that she live (rather than with him?). (NTL 56)

* He gives **Miss Merriman**, Lady Pomfret's former companion, a bag of gold coins for her wedding to **Mr. (Herbert) Choyce**. (ADA 57)

* Still going strong and *still* over eighty. (LAAA 59)

* Rising Castle is the mansion built by his great-grandfather from the stones of the Norman era Rising Castle. He opens

the High Rising Agricultural and presides at the rally to save **Wiple** Terrace. He has had youthful amours, including during his time at King's and when he was attached to the Embassy in Paris. He once half-proposed to Mrs. Morland (but this was actually **Lord Crosse**), and now proposes to **Sylvia Gould**, who turns him down. (TSAT 61)

Stoker

❖ Invaluable household help to **Mrs. (Laura) Morland**, and cosseter of **Tony Morland**. She calls herself "Mrs. Stoker" to increase respect, but her father's real name was **Mac-Henry**; he got the other from shoveling coke at the gasworks. Her mother, long dead, was the pious support of a peculiar sect. Her aunt once called out "Henry, Henry" in her sleep, and the next day her Uncle Alf died. (HR 33)

❖ She was born at Plaistow, and is at war with the Vicarage cook. (DH 34)

❖ She doesn't approve of the blackout. (CBI 40)

❖ Her father was a drinker. She and her mother had to identify him at a mortuary on the Tuesday after Easter. She goes back to Plaistow every other year or so. (NTL 56)

❖ **Tucker** is her uncle, by marriage to her determined aunt, who gave him a lovely funeral, and later died of dropsy. (LAAA 59)

❖ Her aunt at Plaistow (who is rising ninety but still active) had been frightened by an organ grinder's monkey while pregnant, and then gave birth prematurely to a feeble-witted boy who is now in a Home and nearly killed a male

S

nurse. Her aunt's cousin's daughter was hit in the eye by an exploding piece of coal and needed an operation. Then her Auntie died after giving her a Mizpah brooch, which she gives to Mrs. Morland for her seventieth birthday. (TSAT 61)

Stonor, Colonel

✤ Father of **Denis** and **Daphne**; a widower (his first wife died in India) who then married **Lilian Middleton**, and himself died. Of the 23rd regiment, the same as **Alister Cameron's** father and as the late **Harry, Lord Mellings**. (BL 39)

Stonor, Daphne

✤ Younger daughter (age twenty-one) of **Colonel Stonor** and his first wife; she died in India, he later on. Sister of **Denis Stonor**; they get on well with their young step-mother, **Lilian Middleton Stonor**. She lost her job as secretary to **Dr. Browning** because of his death. She stays with her stepmother at the White House for the summer, doing some secretary work for **Lady Bond** and falling in love with her son, **C.W.** (though she meanwhile gets herself engaged to **Alister Cameron** when she thinks C.W. is engaged to **Betty Dean**, but eventually breaks it off). She and C.W. are engaged. (BL 39)

✤ She is now Mrs. C.W. Bond, with two little boys aged six and four. They live at the White Cottage, near the **Middletons**. She has a reunion with Denis. (LAR 48)

✤ She is referred to (incorrectly, as **Alured, Lord Bond** later proves to be still alive) as **Young Lady Bond**. (CC 50)

Strelsa, Guido

❖ Brother of **Count Strelsa**. A blackguard, turned out of every gambling hell in Europe. (PT 38)

❖ He gave a little dog, Carlo, to **Lady Agnes**, sister of **Lord Pomfret**. The dog, perhaps a pug she holds in a photo, later died of overeating. (OBH 49)

❖ Still a thoroughly bad egg, though **Ludovic, Lord Mellings** was given "Guido" as one of his names. He used to lend Lady Pomfret *his* villa, the Casa Strelsa in Florence, whenever she wanted it, or every winter; so now he is seen as being the Count. (NTL 56)

❖ As Count Guido, he is now shaky, hairless and toothless, under the care of nuns; the rest of the Strelsa cousins are almost more English than the English. (LAAA 59)

Stringer

❖ Lawyers to **the Bishop**; the firm was involved in that business of the cheque in Bishop Proudie's day (*cf.* Trollope). (CQ 58)

Stringer, Clem

❖ Of Silverbridge; "Horsy fellow that drinks."—**Mr. Wickham**. His great uncle "or someone" got into trouble over a cheque in Silverbridge years ago (*cf.* Trollope). (HRt 52)

Stringer, Mr.

❖ Barchester contractor who built **Mr. Scatcherd's** house, Rokeby, for his old mother. He lost his money by speculation and died three weeks before she did. (PBO 46)

Sub-organist of Barchester Cathedral

❖ "A pupil-teacher or whatever you call him . . . hopeless," according to the **Dowager Duchess of Towers**. There

were rumors about his holiday in Monte Carlo, where he
stayed at the Pensione Smith kept by the widow of a retired
English bank clerk; he blamed being thirty-six hours late
for his return on the Italian trains. But then the next year he
went to Holland, which proved him un-gossip-worthy.
(LAAA 59)

Suffragan Bishop of Kedgeree, the
❖ An old pupil of the vicar of Southbridge, well-known in the
  mission field in India. (PE 47)

Sumpter, Lee
❖ Along with **Sherman Concord**, a beau of **Edith Graham**
  in the States. (ADA 57)

❖ Now spelled "Sumter," he is a lawyer, a cousin of **Franklin,
  Duchess of Towers**, and is variously from South Carolina
  or Virginia. His mother, who is still around, was a Beaure-
  gard. He was once nursed by **Sister Chiffinch**. He exchanges grips with **Mr. Wickham** at the **Oriels'** wedding.
  (LAAA 59)

Sutton, Lottie
❖ Daughter of **Old Sutton** and former scullery maid at
  Rushwater. Now in the county asylum. (WS 34)

Sutton, Old
❖ Caretaker, Rushmere Abbey. Father of **Lottie**. (WS 34)

Swan, Eric
❖ Boy in **Everard Carter's** house, Southbridge School; a
  friend of **Tony Morland**. He has young half-uncles and
  aunts. He visits the **Keiths**, and looks at **Philip Winter**
  through his spectacles. (SH 37)

❖ He is in Everard Carter's old College in Cambridge, waiting for his call-up. (CBI 40)

❖ Just back from Africa. (PBO 46)

❖ Now he is a new master at Philip Winter's Beliers Priory School. He had met the late **Lord Gerald Palliser** in an O.C.T.U. (DD 51)

❖ Now thirty. His mother was **Flora Ramsay**, who has lived with her family in Scotland since his father died, during the war. He has some money, and will have more. His tutor at Paul's in Oxford (but see above; presumably he didn't graduate Cambridge) was **Mr. (Charles) Fanshawe**, and he got a First in Greats. He has written a book on **Fluvius Minucius**. He became a major during the war, and spent time in Germany. He lectures on Sir Walter Scott's Younger Contemporaries at the Barchester Central Library, at the request of **Grace Grantly**, with whom he falls in love; but he has to settle for being best man at her wedding to **Ludovic, Lord Lufton**. (HRt 52)

❖ Now he took a Second at Paul's when the war was over. He chooses to stay on at Philip Winter's school (now at Harefield Park) rather than go for a fellowship at Paul's, and gets engaged to **Justinia Lufton**. (JC 53)

❖ They are now married. (WDIM 54)

❖ He becomes headmaster of Southbridge School when Everard Carter retires. (TSAT 61)

Swan, (Mrs.) Justinia: *See* **Lufton, Justinia**.

Swift-Hetherington, J.W.
+ Seven- or eight-year-old boy who boxes against **A.L. Fair-weather** in a match at Southbridge School. (HR 33)

Swop, Washington
+ He co-stars with **Glamora Tudor** in a revival of *Burning Flesh*. (ESR 55)

Tacker, Mr.
 * Husband of **Mrs. Tacker**. Sexton of Rushwater church. (PBO 46)

Tacker, Mrs.
 * Wife of **Mr. Tacker**. Formerly a housemaid at Rushwater. (PBO 46)

Tadpole, Hermione, Lady: *See* **Bingham, Hermione**.

Tadpole, Lord
 * Of Tadpole Hall, Tadcaster. He married **Hermione Bingham** just before the war, and they have one daughter. (PBO 46)

 * There are suddenly four babies; the most recent to be christened at Tadcaster, where his cousin has a living. (LAR 48)

* One of the children, a girl, was a seven-month preemie; **Nurse Chiffinch** came in to help. (CC 50)

* They have Nurse Chiffinch for the holidays in Shropshire. (HRt 52)

* He is a churchwarden, very estate-minded, and an expert on shire horses. They have **David** and **Rose Bingham Leslie's** children to stay with them. (ESR 55)

Tadstock, Mistress Pomphelia
* Widow of a canon of Barchester, and object of the erotic verses of the **Rev. Thomas Bohun**. She was buried in Barchester cathedral. (ESR 55)

* She had been married three times. (ADA 57)

Talbot, Sir Alwyn, K.C.M.G.
* Ex-principal of the Board of Tape and Sealing Wax, and middle brother between **Dr. Tufnell Talbot** and **Prof. Armorel Talbot**. Deaf and eighty-six years old, he goes with his elder brother on a Christmas visit to their younger brother at The Aloes. They have a row over Europe and Armorel has a slight stroke, so they leave early, to the relief of his nieces, **Marjorie** and **Dolly Talbot**. (NR 41)

Talbot, Professor Armorel
* Of The Aloes. Father of **Marjorie** and **Dolly**. An authority on the medieval church, eighty-three years old. He endures a Christmas visit from his older brothers **Sir Alwyn Talbot** and **Dr. Tufnell Talbot**; they have a row over Europe and he has a slight stroke, so they leave early, to his daughters' relief. (NR 41)

* He has died. (PE 47)

❖ He died (again!) last summer, at age ninety-five, after having been cross, bedridden and senile for five years, but he leaves his daughters comfortably off. (WDIM 54)

❖ He has died yet again, as reported in the *Barchester Chronicle* and by **Mrs. Dunster**. (ADA 57)

Talbot, Miss Dolly

❖ Of The Aloes. Younger daughter of **Professor Armorel Talbot** and sister of **Miss Marjorie Talbot**. She and her sister are volunteer parachute spotters and ardent adherents of the high-church **Father Fewling**, though they have a brief flirtation with the yet-higher **Father Hislop** at Nutfield. They have a trying Christmas when their uncles, **Sir Alwyn Talbot** and **Dr. Tufnell Talbot**, visit, and are relieved when they leave. (NR 41)

❖ Their father has died, and they take in occasional lodgers, such as **Mrs. (Verena) Villars'** aunt with arthritis. She volunteers as a Red Cross Library bookbinder. (PE 47)

❖ After having been cross, bedridden, and senile for five years, their father died again last summer. They are left comfortably off, and work on the Coronation festivities. (WDIM 54)

❖ Their father has died yet again, as reported in the *Barchester Chronicle* and by **Mrs. Dunster**. (ADA 57)

Talbot, Miss Marjorie

❖ Of The Aloes. Elder daughter (so usually called "Miss Talbot") of **Professor Armorel Talbot**, and sister of **Miss Dolly Talbot**. She and her sister are volunteer parachute spotters and ardent adherents of the high-church **Father**

Fewling, though they have a brief flirtation with the yet-higher **Father Hislop** at Nutfield. They have a trying Christmas when their uncles, **Sir Alwyn Talbot** and **Dr. Tufnell Talbot**, visit, and are relieved when they leave. (NR 41)

❖ Their father has died, and they take in occasional lodgers, such as **Mrs. (Verena) Villars'** aunt with arthritis. (PE 47)

❖ After having been cross, bedridden and senile for five years, their father died again last summer. They are left comfortably off, and work on the Coronation festivities. (WDIM 54)

❖ Their father has died yet again, as reported in the *Barchester Chronicle* and by **Mrs. Dunster**. (ADA 57)

Talbot, Dr. Tufnell, F.R.P.S.
❖ Eldest brother of **Sir Alwyn Talbot** and **Prof. Armorel Talbot**. He is eighty-eight, and has been a widower for fifty-two years. He goes with his middle brother on a Christmas visit to their younger brother at The Aloes. They have a row over Europe and Armorel has a slight stroke, so they leave early, to the relief of his nieces, **Marjorie** and **Dolly Talbot**. (NR 41)

Tall Dark Girl from the Upper Sixth, the
❖ At the Hosiers' Girls' Foundation School. She plays Oliver in *As You Like It*, completely in monotone. (TH 44)

Tebben, Mr. Gilbert
❖ Husband of **Mrs. (Winifred) Tebben**, father of **Richard** and **Margaret**. A civil servant and expert in Icelandic sagas, mainstay of the Snorri Society. He was at Paul's College

Oxford, and met his wife on a cruise to Norway. Their country place is Lamb's Piece, where they have a cat Gunnar and a donkey Modestine (Neddy). (AF 36)

* He and his wife attend the meeting about Pooker's Piece. He visits **Lord Stoke** to see the (putative) bones of **Thorstein Longtooth**. (BL 39)

* He lectures the convalescent soldiers at Beliers Priory on the *Elder Edda*. (GU 43)

* Modestine is dead, and they now keep a nanny goat. (MB 45)

* He is lately retired. In World War I, he was in the censor's department on Scandinavian affairs. They stand up to their son Richard. (LAR 48)

* They vacationed with Richard and his new wife **Petrea Krogsbrog** in Sweden in June. (OBH 49)

* They summered with them in Sweden again. (DD 51)

* In the Worsted coronation pageant, he does a scene of the English driving out the Danes. (WDIM 54)

Tebben, Margaret
* Younger child of **Mr. (Gilbert)** and **Mrs. (Winifred) Tebben**, sister of **Richard**. She has been living abroad as an *au pair*, first in Germany, then in Grenoble, where she met **Laurence Dean**. She summers with her parents at Lamb's Piece, where Laurence flirts with her. She backs out of playing Phaedra in *Hippolytus*, due to **Mrs. (Louise) Palmer's** outburst, and that causes Laurence to twist his ankle, but they are engaged as a result. (AF 36)

* She has another baby, a girl this time. They are all with Laurence in Scotland. (GU 43)

* They and the "little brood" are at home. (MB 45)

* They have four children. (PE 47)

* They live abroad. Their son at Beliers Priory School is **Young Dean**. (LAR 48)

* They now live in Worsted. (WDIM 54)

Tebben, Richard

* Elder child of **Mr. (Gilbert)** and **Mrs. (Winifred) Tebben**, brother of **Margaret**. Having gotten only a poor Third at St. Jude's College, Oxford, he summers with his (despised) parents at Lamb's Piece. There he falls in calf love with **Mrs. (Rachel) Dean**, trains the chorus for **Mrs. (Louise) Palmer's** *Hippolytus*, makes an extraordinary catch at the cricket match, and saves **Jessica Dean** from a bull. In gratitude, **Mr. (Frank) Dean** offers him a job in his firm. (AF 36)

* He is on a three-year job for Mr. Dean in South America. (BL 39)

* He is in Cairo (which is "just like Piccadilly"), presumably in the Army. (GU 43)

* He is out of the Army with a stiff knee. He learned Spanish on his South American job, which was in Argentina. He is offered a job in **Sam Adams'** works. (MB 45)

* At thirty-three or thirty-four, he is second in command of Mr. Adams' Stockholm agency. He brings **Petrea Krogsbrog** from Sweden to England for a visit. She disciplines

him about respecting his parents, and they get engaged. (LAR 48)

❖ They are married and live in Sweden. He is very successful on the commercial side. (OBH 49)

❖ He wrote a scene on Beliers Abbey for the Worsted coronation pageant. (WDIM 54)

Tebben, Mrs. Winifred (née Ross)

❖ Wife of **Mr. Gilbert Tebben**, mother of **Richard** and **Margaret**. She was at St. Mildred's College, Oxford, and was a fellow student of **Effie Pitcher-Jukes**, whom she beat out for the Octavia Crammer Prize. She took a First in Economics, was a tutor, and now writes textbooks. She met her husband on a cruise to Norway. Their country place is Lamb's Piece, where they have a cat Gunnar and a donkey Modestine (Neddy). She is obsessed with using up leftover food, and plays the Nurse in **Mrs. (Louise) Palmer's** production of *Hippolytus*. (AF 36)

❖ She and her husband attend the meeting about Pooker's Piece. (BL 39)

❖ Modestine is dead, and they now keep a nanny goat. (MB 45)

❖ They stand up to their son Richard. (LAR 48)

❖ She is close to Richard's new wife **Petrea Krogsbrog**. They vacationed with them in Sweden in June. (OBH 49)

❖ They summered with them in Sweden again. (DD 51)

Ted, Old

❖ A nasty thing happened to him with a pig when he was young; as a result, he wore the pig's tooth on his watch

chain on Sundays. Later he worked for **Lord Stoke's** father
at Rising Castle. He went where bees swarmed because
their stings cured the rheumatics. (BL 39)

Tempest, Canon
* An angry elderly clergyman, retired but takes Sundays at
Lambton. **Octavia Crawley's** godfather. He lives with his
niece, but wants to get away to Devonshire. (GU 43)

Tempest, Mr.
* Vicar of St. Ewold's before **Mr. (Justin) Miller's** appointment. He was of good Barsetshire family with private
means, and kept the church traditional. (HRt 52)

Thatcher
* Would have won first prize in vedge at the High Rising
Agricultural if his little boy hadn't carved "Teechers A
Fule" on his prize marrow. (TSAT 61)

Thatcher, Sergeant Alf
* Of Grumper's End and the Barsetshire Regiment. All the
Grumper's End Thatchers are intermarried and full of
gypsy blood. His mother ran off with a commercial traveler,
his father drank, and he was brought up by an unlikeable
uncle and aunt. He won the George Cross for bravery, but
is now serving seven years because he and his friends beat
up an old pawnbroker in Limehouse whom they suspected
of having a concealed fortune. (CC 50)

Thatcher, Bessie
* From Grumper's End; cousin to **Edna** and **Doris
Thatcher**. Formerly nurse with **Mrs. (Jane) Gresham** at
Hallbury. Goes to Stories to be **Mrs. Peggy Arbuthnot**
Brandon's childrens' nurse. (HRt 52)

Thatcher, Doris

❖ Of Grumper's End. One of **Mr. and Mrs. Thatcher's** four boys (including **Herb, Jimmy,** and **Teddy**) and three girls; her eldest sister is **Edna**. She has an illegitimate baby, **Glad** (for Gladys). (TB 39)

❖ Now there are eight brothers and sisters (including **Ernie**), plus most of the evacuees. She and Edna are working as daily helps at the Cow and Sickle. (CBI 40)

❖ They had an outbreak of measles in the summer that **Miss (Amelia) Brandon** died, due to a forgotten cesspool in their back yard. (MB 45)

❖ She and Edna have been working for **Rector (Septimus)** and **Mrs. (Mary) Grantly** since shortly after the Peace. She now has four children of various fathers: Glad, **Sid, Stan,** and **Glamora**. (OBH 49)

Thatcher, Edna

❖ Of Grumper's End. Oldest of **Mr.** and **Mrs. Thatchers's** four boys (including **Herb, Jimmy,** and **Teddy**) and three girls; her closest sister is **Doris**. She had an illegitimate baby, **Purse** (for Percy), in 1936. (TB 39)

❖ Now there are eight brothers and sisters (including **Ernie**), plus most of the evacuees. She and Doris are working as daily helps at the Cow and Sickle. (CBI 40)

❖ They had an outbreak of measles in the summer that **Miss (Amelia) Brandon** died, due to a forgotten cesspool in their back yard. (MB 45)

❖ She and Doris have been working for **Rector (Septimus)** and **Mrs. (Mary) Grantly** since shortly after the Peace. She named Purse (now twelve) after an Army Service Corps corporal. (OBH 49)

Thatcher, Ernie

❖ Of Grumper's End. Perhaps the unnamed son of **Mr.** and **Mrs. Thatcher's** four boys (including **Herb, Jimmy**, and **Teddy**) and three girls (including the eldest, **Edna**, and **Doris**). (TB 39)

❖ Now there are eight children (including him by name), plus most of the evacuees. (CBI 40)

❖ They had an outbreak of measles in the summer that **Miss (Amelia) Brandon** died, due to a forgotten cesspool in their back yard. (MB 45)

Thatcher, Glad (Gladys)

❖ Illegitimate child of **Doris Thatcher**. (TB 39)

❖ She now has siblings **Sid, Stan**, and **Glamora**, of various fathers. (OBH 49)

Thatcher, Glamora

❖ Youngest illegitimate child of **Doris Thatcher**. Her elder siblings are **Glad, Sid**, and **Stan**, of various fathers. (OBH 49)

Thatcher, Herb

❖ Of Grumper's End. One of **Mr.** and **Mrs. Thatcher's** four boys (the others include **Jimmy** and **Teddy**) and three girls (including the eldest, **Edna**, and **Doris**). (TB 39)

❖ Now there are eight children, including **Ernie**, plus most of the evacuees. (CBI 40)

❖ They had an outbreak of measles in the summer that **Miss (Amelia) Brandon** died, due to a forgotten cesspool in their back yard. (MB 45)

Thatcher, Jimmy
❖ Of Grumper's End. One of **Mr.** and **Mrs. Thatcher's** four boys (the other include **Herb** and **Teddy**) and three girls (including the eldest, **Edna**, and **Doris**). He serves as acolyte to **Mr. (Justin) Miller** at the Pomfret Madrigal church, and wants to be a dentist. He gets appendicitis at the Vicarage Fete and has to be rushed to hospital, but under the aegis of **Miss (Ella) Morris** he recovers. (TB 39)

❖ Now there are eight children, including **Ernie**, plus most of the evacuees. (CBI 40)

❖ They had an outbreak of measles in the summer that **Miss (Amelia) Brandon** died, due to a forgotten cesspool in their back yard. (MB 45)

❖ He is now eighteen and has a University Scholarship to the Great Western University. (CC 50)

❖ He is in the Air Force at Cologne. (HRt 52)

Thatcher, Lance-Corporal
❖ Of Grumper's End. All the Thatchers there are intermarried and full of gypsy blood. His career in the Barsetshire regiment had mostly been under arrest, for pinching stores. (CC 50)

Thatcher, Mr.
❖ Of Grumper's End. Husband of **Mrs. Thatcher**, and father of four boys (including **Herb, Jimmy,** and **Teddy**) and three girls (including the eldest, **Edna**, and **Doris**). He has a bad leg. (TB 39)

❖ Now there are eight children (including **Ernie**), plus most of the evacuees. He gambles and drinks. (CBI 40)

❖ They had an outbreak of measles in the summer that **Miss (Amelia) Brandon** died, due to a forgotten cesspool in their back yard. (MB 45)

❖ All the Grumper's End Thatchers are intermarried and full of gypsy blood. (CC 50)

Thatcher, Mrs.

❖ Of Grumper's End. Wife of **Mr. Thatcher**, and mother of four boys (including **Herb, Jimmy,** and **Teddy**) and three girls (including the eldest, **Edna**, and **Doris**). She gets hysterical when Jimmy gets appendicitis at the Pomfret Madrigal Vicarage Fete. (TB 39)

❖ Now there are eight children (including **Ernie**) plus most of the evacuees. She works as a char. (CBI 40)

❖ They had an outbreak of measles in the summer that **Miss (Amelia) Brandon** died, due to a forgotten cesspool in their back yard. (MB 45)

❖ All the Grumper's End Thatchers are intermarried and full of gypsy blood. (CC 50)

❖ When **Mr. (Theodore) Parkinson** had pneumonia, she sent her niece to the vicarage to help out. (HRt 52)

Thatcher, Purse (Percy)

❖ Illegitimate child of **Edna Thatcher**, born in 1936. (TB 39)

❖ He was named after an Army Service Corps corporal. He is now twelve, and good with cars. (OBH 49)

* He has a scholarship to the County Technical School. Now the success of **Miss (Hilda) Sowerby's** *Palafox borealis* is attributed to his skill with the radio rather than that of his cousin **Sid Thatcher**. (HRt 52)

Thatcher, Sid

* Illegitimate child of **Doris Thatcher**. His elder sibling is **Glad**, the younger ones are **Stan** and **Glamora**, of various fathers. He is very good with plants, and grows **Miss Sowerby's** *Palafox borealis* to blooming with the aid of the radio. (OBH 49)

* The success of *Palafox* is now attributed to his cousin **Purse Thatcher's** skill with the radio. (HRt 52)

* They got fifty pounds for the *Palafox* seeds, which went into his post office account. **Sam Adams** has his eye on him as a gardener for Adamsfield. (TSAT 61)

Thatcher, Stan

* Illegitimate child of **Doris Thatcher**. His elder siblings are **Glad** and **Sid**, the youngest is **Glamora**, of various fathers. (OBH 49)

Thatcher, Teddy

* Of Grumper's End. One of **Mr.** and **Mrs. Thatcher's** four boys (the others include **Jimmy** and **Herb**) and three girls (including the eldest, **Edna**, and **Doris**). He is disqualified from the sack race at the Pomfret Madrigal Vicarage Fete due to poor sportsmanship. (TB 39)

* Now there are eight children, including **Ernie**, plus most of the evacuees. (CBI 40)

* They had an outbreak of measles in the summer that **Miss (Amelia) Brandon** died, due to a forgotten cesspool in their back yard. (MB 45)

Thomas, Miss Dolly
* Daughter of **Dr. Thomas**, younger sister of **Phyllis**. She is in the chorus of **Mrs. (Louise) Palmer's** production of *Hippolytus*. (AF 36)

Thomas, Dr.
* The rector, father of **Phyllis** and **Dolly**. A good classicist, but deaf; he coaches **Betty Dean** for the role of Phaedra in *Hippolytus*. (AF 36)

Thomas, Miss Phyllis
* Daughter of **Dr. Thomas**, elder sister of **Dolly**, so generally called "Miss Thomas." She leads the second chorus in **Mrs. (Louise) Palmer's** production of *Hippolytus*. (AF 36)

Thompson, Rev.
* A clergyman who christens **Fred Wamber's** first child **Zernebok**. (LAAA 59)

Thorne, Admiral
* His Trafalgar monument in Barchester Cathedral has Neptune and a mourning Britannia on it. (CBI 40)

Thorne, Canon
* A peaceable elderly bachelor with High Church leanings. **The Bishop** accused him of Mariolatry, and it is taken as an omen that when the Bishop's cellar flooded, his second-best gaiters washed up on the Canon's front steps. (CBI 40)

* He is indignant about **the Bishop's wife** turning the palace wine cooler into a planter. (PBO 46)

* He dies. **Mr. (Septimus) Grantly** does his funeral service, and **Dr. Joram** gets the Vinery, his house in the Close. (OBH 49)

* He was reclusive in his last years, while writing a commentary on the *Pastoral Charges* of **Hippocampus**. His widowed sister wrote a Life of him, privately printed, in which she remembers sitting in a carriage with her great-aunt Miss (Monica) Thorne (*cf.* Trollope) and waiting for the footman to being them ices from Gunter's. (CC 50)

* He used to imitate Regency speech with the late **Lord Lufton**. When he was vicar of St. Paradox, he kept two curates out of his own private funds to visit in the parish. (HRt 52)

* Apparently he has been resurrected. "He is now immune to all mundane matters except his meals and the intromissions of the Bishop." (CQ 58)

Thorne, Edith: *See* **Pomfret, Edith, Lady**.

Thorne, Mr.
* Conservative Member of Parliament for Barchester. He can't stand for re-election due to a heart condition, so he hands it to **Sir Robert Fielding**. (PBO 46)

Thorne, Young
* A farmer with his father near Chaldicotes. He wins the Silver Challenge Cup as an outstanding rider at the Nutfield Gymkhana. (TSAT 61)

Tidden, Horace
* Mentally defective son of the marriage between cousins **Ned Tidden** (a bit dotty) and **Lily Tidden** (illegitimate

and insane). He was a laborer on **Lord Pomfret's** estate, but he killed the old uncle and aunt he lodged with, then threw himself down a well. (TB 39)

Tidden, Lily

❖ Illegitimate, she married her cousin **Ned Tidden**, and produced a mentally defective son, **Horace**. She nearly killed a nurse at the County Asylum, and then became quite happy and quiet. (TB 39)

❖ She is still alive, and **Dr. Ford** sees her at the Asylum. (OBH 49)

Tidden, Ned

❖ From **Lord Pomfret's** estate. He was a bit dotty, married his cousin **Lily Tidden**, and produced a mentally defective son, **Horace**. (TB 39)

Todd, Anne

❖ Daughter of **Mrs. Todd**, whom she lives with and cares for (with the help of their maid **Louisa**). Fortyish, she is a great fan of **Mrs. (Laura) Morland's** books, and does secretarial work for her. They are very badly off, and **Dr. Ford** visits her mother with as little cost as her pride allows. She masterminds the downfall of **Una Grey**. When her mother dies, she breaks down; **Dr. Ford** proposes to her, but she refuses him and accepts **George Knox**. (HR 33)

❖ Now married, she gives a tea for **Adrian** and **Sibyl Knox Coates** and **Tony Morland** and his mother. (DH 34)

❖ She is W.V.S. Secretary, and a friend of **Mrs. (Catherine) Middleton**. (MB 45)

* She invites the **Grahams** (including **Edith Graham's** beaux) to punt on their bit of river. (NTL 56)

* When her father had died, she and her mother were left badly off, and she had had to sell her pony. (LAAA 59)

Todd, Mrs.
* Mother of **Anne Todd**, who lives with and cares for her (with the help of their maid **Louisa**). She is gently mad, and has a heart condition. They are very badly off, and **Dr. Ford** visits her with as little cost as pride allows. She dies. (HR 33)

* She and Anne were left badly off when her husband died. (LAAA 59)

Tomkins
* Engineer of the *Rising Castle*, disheartened at wartime measures. (GU 43)

Tomkins
* Woodman for **Lord Pomfret**, Pomfret Towers. (LAAA 59)

Tomkins
* Former boot-and-knife man at **the Bishop's** Palace, Barchester. He brought back a French wife, **Madame Tomkins**, from his service in World War I, then left for New Zealand due to her temper. (MB 45)

* His father is **Old Tomkins**. (PBO 46)

* He was married in 1917; he is sometimes vaguely heard of in South Africa and Australia. (OBH 49)

* By now, he is almost mythical. (LAAA 59)

Tomkins, Madame

✢ Dressmaker, of Barley Street, Barchester. French wife of **Tomkins**, who brought her back from his service in World War I, but left due to her temper. (MB 45)

✢ **Old Tomkins** is her father-in-law. She argues with **Mrs. Betts** because she rented out a room for the Clothing Exchange. (PBO 46)

✢ She makes **Anne Fielding's** wedding gown. (LAR 48)

✢ She was married in 1917; Tomkins is sometimes vaguely heard of in South Africa and Australia. (OBH 49)

✢ **Jennifer Gorman** is working as her assistant. By now, Tomkins is almost mythical, and a *commis-voyageur* in the silk trade has his eye on her (or, she thinks, on her savings). (LAAA 59)

Tomkins, Old

✢ Father of **Tomkins**, and father-in-law of **Madame Tomkins**. Jobbing gardener of the Close, Barchester. (PBO 46)

✢ "I'm no gardener, I'm a sexton I am." He finds the bell that used to be rung by the fish in the Palace pond, and which **the Bishop and his wife** had had removed. He and the young **Grahams** and **Leslies** rehang it. (CC 50)

✢ His son is verger of the Cathedral, and will allow **Leslie Minor** to climb the Palace tulip tree when the Bishop and his wife are out of the way. (ESR 55)

Tompion, Mr.

✢ Low-church vicar of Little Misfit. Famed for his bad luck, but in January he married a colonel's daughter from Leamington. (TB 39)

✤ She was a **Miss Parkinson**. He is now abroad as chaplain of the Barsetshire Regiment. (CBI 40)

✤ His service is delightful. (MH 42)

Tone, Mars

✤ Artist, leading light of the Phallo-Hexagonal Group. He proposed a bas-relief of "Knowledge and Ignorance" for the new "functional" school hall at Southbridge School. (PE 47)

Toothbane, Lord: *See* Aelthwithric, Bishop of Barchester.

Topham, (Mrs.) Betty: *See* Betty.

Topham, Captain ("Topsy")

✤ He is billeted on the **Villars**, Northbridge Rectory. His pre-war interests had been the Turf and the Stage. He is engaged to **Mrs. (Poppy) Turner's** niece **Betty**. His uncle in Norfolk dies and he becomes Squire. (NR 41)

✤ Married and living in Hacken's Fen, Norfolk. Mrs. Turner comes to live with them, and **Effie Arbuthnot** comes for the birdwatching. (PE 47)

✤ They mainly spend their time birdwatching. He is the East Anglian delegate to the Birdwatcher's Congress in Mixo-Lydia. (WDIM 54)

Tory, Greta

✤ Postwoman at Hallbury. **Mrs. Tory** is her aunt. She gives her spare wages to her mother, who is caretaker at Hall's End when the **Fieldings** are in Barchester. She wins a goat in the Cottage Hospital Raffle. (MB 45)

* Now she is a waitress at the White Hart. (LAR 48)

* She is back to being postwoman. (CQ 58)

Tory, Mrs.
* Cook to **Admiral Palliser** at Hallbury House. **Greta Tory** is her niece. She has a feud with the gardener **Chaffinch**. (MB 45)

Towel, E.G.
* Writes hate mail to **Mrs. (Laura) Morland**. (LAR 48)

Towers, the (previous) Duke of
* Husband of a **Miss Foster**, who was cousin of the **Sixth Earl of Pomfret**; their second daughter was **Dorothy "Dodo" Bingham**. There were no sons, so the title went to a nephew. (PBO 46)

* The current duke, **Rose Bingham's** Uncle Tom, is now impoverished. (LAR 48)

* Thereafter, see the **Harcourts**. An earlier, related branch of their family included a bad duke in the Diplomatic and his wife Mary Seraskier (*cf.* Trollope); their only son died and she separated form him; when he died, the present, respectable branch of the family came in. (ADA 57)

Towers, the (current) Duke of
* Nephew and successor of **the (previous) Duke of Towers**. (PBO 46)

* The current duke, **Rose Bingham's** Uncle Tom, is now impoverished. (LAR 48)

* The family name is identified: *See* **Thomas Harcourt, (the Old) Duke of Towers**. An earlier, related branch of their

family included a bad duke in the Diplomatic and his wife Mary Seraskier (*cf.* Trollope); their only son died and she separated from him; when he died, the present, respectable branch of the family came in. (ADA 57)

Tozer, Mr.

* Of Scatcherd and Tozer, Caterers, of Barchester. He was a mess waiter on Salisbury Plain from 1914 to 1918. He is on hand for **Rose Birkett's** wedding. (CBI 40)

* He caters **Sam Adams'** garden party at the Old Bank House. (OBH 49)

* He caters both the Palace garden party and the Conservative Do at Gatherum. **Old Mr. Scatcherd** is his partner. (CC 50)

* His cousin owns the Maison Tozier, Barchester's best beauty parlor, where **Miss Dahlia** works. (JC 53)

* He caters the reception at Holdings for **Miss Merriman's** wedding. Mr. Scatcherd is still in charge. (ADA 57)

* He caters the reception for the **Oriels'** wedding at the Vinery. (LAAA 59)

* He caters the High Rising Agricultural, and **Mrs. (Laura) Morland's** seventieth birthday tea at the Old Bank House. He has not missed a major event in Barsetshire for almost forty years. (TSAT 61)

Traill, Mr. Donald

* Assistant master at Southbridge School. No first name. A bachelor, recently demobilized, whose family lives in a big

house in South Kensington. He lives in Maria in **Wiple Terrace**, and plays his radio loudly. (PE 47)

❖ He is an usher at **Anne Fielding's** wedding. (LAR 48)

❖ Now he plays records loudly, and **Mr. Feeder** plays the radio. (CC 50)

❖ They could hear each other's music so clearly because their two houses had once been joined, so they rejoin them with communicating doors. His first name is given. (CQ 58)

Tristam, Professor
❖ He goes hunting in churches for frescoes that aren't there; see also **Professor Lancelot**. (WDIM 54)

Tropes, Mrs.
❖ Dresser to **Jessica Dean**. Her husband was in "the profession," and a drinker. Her sisters all went to the bad and did very nicely. She dresses **Lucy Marling** for her wedding. (CC 50)

Trotter, Mrs.
❖ She was cook at the Deanery for twenty years, and now has a house in Barchester and takes temporary jobs. She cooks for **Philip** and **Leslie Waring Winter** at the Priory School. (LAR 48)

Troubridge
❖ When **Tom Buckley** is fined for not voting in the Federal Election, he (along with **Mr. Wickham** and **Jim Brentwood**) puts up the money for the fine (and a few drinks afterward). (HRt 52)

Trouncer, Old Mrs.

❖ She says she'll live to be one hundred to spite **Mr. Hibberd** the sexton. She dies at ninety-nine, but Mr. Hibberd has the flu, so **Bunce** has to dig the grave. (NR 41)

Trowel

❖ Builder at Northbridge. The son of **Fitchett** the grocer is his apprentice. (NR 41)

❖ He is to play a Druid in the Northbridge Pageant of History for the Coronation. (WDIM 54)

Trowell, Norma

❖ Old Trowell's girl. She runs the Northbridge telephone exchange, and is bribed with chocolates by **John Villars**. (NR 41)

Tucker

❖ **Stoker's** uncle, by marriage to her determined aunt, who gave him a lovely funeral, and later died of dropsy. (LAAA 59)

Tucker, Mrs.

❖ Of Starveacres Hatches. She has three retarded invalid children, and is the object of **Edith, Lady Pomfret's** charity. **Gillie Foster** gets her cottage repaired. (PT 38)

Tuckwell, Lilian

❖ Author of *The Truth About Byron*; also *The Truth About* Shelley, Keats, the Brownings, and many other popular works. (CBI 40)

Tudor, Glamora

❖ Known in Hollywood as "The Woman Who Cannot Love." She plays Princess Alix in *Moonlight Passion*. (TB 39)

* Her latest is *The Flames of Desire*. (BL 39)

* She plays Elizabeth Barrett Browning in *Lips of Desire*. (CBI 40)

* She is Columbine in *Loves of a Court Painter* (Watteau, during the French Revolution) and stars in *Virgin Flesh*, about the love life of Florence Nightingale. (NR 41)

* She plays a factory worker in *Inglorious Hampdens* (according to **Greta Tory**) or *In Glorious Hampton* (according to **Ernie Freeman**). (MB 45)

* She stars in *Burning Flesh*. (PBO 46)

* Plays Queen Henrietta Maria in *Mayflower Madness*. (PBO 46)

* *She Kissed and Told*. (LAR 48)

* Stars with **Hastings Pond** in *What Men Desire* (about the love life of Marcus Aurelius), and with **Croke Hosskiss** in both *Love and Lust* (about New York gangsters) and *The Ladies' Man* (about Casanova). (OBH 49)

* Plays Tamar in *Too Close for Love*, a Mammoth Scenario of King David's Court, with **Crab Doker** as Amnon. Also in *Honka-Tonka-Bodyline* and *Renunciation* (as La Gioconda). (CC 50)

* In *Legs Round Your Neck*, featuring **Croke Scumper**; and with the new actor **Phil Kreelson** in *One Night in the Vatican*. (HRt 52)

* Stars with **Hake Codman** in *Moslem Love*. (JC 53)

* With **Washington Swop** in a revival of *Burning Flesh*. (ESR 55)

* She is in a remake of Tristan and Isolda called *They Loved Too Well*; and in *Love in a Bath*, the true story of Marat and Charlotte Corday, with **Buck Follanbee**. (NTL 56)

* She plays Cora Pearl in *Pearl of Paris*, featuring **Buck Pickaback**, the scion of an old Pennsylvania Dutch family. (ADA 57)

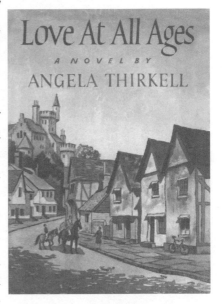

* She is Cleopatra in *Daughter of the Pyramids* (with **Hank Hawksfoot**), and co-stars with **Pietro Nasone** in a **Czemschk Kpozcz** production about Cyrano de Bergerac. (CQ 58)

* She is in *Hearts Aflame* (in Glorious Technicolor), and with her new co-star **Hick Pilldozer** in *The Cardinal's Mate, A Factual Comment on Life Under the Borgias*. (LAAA 59)

* "That ageless vedette" is now starring in *A Mistress of Voltaire*, with **Hank Pilsener** as Voltaire. (TSAT 61)

Turner, Cecil
* Late husband of **Mrs. (Poppy) Turner**, and a distant relation of **Mrs. (Laura) Morland's**. A cad, waster, and drunkard, he died after a year of marriage. (NR 41)

Turner, Mrs. Poppy
* Of the Hollies, Northbridge. She runs and raises money for the Communal Kitchen. (CBI 40)

* Widowed after a year of marriage to the very unsatisfactory **Cecil Turner**. She has raised her nieces, **Betty** and **the Other Niece**, after their parents died of influenza; she also boards evacuee children, including **Derrick Pumper, Derrick Farker**, and their cousin **Ron**. Both her nieces get engaged, and she gently turns down the proposal of **Mr. (Harold) Downing**. (NR 41)

* She moves to Hacken's Fen in Norfolk to live with Betty and her husband **Mr. Topham**. (PE 47)

* She was at school with **Sister Chiffinch**. She comes back to Northbridge for a visit and decides to stay. She gets back both the Hollies and Mr. Downing; they will marry and go to America in October. (WDIM 54)

* Now happily married to Mr. Downing. (NTL 56)

* They travel together as he lectures in Europe and America. (ADA 57)

Turpin
* Gardener to the **Brandons**, Stories. He is a nephew of an Old Turpin; his father was ninety-three and his grandfather almost one hundred when they died. **Hettie** may be his daughter, but *see* below. He grows a giant marrow for the harvest festival, but **Delia Brandon** carves **Hilary Grant's** name into it. (TB 39)

* He and Mrs. Turpin have no children. They have Hilary and Delia Grant and their boys to stay at their cottage for ten days. (HRt 52)

Turpin, Hettie
* Also known as Mr. **Turpin's** Hettie (his daughter?). Housekeeper to **Mr. (Justin) Miller** at the Vicarage, Pom-

fret Madrigal. She has to hurry with her voyle for the Feet. (TB 39)

* She can't be Turpin's daughter because he has no children. (HRt 52)

Twicker, Mr.
* Husband of **Nanny Twicker** and gardener to the **Keiths**, Northbridge Manor. They got married when **Robert Keith** was four, and all their children are grown and gone. They let rooms in their cottage to **Tony Morland, Eric Swan**, and **Percy Hacker**. (SH 37)

* They are misnamed **Twitcher**. He finds **Philip Winter's** engagement ring for **Rose Birkett** in the stream channel from the pool where Philip dropped it. (GU 43)

* He is getting rather old for gardening. (PE 47)

* He died a few years ago. (LAAA 59)

Twicker, Nanny
* Wife of **Mr. Twicker** and nurse to the **Keiths**, Northbridge Manor. They got married when **Robert Keith** was four, and all their children are grown and gone. She is a farmer's daughter from Westmorland (the north country). They let rooms in their cottage to **Tony Morland, Eric Swan**, and **Percy Hacker**. (SH 37)

* They are misnamed **Twitcher**. (GU 43)

* She takes in **Harry Merton** when **Lydia Keith** Merton gets measles. (PE 47)

* Her husband died a few years ago. (LAAA 59)

Twitcher: *See* **Twicker**.

Umblebys, the

* Agents and lawyers to the **Greshams** of Greshamsbury House. They let their house, the Laurels, to some nice uninteresting people named **Green**, who sublet it to **John** and **Rose Birkett Fairweather**. An Umbleby is still a churchwarden. (JC 53)

* They had owned their house for over a hundred years, and now let the coachhouse and stables to a riding school. They have three children. (CQ 58)

Umbleby, Old Canon

* He left the town of Greshamsbury in a curate's care for seven years. (CQ 58)

Umbleby, Yates

* Relation of the legal **Umblebys** of Greshamsbury. (CQ 58)

Uncle Oswald: *See* **Oswald, Uncle**.

Updike, Mrs. Betty

❖ Wife of **Mr. (Philip) Updike**, of Clive's Corner. They have four children between fifteen and twenty-five: **the Elder Boy, the Elder Girl, the Younger Boy**, and **the Younger Girl**. She is highly accident prone, but charming. (TH 44)

❖ She is doing a first aid course but couldn't take the exam because she pulled up a stake that turned out to be marking a wasps' nest. (LAR 48)

Updikes' Elder Boy, the

❖ One of the four children between fifteen and twenty-five years old of **Mr. (Philip)** and **Mrs. (Betty) Updike**. He is a colonel. (TH 44)

❖ He is now a solicitor. (LAR 48)

❖ He left the service as a lieutenant colonel, and has gone into partnership with his father. He and the elder girl live at home and keep an eye on their mother. (DD 51)

Updikes' Elder Girl, the

❖ One of the four children between fifteen and twenty-five years old of **Mr. (Philip)** and **Mrs. (Betty) Updike**. She is in the WAAFs. (TH 44)

❖ She runs a domestic science school. (LAR 48)

❖ She is now head of the Barchester Public Library. She and the elder boy live at home and keep an eye on their mother. (DD 51)

❖ She comes in as temporary secretary-help to **Lord** and **Lady Pomfret** after **Miss Merriman** leaves. (NTL 56)

❖ Her job with the Pomfrets is now permanent. (ADA 57)

Updike, Mr. Philip

* Husband of **Mrs. (Betty) Updike**, of Clive's Corner; a solicitor. They have four children between fifteen and twenty-five: **the Elder Boy, the Elder Girl, the Younger Boy**, and **the Younger Girl**. His family has been solicitors to the **Beltons** since **the Nabob**. (TH 44)

* He acts for **Margot Phelps** Macfadyen on **Mr. (Donald) Macfadyen's** will. (CQ 58)

Updikes' Younger Boy, the

* One of the four children between fifteen and twenty-five years old of **Mr. (Philip)** and **Mrs. (Betty) Updike**. He is at Southbridge School, and gets scholarships. (TH 44)

* He is about to do his military service, and has a bag of scholarships for Oxford. (LAR 48)

* He is almost a chartered accountant, and is seldom home. (DD 51)

Updikes' Younger Girl, the

* One of the four children between fifteen and twenty-five years old of **Mr. (Philip)** and **Mrs. (Betty) Updike**. She is at St. Perdida's school. (TH 44)

* She has a research scholarship at Cambridge. (LAR 48)

* She works in a large travel agency, and is seldom home. (DD 51)

Valoroso, Marleen
> ❖ One of a theatrical family; daughter of **Mr.** and **Mrs. Valoroso** and sister of **Ruby**. She and her sister are tap dancers, and they and their mother are evacuated to Barchester. (MH 42)

Valoroso, Mr.
> ❖ One of a theatrical family; husband of **Mrs. Valoroso** and father of **Ruby** and **Marleen**. He is an acrobat, now stationed in the Middle East. (MH 42)

Valoroso, Mrs.
> ❖ One of a theatrical family; wife of **Mr. Valoroso** and mother of **Ruby** and **Marleen**. She and her daughters are evacuated to Barchester. **Bishop Joram** drinks her under the table. (MH 42)

Valoroso, Ruby
> ❖ One of a theatrical family; daughter of **Mr.** and **Mrs. Valoroso** and sister of **Marleen**. She and her sister are

tap dancers, and they and their mother are evacuated to
Barchester. (MH 42)

Vance, Miss

* Unnamed **Nurse** to **Mrs. (Lavinia) Brandon's** family,
Stories. She is always altering **Delia Brandon's** undergar-
ments, and vies with **Rose** in tyranny and devotion to Mrs.
Brandon. (TB 39)

* She is busy with the evacuated nursery school run by **Miss
Feilding (or Fielding)** and **Miss Driver** at Stories. (CBI
40)

* Now identified by name, she came to Stories when **Francis
Brandon** was six weeks old. She is still hanging on to three
babies of the nursery school, but they leave. (PE 47)

* She feuds with the **Nannie** of Francis and **Peggy Arbuthnot** Brandon, and outlasts her at Stories, taking over Francis and Peggy's three children. (CC 50)

* She leaves to become nurse to **Lady Glencora Palliser**
Waring at Beliers Priory. (HRt 52)

* She runs a sort of Small Child Hotel at the seaside. (LAAA
59)

van Dryven, (Mrs.) Betty: *See* **Dean, Betty**.

van Dryven, Cutsam Porck

* Father of **Woolcott Jefferson van Dryven**. Former
American minister at the Grand Ducal Court of Schauer-
Antlitz, where he met **Miss (Juliana) Starter**. (BL 39)

van Dryven, Woolcott Jefferson

* American fiancé of **Betty Dean**, son of **Cutsam Porck van
Dryven**, of New York. He took a Classical Excavation

Diploma at Pittsburgh in three months, and now looks after his money. (BL 39)

❖ Now married, he visits England on a commission to reorganize the peanut industry after the war. (GU 43)

❖ He was on the Peanut Control Board through the war; his wife is his right-hand man in reorganizing the peanut export trade. They have three children. (PE 47)

❖ They live in New York. They visit England to study the peanut cartel. (LAR 48)

❖ They are almost millionaires, and have a place on Long Island and a ranch in Texas as well as the New York penthouse. (WDIM 54)

❖ They are now multi-millionaires. He buys at auction in New York a celebrated **Guido Guidone**, a primitive by **Pictor Ignotus**, an Etruscan statue, and the *Très Jolies Heures* of St. Panurge from **Harcourt, the Duke of Towers**. (LAAA 59)

van Pork, Cutsam
❖ **Franklin Harcourt, Duchess of Towers**, arranged his wedding in Baltimore. (LAAA 59)

Verger
❖ Butler at the Deanery to the **Crawleys**. (PE 47)

❖ Toastmaster of the Club of the Upper Servants in the Close. (ADA 57)

Vicar and his Aunt, the: *See* **Horton, Dunstan** and **Monica**.

Vicar's Aunts, the

* Residents of Maria and Editha in **Wiple** Terrace. One goes to Gibraltar to join her husband and lets Maria to the **Bissells**, the other is a widow. (CBI 40)

Vidlers, the

* Of Northbridge. An extended clan, of which two nieces wheel their aunt and uncle in perambulators. (ESR 55)

Vidler, Bill

* One of the **Vidlers** of Northbridge. (ESR 55)

Vidler, Jno.

* Spelling on John Vidler's tombstone. He was struck by lightning. (ESR 55)

Vidler, Mr. ("the Fish")

* Poulterer, Northbridge. (NR 41)

* He also sells fish. (PBO 46)

* He is to recite for the Coronation festivities, Northbridge. His sister-in-law is **Mrs. Vidler** of the Mitre. (WDIM 54)

* His son **Young Vidler** is well over forty. (NTL 56)

* His mother and father had been married and childless for eighteen years, until the old woman over Starveacres way sold them a charm and he was born. They're long dead now. (ADA 57)

Vidler, Mrs.

* Proprietress of the Mitre, Northbridge. Her brother-in-law is **Mr. Vidler the Fish**. (WDIM 54)

* She has a Nasty Finger. (ESR 55)

Vidler, Percy

❖ Son of a **Vidler** who does odd jobs. He teaches his younger illegitimate brother to read off **Jno. Vidler's** tombstone. (ESR 55)

Vidler, Young

❖ Son of **Vidler the Fish**; he is well over forty. (NTL 56)

Villars, Mr. Gregory

❖ Husband of **Mrs. (Verena) Villars**, and rector of Northbridge. Their elder son, twenty-six, is an engineering professor at a provincial university, and their younger is **John Villars**. He was formerly headmaster of Coppin's School. They billet an office of the Barsetshire regiment under **Colonel Passmore**. (NR 41)

❖ They have grandchildren. (PE 47)

❖ He came to Northbridge after leaving Coppin's in 1937, and now wants to leave. He becomes a canon of Barchester. (CQ 58)

❖ They are living in Barchester. (LAAA 59)

Villars, John

❖ Younger son of **Mr. (Gregory)** and **Mrs. (Verena) Villars**, with one elder brother, twenty-six. He is a wing commander in the R.A.F. (NR 41)

❖ He has bombed Italy six times. (GU 43)

❖ He now has two little girls. (JC 53)

❖ He was twenty-one in 1939. (CQ 38)

Villars, Mrs. Verena

❖ Wife of **Mr. (Gregory) Villars**, of Northbridge Rectory. Their elder son, twenty-six, is an engineering professor at a

provincial university, and their younger is **John Villars**.
They billet an office of the Barsetshire regiment under
Colonel Passmore. One of the officers, **Captain Holden**
is smitten with her. (NR 41)

* She is a cousin of **Sir Harry Waring**. (GU 43)

* She stands as godmother to one of **Effie Bunce's** children
  of shame and to a cow at Northbridge Manor. She is
  conceited about having grandchildren. (PE 47)

* She is not so healthy, but helps on the Northbridge Coronation Committee. (WDIM 54)

* Her husband becomes a canon of Barchester. (CQ 58)

* They are living in Barchester. (LAAA 59)

Violante
* A nun seduced by **Cosimo di Strelsa**; she bore a male child
  who may have become the painter **Giacopone Giacopini**.
  (NR 41)

Vivien
* She and her husband **Joe** are acquaintances of **Charles
  Belton**. She is twenty-one, they have two babies, and they
  live in two rooms in Chelsea. He has no job, and spent all
  his money on the honeymoon; she quarreled with her
  family and went on the stage. (LAR 48)

von Storck, Lieutenant
* When **Rose Birkett** was sent to school in Munich, she got
  engaged to him and to a band conductor (**Herr Lob**) at the
  same time. (SH 37)

Wagstaffe, Mr.

❖ Of the Signal Corps, stationed at the Hush-Hush camp at the Dower House. (GU 43)

Walker, Mr.

❖ Master at Southbridge School; deals out "the very highest mathematics to a privileged and harassed few." Popularly supposed to be coeval with the late Queen Victoria. (CBI 40)

Walter

❖ Footman at Rushwater House. Found skylarking with **Ivy** in the pantry. (WS 34)

Walton

❖ Butcher in Northbridge. (NR 41)

Wamber, Fred

❖ Laborer and cottager. He had **Rev. Thompson** christen his first child **Zernebok**, after his great-grandfather. A possible lineal descendant of Wamba the Witless (*cf. Ivanhoe*). (LAAA 59)

Wamber, Zernebok
- ❖ Great-grandfather of **Fred Wamber**, who names his first child after him. (LAAA 59)

Wandle, Mr.
- ❖ Butcher in the Old Town, Hallbury. (MB 45)

Warburg or **Warbury**: name given in later editions to the **Gissings** (*q.v.*).

Ward, Nurse ("Wardy")
- ❖ A nurse who shares a flat with her pals Heathy (*see* **Nurse Heath**) and Chiffy (*see* **Nurse Chiffinch**). (DH 34)

- ❖ She, Heathy, and Sister Chiffinch want to run a small nursing home for the wealthy after the war. (MB 45)

- ❖ She and Miss Heath took the cottage Punshions after **Miss (Ianthe) Pemberton** died. She has worked with Miss Heath since Knight's, and nurses **Mr. (Leonard) Halliday** with her. (NTL 56)

- ❖ Perhaps she is not living at Punshions with Nurse Chiffinch and Miss Heath. (ADA 57)

- ❖ She is sharing the cottage with both Heathy and Chiffy. (CQ 58)

Wardy: *See* **Ward, Nurse**.

Waring, Cecil
- ❖ Nephew of **Sir Harry** and **Lady Harriet Waring**, and brother of **Leslie Waring**. Heir to Beliers Priory and a

lieutenant commander in the Royal Navy. After a long delay with no word from him, he turns up in Washington, D.C. (GU 43)

❖ After Sir Harry's death, he inherits the baronetcy and becomes Commander Sir Cecil Waring. He also inherited through his mother a large fortune at an early age, which he invested in good farmland around the Priory. He was lately in the East. Due to a bit of metal left in him from D-day, he is at home on half pay, and is thinking of using the Priory as a home for orphans of naval ratings. Persuaded by **Lady Glencora Palliser** and seconded by his lawyer **Mr. Winthrop**, he lets the Lodge at Silverbridge (which he inherited from an uncle) to **Jeffrey** and **Isabel Dale Palliser**, the Silverbridges, instead of to **Geoffrey Harvey's** office. When he tries to dredge the Dipping Pond his injury is disturbed, and Lady Cora has to drive him to Barchester General for an emergency operation. They get engaged. (DD 51)

❖ They are married, have a baby (**"the future Bart"**) a little early, and name him Harry (for now). He is doing well, selling produce to **Mr. (Donald) MacFadyen's** Amalgamated Vedge, and sold some distant land to the Barsetshire Golf Club. An old cousin of his who lived in a cottage on the grounds died of rage after the General Election, under the illusion that Mr. Gladstone had beaten Lord Salisbury. (HRt 52)

❖ He is helping with the Sea Scouts. The future Bart is now named Plantagenet Cecil, or "P.C." (WDIM 54)

❖ His wife is pregnant again. (ESR 55)

> ✦ They have more than two children. (CQ 58)

Waring, Lady Cora: *See* **Palliser, Lady Glencora.**

Waring, "the future Bart"
> ✦ Eldest child of **Sir Cecil** and **Lady Glencora Palliser Waring.** At first named Harry. He was born a little early. (HRt 52)

> ✦ He is now named Plantagenet Cecil, or "P.C." (WDIM 54)

> ✦ There are more than two children in the family. (CQ 58)

Waring, George
> ✦ Only son and heir of **Lady Harriet** and **Sir Harry Waring,** born in 1900 and named for his grandfather. He went to Southbridge School, and was fond of **Dean** and **Mrs. Crawley's** eldest daughter. A second lieutenant, he was killed in 1918. (GU 43)

Waring, Lady Harriet
> ✦ Wife of **Sir Harry Waring** (married June 1899); of Beliers Priory, which is now quartered with convalescent soldiers. Their only son **George** was killed in 1918. She is the aunt of **Cecil** and **Leslie Waring.** A staunch committeewoman. (GU 43)

> ✦ Her husband died during the winter, and she herself not long after. (DD 51)

Waring, Sir Harry
> ✦ Husband of **Lady Harriet Waring** (married June 1899); general of the 408th Regiment, and baronet; of Beliers Priory, which was built by his grandfather and his beautiful City-heiress wife. His only son **George** was killed in 1918.

He is the uncle of **Cecil** and **Leslie Waring**, and the former is his heir. He is also cousin to **Mrs. (Verena) Villars**, and had a spinster aunt who was an invalid at forty by choice. Now seventy-six years old, with a houseful of convalescent soldiers. (GU 43)

* Now called Sir Henry, he tells well-worn anecdotes of the Boer War. He was attached to **Fred Arbuthnot's** regiment in '93 under **Colonel Barc**, for whom they were known as the Polar Bears. (PE 47)

* He allows Leslie and her husband **Philip Winter** to start a school in the Priory. (LAR 48)

* He died during the winter, and his wife not long after. (DD 51)

Waring, Leslie

* Niece of **Sir Harry** and **Lady Harriet Waring**, and sister of **Cecil Waring**. She has been secretary of a large naval charity organization for three years. She was in London and Portsmouth during the bombing, and after her second visit to America her ship was torpedoed and she was in a boat for two days. When she has a breakdown, she comes to her aunt and uncle at Beliers Priory for three months, where she worries over her brother's not writing. With **Lydia Keith Merton's** help, she gets engaged to **Philip Winter**. (GU 43)

* They are married while he is on twenty-four hours' leave. (MB 45)

* They plan to start a prep school at Beliers. (PBO 46)

* They start the Beliers Priory School, and she has a baby boy. (PE 47)

* The boy is named **Noel**, and she is pregnant again. (LAR 48)

* Their second child is **Harriet**. The school is a success, and they plan to enlarge it by moving it to the **Beltons'** Harefield House. (DD 51)

* The move is finally accomplished. (JC 53)

Watson, Mr. Charles

* Husband of **Mrs. (Molly) Watson** and father of **Tom**. A Hallbury solicitor, of a family respected there for several generations. Machinery mad, he finds a friend in **Heather Adams**. (MB 45)

Watson, Clare

* Second child of **Lettice Watson** and the late **Robert Watson**; her elder sister is **Diana**. Three years old, and celebrates her fourth birthday while the family is staying with her mother's parents **Mr. (William)** and **Mrs. (Anabel) Marling**. Her mother gets engaged to **Captain Tom Barclay**. (MH 42)

* They are all living in Yorkshire. (MB 45)

* She and her sister are at prep school; they have two younger half-brothers. (CC 50)

Watson, Diana

* Eldest child of **Lettice Watson** and the late **Robert Watson**; her younger sister is **Clare**. She is five years old, and the family is staying with her mother's parents **Mr. (William)** and **Mrs. (Anabel) Marling**. Her mother gets engaged to **Captain Tom Barclay**. (MH 42)

* They are all living in Yorkshire. (MB 45)

✤ She and her sister are at prep school; they have two younger half-brothers. (CC 50)

Watson, Mrs. Lettice (née Marling)

✤ Second child of **Mr. (William)** and **Mrs. (Anabel) Marling**; her elder brother is **Bill**, her younger siblings are **Oliver** and **Lucy**. Her husband, Robert, was killed at Dunkirk, leaving her with two daughters, **Diana** (five) and **Clare** (three going on four). She stays with her parents at Marling Hall, where she meets and gets engaged to **Captain Tom Barclay**. (MH 42)

✤ They are living in Yorkshire with the children. (MB 45)

✤ They have two more children, both boys. (CC 50)

Watson, Mrs. Molly (née Glover)

✤ Wife of **Mr. Charles Watson** and mother of **Tom**. She is of good sub-county stock and has a good elderly maid, so she takes over the local committees when the doctor's wife is widowed and goes back home to Ayrshire. She runs working parties in their own Drill Hall. At Fairlawns School, she was a friend of **Miss (Cicely) Holly** and formerly a particular friend of **Hilda Cowman**. (MB 45)

Watson, Mr.

✤ A master at Southbridge School, husband of **Mrs. Watson** and father of **Young Watson**. At the school boxing match, he leaves the judges' table for the duration of his son's contest. (HR 33)

Watson, Mrs.

✤ Wife of **Mr. Watson** of Southbridge School, and mother of **Young Watson**. At the school boxing match, she leaves the hall until the boxing is over because her son might bleed. (HR 33)

Watson, Mr. Robert

❖ The late husband of **Lettice Watson**, and father of **Diana** and **Clare**. Killed at Dunkirk. (MH 42)

Watson, Tom

❖ Son of **Mr. (Charles)** and **Mrs. (Molly) Watson**, and friend of **Frank Gresham**. (MB 45)

Watson, Young

❖ Student at Southbridge School, son of **Mr.** and **Mrs. Watson**. His tender-hearted parents leave the school boxing match while he fights, but he loves boxing. (HR 33)

Weaver, Sir Hosea

❖ Master of the Hosiers' Company; his wife is Lady Weaver. He had scholarships in grammar school and college, and took a First in Political Economy at Cambridge. To celebrate Bobbin Day at the Hosiers' Girls' Foundation School, he brings the Remembrancer, the Almoner, six Free Hosiers, four Indentured Prentice Hosiers, the Hosiers' Wardmote Bailiff, and the Master's Apparitor of Worship (**Mr. Simnet**) with him to Harefield Park. (TH 44)

❖ As a second lieutenant during the war, he worked with **Philip Winter** on a hush-hush job at the Dower House. Now a Past Master of the Hosiers' Company, he arranges the transition of Harefield Park from the Hosiers' Girls' School to Philip and **Leslie Waring** Winter's Priory School. (DD 51)

Welk, Harold

✤ Descendant of a North Barsetshire line of woodsmen and bodgers, he served in the Boer War as a trooper in the Barsetshire Yeomanry under **Sir Edmund Pridham**. His fiancée's father said she shouldn't marry a gypsy and so brought him into his own funeral business, as there was no son. He became the father of **Mr. (Harold) Welk**. (HRt 52)

Welk, Mr. Harold

✤ An undertaker, father of **Mavis Welk**, and very generous to her fianceé **Teddy Parkinson**. (PE 47)

✤ His daughter's first child was named after him. He did funeral work for an American hospital during the war. (CC 50)

✤ He is a widower, member of the Conservative Club, and former boxer. His family were woodsmen and bodgers from North Barsetshire, down to his father, **Harold Welk**. **Sir Edmund Pridham** convinces him to make over some capital to his daughter and son-in-law. (HRt 52)

✤ He is taking the Parkinsons to France. Mrs. Welk died at age twenty-seven when Mavis was a toddler. (CQ 58)

Welk, Mavis

✤ Daughter of **Mr. (Harold) Welk**; engaged to **Teddy Parkinson**. (PE 47)

✤ Now married, with two skinny children, **Harold**, after her father, and **Connie**, after his mother. He is appointed vicar of Pomfret Madrigal to replace **Mr. (Justin) Miller**. (CC 50)

* They met at a Young Conservatives meeting (their son's full name is Harold Winston). Though poor, they are well-respected in the village; she is secretary of the Pomfret Madrigal Women's Institute. She delivers their third child quite suddenly, and they name him **Josiah**, as **Dean Crawley** will be his godfather. (HRt 52)

* Her mother died at age twenty-seven, when she was still a toddler. Her husband is now vicar of Greshamsbury New Town, and doing well, though they are still poor. **Mary Preston** Leslie gives her a winning lottery ticket for a new washing machine. Her father takes the family to France. (CQ 58)

* They are now in a comfortable new house. (TSAT 61)

Welper
* A chicken farmer, ruined by grain rationing. His baby is inoculated by **Dr. March**. (MH 42)

Wesendonck, Robert ("Donk" or "Donkey")
* A shrimplike boy in spectacles who wins all the prizes at Southbridge School. He stays with **Tony Morland** over the holidays. (HR 33)

* He has three sisters, plays the harmonica, and visits **Mrs. (Laura) Morland** and Tony again. (DH 34)

* He later swam on the Olympic team. (TSAT 61)

Weston
* Chauffeur to the **Leslies**, Rushwater House. (WS 34)

Wheeler
* Second housemaid to the **Pomfrets**, Pomfret Towers. Her uncle is the under-gardener, her cousin is **Bill Wheeler** the

chimney sweep. Her married sister **Esme** fills in as a housemaid during the flu epidemic. (PT 38)

Wheeler
 ❖ Runs the garage at Pomfret Madrigal, with his sons **Bert** and **Harry**. He had some unpleasantness with the **Spindlers** over a cask. (TB 39)

Wheeler
 ❖ Groom for the **Pomfrets**, Pomfret Towers. He is a nephew of **Old Wheeler** and of **Bill Wheeler**. (OBH 49)

Wheeler
 ❖ Head carpenter to the **Pomfrets**, Pomfret Towers. (NTL 56)

Wheeler, Bert
 ❖ Works for his father, **Wheeler**, at the garage, Pomfret Madrigal. His brother is **Harry**. (TB 39)

Wheeler, Bill
 ❖ Chimney sweep of Little Misfit, the only man who understands the **Pomfret** Towers chimneys. His cousin is **Wheeler** the second housemaid there. (PT 38)

 ❖ Another cousin is **S. Wheeler**. (TH 44)

 ❖ He is now retired; his ninety-year-old sister is **Old Mrs. Freeman**. (MB 45)

 ❖ He is still a bachelor, with lots of money. He once walked out with **Selina Allen** but **Nannie Allen** put a stop to it. (LAR 48)

 ❖ He never cleans his own chimney; he would put a goose up it if all his geese hadn't been stolen by black marketers last year. His nephew is **Wheeler** the groom. (OBH 49)

* He is now cleaning the Gatherum Castle chimneys for the **Pallisers**. (CC 50)

* He is a cousin of **Sid Wheeler** of the Nabob, Harefield. (HRt 52)

* His great-aunt, who was toothless and hairless but would eat anything, dies in Barchester General Hospital. (WDIM 54)

Wheeler, Ernie
* An evacuee boarded by **Mr. and Mrs. Gibbs**. (NR 41)

Wheeler, Florrie
* Maid for the **Beltons** at Arcot House, working under **S. Wheeler**. Sixteen years old. (TH 44)

* S. Wheeler is her aunt, and she is niece (or second cousin twice removed) to **Sid Wheeler** of the Nabob. (HRt 52)

Wheeler, Harry
* Works for his father, **Wheeler**, at the garage, Pomfret Madrigal. His brother is **Bert**. (TB 39)

Wheeler, Old
* A tenant on the **Pomfret** estates whose cowshed is falling down. His nephew is **Wheeler** the groom. (OBH 49)

* His family have lived rent-free at Starveacres Hatches for the last eight hundred years or so. (WDIM 54)

Wheeler, S.
* Former nurse to the **Beltons**, and later houseparlormaid. **Florrie Wheeler** is her assistant. Her cousin is **Bill Wheeler** the chimney sweep, and her uncle is **Sid Wheeler**

of the Nabob. Her mother was a laundress, her father did odd jobs. She is secretive about her first name, which is revealed to be Sarah. (TH 44)

* Her duties have increased to general utility. (LAR 48)

* She is aunt to **Ellen Humble**. (CC 50)

* She once served as under-nurse to **Nannie Allen**. (DD 51)

* She is now housekeeper, and Florrie Wheeler is her niece. She was originally **Mrs. Belton's** old nurse. Sid Wheeler becomes her cousin, not her uncle. (HRt 52)

* She is back to being Sid Wheeler's niece. Her male cousin at Southbridge does odd jobs for **Admiral Phelps**, and **P.C. Haig Brown's** mother is her cousin, too. (CQ 58)

Wheeler, Sid

* Landlord of the Nabob, Harefield. He also runs, and sometimes drives, a taxi service. **S. Wheeler** at the **Beltons'** is his niece. (TH 44)

* He is a cousin of **Bill Wheeler** the chimney sweep, and **Florrie Wheeler** at the **Beltons'** is his niece (or second cousin twice removed). S. Wheeler becomes his cousin, not his niece. (HRt 52)

* S. Wheeler is his niece again. (CQ 58)

Wickens, Mr.

* He and his wife **Mrs. Wickens** are housekeepers for **Mr. Sidney Carton** at Assaye House, Harefield. He is an ex-scout from St. Jude's, with a game leg. (TH 44)

* Now he is an ex-scout of Paul's. (HRt 52)

Wickens, Mrs.

❖ She and her husband **Mr. Wickens** are housekeepers for **Mr. Sidney Carton** at Assaye House, Harefield. She is very deaf. (TH 44)

Wickham, Mr. ("Wicks")

❖ Estate agent to the **Keiths**, Northbridge Manor. A bachelor, nearly fifty, from an old Barsetshire family out Chaldicotes way. His father was a farmer. He was in the navy and reached second lieutenant on the East India Station, left the service to farm after World War I, rejoined in 1939, and was invalided out after Dunkirk (where he met **Aubrey Clover**). He stayed on at Northbridge after **Noel** and **Lydia Keith Merton** bought it from **Robert Keith**. His hobbies are birdwatching, shooting, and providing drinks. He gets **Effie Arbuthnot's** bird book for his cousin, **Mr. Johns** the publisher, and then proposes to her, but is turned down. (PE 47)

❖ Now Mr. Johns is "sort of an uncle" of his. He knew **Isabel Dale's** late fiancé **John** in Italy, and **Lady Glencora Palliser** in the London blitz. **Pinky Smith** sends him rum from the West Indies, and **Joe Hodgkins** sends him Marsala. He proposes to Isabel Dale to make her feel better, but is turned down. (CC 50)

❖ When **Tom Buckley** is fined for not voting in the Australian Federal Election, he, along with **Troubridge** and **Jim Brentwood**, puts up the money for the fine (and a few drinks afterward). (HRt 52)

❖ His mother's stingy brother, a farmer down Chaldicotes way, dies and leaves him everything. A fellow drinker,

Tommy Prescott, stripped his car's gears. He proposes to **Margot Phelps** out of naval solidarity, but is turned down. (JC 53)

* He was in North Africa in World War I. He doesn't propose to anyone. (CQ 58)

* He attends the **Oriels'** wedding reception, bringing two bottles of brandy sent by his friend **"Sheep" Scrimageour**. He exchanges grips with **Lee Sum(p)ter** as he had with his naval friend **Fritz Beverley**. (LAAA 59)

* He buys **Mr. Scatcherd's** sketch of "The Girls" for **Wiple** Terrace. (TSAT 61)

Wicklow, Alice *or* Mrs. Roddy: *See* Barton, Alice.

Wicklow, Young Alice

* Unnamed and unsexed third of three small children of **Roddy** and **Alice Barton Wicklow**. (PE 47)

* She and her siblings are named: the two elder are **Guy** and **Phoebe**. She is in the pram. (OBH 49)

* She and Phoebe have measles. Their nurse is **Nannie Peters**, whose brother used to be the butler at **Pomfret** Towers (**Peters**). (WDIM 54)

* All the children are at **Miss Vance's** Small Child Hotel at the seaside. (LAAA 59)

* All the children are now young adults. She is at Barchester High School, and is unsure whether to become a ballet dancer or a vet; likely the latter, as their dogs win prizes at the Nutfield Gymkhana. (TSAT 61)

Wicklow, Guy

✤ Unnamed and unsexed elder of two children of **Alice Barton** Wicklow and **Roddy Wicklow**. (GU 43)

✤ Now there are three small children. (PE 47)

✤ He and his siblings are named: the two younger are **Phoebe** and **young Alice**. (OBH 49)

✤ All the children are at **Miss Vances's** Small Child Hotel at the seaside (though Guy and Phoebe must be at least sixteen!). (LAAA 59)

✤ All the children are now young adults. He is learning forestry, and summers with friends in Sweden. (TSAT 61)

Wicklow, Mr.

✤ Husband of **Mrs. Wicklow**, father of **Roddy** and **Sally**. Junior partner of **Mr. (Walter) Barton** in the architectural firm of Barton and Wicklow. They live in Nutfield. He and his wife are very sensible parents who know their place. They go on a cruise to Madeira, and so have to be informed of Sally's engagement later. (PT 38)

✤ On a family note, Roddy and Sally's great grandmother had ten children, and when one got measles, she shut them all up in the nursery; half got it (and two died), the other half didn't and all had it at different times later, and then she had an eleventh baby. (WDIM 54)

Wicklow, Mrs.

✤ Wife of **Mr. Wicklow**, mother of **Roddy** and **Sally**. They live in Nutfield. She and her husband are very sensible parents who know their place. They go on a cruise to Madeira, and so have to be informed of Sally's engagement later. (PT 38)

Wicklow, Phoebe

* Unnamed and unsexed second of two children of **Alice Barton** Wicklow and **Roddy Wicklow**. (GU 43)

* Now there are three small children. (PE 47)

* She and her siblings are named: her elder brother is **Guy** and her younger sister is **young Alice**. (OBH 49)

* She and young Alice have measles. Their Nanny's brother used to be the butler at Pomfret Towers (**Peters**). (WDIM 54)

* All the children are at **Miss Vance's** Small Child Hotel at the seaside (though Guy and Phoebe must be at least sixteen!). (LAAA 59)

* All the children are now young adults. She is at art school in London. (TSAT 61)

Wicklow, Roddy

* Son of **Mr.** and **Mrs. Wicklow**, elder brother of **Sally**. He went to Cambridge, then took an agricultural course and went into **Mr. Hoare's** office as agent to **Giles, Lord Pomfret**. He wards off **Julian Rivers** from **Alice Barton**, and then gets informally engaged to her. (PT 38)

* He and Alice are formally engaged. (BL 39)

* They are married. (CBI 40)

* They have two children. He has a wounded leg, which keeps him out of active service. (GU 43)

* He is at home on leave. (TH 44)

* Back again, on leave from Belgium. (MB 45)

* Now there are three small children, several dogs and some puppies. (PE 47)

* The **Wicklow** children are **Guy, Phoebe**, and **young Alice** in the pram. They live at Nutfield. He helps and advises **Tom Grantly**. (OBH 49)

* Their Nutfield house is the one his parents lived in. (LAAA 59)

* He is teaching the local youth in the pony club. (TSAT 61)

Wicklow, Sally

* Daughter of **Mr.** and **Mrs. Wicklow**, younger sister of **Roddy**. She raises dogs (Wuffy, Chips, Chloe, and Hero) and runs the beagles. She is a friend of **Alice Barton** and gets engaged to **Gillie Foster**, heir to **Giles, Lord Pomfret**. (PT 38)

* Now married, they take Lord Pomfret on a cruise. (TB 39)

* Their baby, Giles (later Ludovic) is six months old. They vacation at Cap Martin. (BL 39)

* At Lord Pomfret's death, she becomes the **Countess of Pomfret (Lady Pomfret)**. She and Gillie have two sons (but later there's a daughter between the two, *see* below). (CBI 40)

* Their children are **Ludovic, Lord Mellings**, age four-and-a-half; **Lady Emily**, three; and **the Honourable Giles**, six months. She is head of the Barsetshire W.V.S. (TH 44)

* She worked for the Red Cross and St. John through the war, and is made a Lady of Grace of St. John for it. She is

now county chairman of the Red Cross Hospital Libraries. They have a fourth child, **Lady Agnes**, who never appears again. (PE 47)

* She is County President of Red Cross Libraries. (LAR 48)

* She has **Eleanor Grantly**, who works under her at the Red Cross Libraries, to visit at Pomfret Towers. The family visits **Lord** and **Lady Ellangowan** in shooting season. (OBH 49)

* There are disagreeable differences at the Hospital Libraries, and she resigns for six months, and perhaps permanently. The whole family goes to Cap Ferrat for the winter. (CC 50)

* They have a villa at Cap Ferrat, which they lend to **Charles** and **Clarissa Graham Belton** for their honeymoon. (HRt 52)

* They'll stay with Gillie's aunt in Smith Street, London, for the Coronation. (WDIM 54)

* She has given up hunting. (ADA 57)

* She is godmother to **Edith Graham** Harcourt's baby girl, **Gwendolen Sally**. (LAAA 59)

Wicks: *See* **Wickham, Mr.**

Wife of the Master of Barabbas College: *See* **Barabbas College, Wife of the Master of.**

Wife of the Master of Lazarus: *See* **Lazarus, Wife of the Master of.**

Wilson

* Friend of **Leslie Minor** from Southbridge School days.
  His uncle in America sent him a pen that wrote in three
  different inks. He was disciplined by both **Mr. Stanhope**
  and **Everard Carter**. Later, at Oxford, he did the Muff's
  Walk at Paul's and was disciplined by **Mr. (Charles) Fanshawe**. (CQ 58)

Wimple, Lady

* Of Wimple Hall. A weekend guest of **Lord** and **Lady
  Pomfret**. She did tapestry covers for three sofas and forty-
  five chairs, and she and her husband have read aloud to
  each other every night for nearly fifty years. (PT 38)

Winter, Harriet

* Second child of **Philip** and **Leslie Waring Winter**; her
  brother is **Noel**. (DD 51)

Winter, Noel

* Unnamed baby boy of **Philip** and **Leslie Waring Winter**.
  (PE 47)

* He is named. (LAR 48)

* He gets a sister, **Harriet**. (DD 51)

Winter, Philip

* Junior classics master at Southbridge School, trying to
  control **Eric Swan, Tony Morland**, and **Percy Hacker**.
  His politics are Communist, and his book on Horace's
  Epistles is published by Oxbridge. He is engaged to **Rose
  Birkett**, but when she breaks it off he drops her ring in the
  Keiths' pond. He succeeds to the Classical Sixth when **Mr.
  Lorimer** dies, and instead of going to Russia, goes to

Austria on his holidays with **Colin Keith** and **Noel Merton**. (SH 37)

* Now senior classical master, he attends the party before Rose's wedding to **John Fairweather**. He joins the Territorials as a captain. (CBI 40)

* His aunt died and left him some money; he is now a lieutenant-colonel. Using Rose's ring (rediscovered by **Mr. Twicker**), he gets engaged to **Leslie Waring** just before being sent abroad. (GU 43)

* They are married while he is on twenty-four hours' leave. He is now a colonel, serving in Holland. (MB 45)

* He and Leslie plan to start a prep school at Beliers Priory. (PBO 46)

* They start the Beliers Priory School, and she has a baby boy. (PE 47)

* The boy is named **Noel**, and she is pregnant again. He is the author of a new Latin grammar to succeed Mr. Lorimer's. (LAR 48)

* Their second child is **Harriet**. The school is a success, and they plan to enlarge it by moving it to the **Beltons'** Harefield House. (DD 51)

* The move is finally accomplished. (JC 53)

Winthrop, Mr.
* Solicitor, of the firm of Walker and Winthrop (or vice versa). An elderly bachelor who lives in Silverbridge over the office. Lawyer for **Cecil Waring** regarding his letting the Lodge, he also does **Lady Glencora Palliser's** settlements. (DD 51)

Wiple, Mr.

 ✦ A small master builder of Southbridge. In 1820, he built
   Wiple Terrace, whose four houses are monuments to
   his daughters, Maria, Adelina, Louisa, and Editha. The
   houses are owned by Paul's College, Oxford. (CBI 40)

 ✦ His work is endangered, as **Lord Aberfordbury (Sir
   Ogilvy Hibberd)**, via a new Labour bursar of Paul's, wants
   to take over the Terrace to build a factory for **his son's**
   unsuccessful National Rotochrome Polychrome Universal
   Picture Post Card Company. But he is ousted by a Syndi-
   cate led by **Sam Adams** and **Gradka Bonescu**, the Mixo-
   Lydian Ambassador. **Mr. Scatcherd** the artist does an
   "Abstrack Conception" of the four Wiple girls which is
   bought by **Mr. Wickham** and placed as a monument in the
   Terrace. (TSAT 61)

Wixett, Miss

 ✦ First headmistress of the Barchester High School, now
   retired at Lyme Regis. (CBI 40)

Woollff, Hector

 ✦ Band leader; his orchestra is the Happy Hectorians. (ESR
   55)

Wren, the

 ✦ Daughter of an Admiral; she and **Freddy Belton** were in
   love. She is killed in an air raid on the East Coast. (TH 44)

Wyckens, Bishop

 ✦ He made himself unpopular at the Abbey over the waste
   land at Starveacres, and so may be the upside-down figure
   in the murals by **Nicholas de Hogpen** in Pomfret Madrigal
   church. (TB 39)